1000
바바차 5426067
한국은행권
천원
율곡 이이
1536-1584
26067
1000
5672 사
5000

KOREA

THE NEXT STEP

KOREA

THE NEXT STEP

Peter Stewart

Published by
Euromoney Books

in association with
Coryo Securities Corporation
Daewoo Securities Co., Ltd.
Korea Development Securities Co., Ltd.
Korea Exchange Bank

Published by
Euromoney Publications PLC
Nestor House, Playhouse Yard
London EC4V 5EX

ISBN 1 85564 243 3

The pictures in the text were provided by Neil Beer, Capstone Design. The co-publishers provided their own pictures.
The map was supplied by Draughtsman Ltd, London.

Typeset by Euromoney Books & PW ReproSharp, London.
Printed in Malaysia by Times Offset (Malaysia).

Contents

구
찜
쌈
밥
12
月
25
日
가요주점
광화문가든
냉면
전파사
구천동
국제
광화문

Foreword

In-Kie HONG
Chairman and CEO, Korea Stock Exchange

The year 1994 will be a banner year for all of us. The world economy is showing signs of emerging from the long tunnel of stagnation. Major international forecasters are predicting that global GDP will record a growth rate of over 2.5 per cent this year, supported by lower international interest rates and oil prices. The world-wide boom in stock markets underlines these optimistic projections. Global stock markets posted an unprecedented performance in 1993 and the bullish trend has continued into this year. The trend toward globalisation will also foster growth in the world economy at large.

The Uruguay Round of multilateral trade talks, which heralds a new world economic order for the 21st century, was concluded after seven years of negotiation. This global development will facilitate borderless trading and intensify competition among countries. Simultaneously, a trend toward regionalism is emerging. The European Union and the North American Free Trade Zone took shape. Asian-Pacific Economic Cooperation (APEC) suggests the possible formation of an economic bloc among the Asia-Pacific Rim countries.

In the face of an age of unbounded economic competition, Korea placed its top priority on strengthening national competitiveness. Since the late 1980s, the competitiveness of Korean-made products has eroded substantially due to wage hikes and the steep rise in real estate prices. This caused sizeable current account deficits until 1992. The task of regaining international competitiveness calls for extensive reforms in every facet of our society and for the globalisation of our economy. Reform and globalisation will pave the way for the country's second economic take-off.

Since the new government was inaugurated in February 1993, Korean society has experienced many changes as part of the extensive reform drive. The Real Name Financial Transaction System was implemented, hastening the introduction of transparency in economic activity and economic justice. Many deregulatory measures have been taken to foster a healthier and more vigorous business climate and internationalise the economy.

The Korean economy is coming out of a protracted slump. The GNP growth rate for the last quarter of 1993 is expected to hit 6.5 per cent compared with 2.8 per cent over the same period of 1992. Last year saw a current account surplus, albeit a small one. Both industrial output and corporate facility investment are picking up. Boosted by improving economic fundamentals, the stock market is showing an upward trend. The

Korea Composite Stock Price Index (KOSPI), which registered a gain of 27.7 per cent last year, exceeded 970 in February for the first time in nearly five years. Foreign companies, having been scared off by the country's unfavourable business climate, are coming back to Korea. At the same time, Korean entrepreneurs are moving briskly to exploit new business opportunities.

As a part of strengthening the competitiveness of Korea's economy, the government has been actively encouraging foreign investment in technology-intensive and high value-added industries. To this end, it drew up the Foreign Investment Liberalisation Plan, under which 132 of the 224 currently restricted businesses will be opened to foreign investment by 1997. To provide a better business climate for foreign companies, the government curtailed foreign investment formalities and offered reduced tax burdens and financial assistance. Beginning this year, it allowed foreign companies in Korea to acquire land for business purposes and has also constructed industrial parks for their exclusive use.

In line with efforts to globalise Korea's economy, outbound direct investment by domestic companies has been encouraged. In the same vein, the government greatly relaxed restrictions on investment overseas and cut back foreign exchange regulations. Big trading firms were allowed to acquire real estate in foreign countries and to hold foreign currency up to US$300 million. The paperwork for outbound investment was reduced substantially, while financial assistance and an information service were offered.

At the core of these changes lies the financial industry. Extensive financial reform is underway to improve market efficiency and quality of service, thereby enhancing the Korean financial industry's competitiveness. The "Blueprint for Financial Liberalisation and Market Opening" announced in June 1993 details the schedule of financial reform to be implemented during 1993 to 1997. Following the blueprint, the Korean government has taken a host of measures further to liberalise, globalise, and restructure the financial markets.

The most significant moves toward financial liberalisation are the steps being taken to deregulate interest rates under the four-stage plan announced in 1991. In line with this plan, the second stage was carried out in 1993, liberalising most lending rates of banks and other financial institutions and the rate for long-term deposits of more than two years. Most interest rates are stabilising around 11 per cent, reducing the cost of financing for companies.

After the regulation of foreign exchange and capital flow was changed from a positive to a negative system in 1991, there has been considerable progress in liberalising the foreign exchange market. As an interim step toward a free-floating exchange rate regime, the intra-day fluctuation band of exchange rates was widened to 1.0 per cent from 0.8 per cent in 1993. The government mapped out the Foreign Exchange Reform Plan this February with the ultimate goal of scrapping the Foreign Exchange Management Act in a few years. This plan relaxes foreign exchange regulation and expands outbound portfolio investment by institutional investors.

The Korean securities market has been in the forefront of the effort to internationalise the financial industry. From the beginning of 1992, the Korean securities market has been open to foreign investors for direct portfolio investment. So far, foreign investors have brought over US$10 billion into the Korean market. The net capital inflow stood at US$7.7 billion at the end of 1993. Currently, foreign shareholding represents about 10 per cent of total market capitalisation.

Since Korea started internationalising its securities market, foreign securities companies have expanded their presence. To date, ten foreign companies from France,

Hong Kong, Japan, the UK and the US have set up branch offices in Seoul. Another 27 companies are maintaining representative offices and two joint venture securities firms are operating.

On the international scene, stock markets are rapidly changing the world over. Driven by the global trend toward deregulation and progress in technology, stock markets are becoming borderless and globalised. Innovative products and sophisticated techniques are fast developing. Most countries are eager to reinforce the competitiveness of their financial markets. They are competing to become international financial centres by reducing regulation, lowering transaction costs, and extending trading hours.

The volume of the Korean stock market has expanded greatly, and the Korea Stock Exchange ranked the 7th and 14th in 1993 in terms of trading volume and market capitalisation, respectively. It is true , however, that the Korean stock market has a long way to go to become a fully-fledged international market. We must build an attractive, accessible market to satisfy the needs of our customers and become a major Asia-Pacific financial centre.

With this goal in mind, the Korea Stock Exchange is moving ahead with a large-scale project to make it a competitive international market in the 21st century. To accommodate increasing volume, the current electronic trading system will be replaced with a highly advanced one, and construction of a new building is underway to provide the necessary facilities. A total of US$120 million is being poured into these two projects. As a part of the effort to reinforce the stock market's infrastructure, the Korea Stock Exchange will also open a stock index futures market no later than early 1996 and an index options market shortly after that. Additionally, it will improve the corporate disclosure system as well as the system for dissemination of market information to foreign users.

With the 21st century close at hand, we are facing two conflicting economic trends: globalism and regionalism. These developments will intensify competition among countries and make international cooperation even more important. In some respects, the coming century may be called an era of competition and cooperation.

In conclusion, Korea will, in the age of competition and cooperation, assume a relevant role and bear proportional responsibility as a member of the international community. To this end, we will not cease our efforts to reform and globalise our society. The ongoing reform and globalisation drive is not an idealistic slogan, but a pressing challenge that the entire nation must meet. I see these goals as clear indications of Korea's next steps toward the 21st century.

KOREA
CHINA
RUSSIA
N
Sea of Japan
Yellow Sea
Korea Strait
P'Yonyang
Kyonggi-do
Ch'unch'on
Kangnung
Uijongbu
Puch'on
Seoul
Inch'on
Kangwan-do
Tonghae
Anyang
Wonju
Suwon
Ch'ungch'ongbuk-do
Ch'ungju
Ch'onan
Ch'ungch'ongnam-do
Chongju
Andong
Kyongsanbuk-do
Kumi
Pohang
Kunsan
Iri
Taegu
Kyongju
Chŏnju
Chollabuk-do
Ulsan
Chongup
Kyongsangnam-do
Chinju
Masan
Ch'angwon
Kwangju
Pusan
Sunchon
Chollanam-do
Mokp'o
Yosu
Cheju-do
Tsushima (JAPAN)
Cheju-haehyŏp
Cheju
Cheju-do
150km south of Mokp'o
Capital
City
City and Port
Major Town
Airport
International Border
State Border
Primary Road
Rail
0
50
100
Kms

Introduction

Hermit or Tiger? South Korea (hereafter referred to as Korea) has developed in the last 30 years from an impoverished nation, torn by a recent war and subsisting largely on agriculture, into one of Asia's most dynamic Newly Industrialising Economies (NIEs). However, Korea remains relatively isolated among Asia's rapidly developing "Tiger" economies: even after hosting the 1988 Olympic Games, it retains some of the features that earned it the sobriquet of "The Hermit Kingdom" in the 19th century.

Korea is less cosmopolitan than Singapore and less sophisticated than Hong Kong; it also lacks the widespread knowledge of English that makes doing business in these two centres so attractive for the western businessman. At the same time, Korea lacks the close cultural association with China (which many expect to be the future economic growth-engine for the region) enjoyed by some of the other Asian NIEs, notably Taiwan and Hong Kong.

Although Korea is heavily dependent on trade with Japan and the United States, many Koreans have mixed feelings about their two more advanced partners. The presence of American troops in Korea since the 1950-1953 Korean War remains an irritation to the patriotic pride of the country's citizens, and the humiliations experienced during the 36 years of Japanese colonial rule preceding the end of World War II have led to a deeply ambiguous relationship with Japan. As a North Asian power it remains in the shadow of Japan, and its heavy military dependence on the United States compromises its potential for political leadership in the Asia-Pacific region.

Whereas the ranks of expatriates swelled to more than one million in Japan during 1993, the foreign community in Korea is tiny in comparison; less than a tenth of the total in Japan, excluding US servicemen in the country according to one off-the-cuff estimate. Most foreign businessmen, moreover, spend only a few days in the country, and generally travel no further than the commercial hub of the capital Seoul. In short, despite hosting the Olympics, Korea remains a country on the fringes in the minds of many non-Koreans.

The government has been making a concerted effort to change this perception. Korea played host to the "Expo 1993" world fair held at Taejon, albeit with mixed results: only an estimated 500,000 foreigners visited the exhibition, with the bulk of visitors coming from Korea. 1994 has been declared "Visit Korea Year", and the tourist authorities are plugging the slogan "Korea is more than Seoul" to encourage more tourists into the beautiful countryside surrounding the capital.

The perception of Korea as a somewhat marginal country belies its huge commercial penetration in both Asia and the West. Many now recognise the country's successes in the fields of consumer electronics and heavy industry. Hyundai cars, Samsung microwave ovens, Goldstar televisions and Daewoo ships have all become household names but few people grasp the extent to which Korea has penetrated the international commercial arena. For example, The Simpsons, the American cartoon series is produced in Korea. The all-American celluloid heroes of this popular family show have been brought to life by the production house A-Kom, whose digitalised ink and paint software allows the process of moving cartoon drawings into a format suitable for television to be done completely by computer. Studios in the United States, Japan and France subcontract work to the Korean houses because they are more competitive; the artwork brings in an estimated US$80 million each year to the Korean firms.[1]

Korea has already made its mark in the computer field, becoming one of the biggest manufacturers of semiconductors and providing parts and assembly for many well-known makes of PC. Increasingly, technology developed by Korea for the export market is being applied domestically, allowing it to diversify business lines and move up the value chain from labour-intensive to capital-intensive production.

As the domestic market develops, however, Korea has come under increasing pressure to liberalise its trade. This has coincided with the government's view that foreign investment is now needed to stimulate technology transfer. The success of this programme depends not only on the removal of trade barriers, but also on social, environmental and cultural factors: despite its outward-looking development strategy, its unrivalled success in building exports, and its heavy dependency on trade, Korea has failed to shake off its rather introverted reputation. In response, government ministries and agencies have made efforts to make relevant information available in English as well as Korean, and a wide variety of publications are available documenting the regulations and procedures for doing business. A thriving English-language press, including two newspapers and half a dozen magazines also help transparency in Korea. The official government statistics are impressive and there is also a wide network of Korean Overseas Trade offices in the main commercial and financial centres, which provide advice on doing business in Korea and details of business opportunities and potential partners (see Appendix on page 173).

However, much of this material is unavailable outside the country (or in the absence of contacts in the relevant bodies), and this book is designed to fill in the gaps as well as providing an overview of the Korean economy, outlining the various industrial sectors and the financial system, and providing enough reference material to allow the reader to pursue his own particular interests further.

The gap this book cannot fill, however, is the cultural and social chasm between Westerners and Koreans. This book does not propose any "secrets for success" on doing business with the Koreans, simply because there are none, although, broadly speaking, a good social relationship is probably more important to doing business in Korea than it is in the West, and meeting business contacts in person, rather than negotiating over the phone, is also essential.

The first chapter of this book provides an overview of Korean history and economic development. Since the reunification of Korea could transform the whole picture at a stroke, a brief review of the potential impact and cost of unification is included. It should also be mentioned here that this chapter, along with subsequent chapters, includes a number of charts and tables where the component data has been drawn from a variety of sources. These sources are cited in the endnotes appended to each chapter.

Chapter 2 aims to orientate the reader in terms of people and places. The geography and climate of Korea have been described and an overview of the physical and human resources of Korea is provided. Korea boasts an educated and hard-working labour force, but wage costs have risen as the country has industrialised.

The third chapter provides an overview of the transportation system in Korea. Infrastructure development has lagged behind economic growth, but the government has ambitious plans to increase infrastructure spending on a series of projects.

Korea remains one of the most trade-dependent countries in the world, due largely to its export-led growth strategy in the 1970s and 1980s. This is the subject of the fourth chapter, where the structure of Korea's imports and exports is detailed and new relationships that will shape the economy in the years up to the end of the century are outlined. Korea's successful transition from labour-intensive to capital-intensive production has been largely the work of the large conglomerates (*Chaebol*) and the changing role of these groups is described.

The financial system is also undergoing a rapid overhaul, but the shadow of years of government guidance and control in this sector remains. The fifth chapter discusses the financial system and outlines the process of deregulation which is vital to the success of the latest five-year plan. The role of the private and foreign banks in the newly liberalised climate is assessed.

Chapter 6 reviews the process of deregulation in the capital markets. The Korean Stock Exchange has been opened to foreign investment and the government plans to raise foreign stockholding limits in the near future and to introduce the trading of derivative products by 1996. Raising capital remains a key concern for many Korean companies, particularly among small- and medium-sized businesses, and liberalising this sector is crucial to the development of the economy as a whole.

Investment is the theme of the seventh chapter. Both inward and outward investment in Korea remain relatively low as a percentage of GNP compared to Korea's international competitors and the government needs to encourage investment in both directions: inward investment is needed to speed technology transfers and to reduce Korean dependence on imported technology; and outward investment is important because of rising domestic labour costs and the need to reduce structural trade imbalances.

The regulatory environment is detailed in Chapter 8 and has been contributed by the major law firm of Shin and Kim. The review of the tax and accounting environment, Chapter 9, has been contributed by Mr Yong Kyun Kim of Samil Accounting Corporation, a part of the international and consulting firm Coopers & Lybrand.

The full liberalisation of Korea's economy is widely held to be a precondition for it playing a wider role on the international stage. The tenth chapter attempts to describe how the winds of change are blowing for Korea in the international arena, as the "Pacific Century" draws near. Korea's bid to internationalise and play a more important role in the development of the regional and other multilateral institutions to which it is affiliated are discussed. The break-up of the Soviet Union and China's move towards a market economy have transformed relations with Moscow and Beijing and these changes could dramatically affect Korea's relations with communist North Korea.

Chapter 10 also discusses the potential effects of these changes on Korea's competitiveness in the years ahead. Economic maturity is just around the corner, but Korea is being squeezed from both top and bottom: from the advanced industrial countries eager to keep their market share in technologically-sophisticated sectors and from newly developing nations which can offer more competitive labour costs.

[1] "Cartoon Capers", magazine article by Peter Crosby.

Chapter One

Historical and economic overview

Korea has emerged painfully from the period of isolation which earned it the name of "The Hermit Kingdom". Since the doors of the country were prised open in the mid-1870s, it has suffered invasion and colonial rule by the Japanese, occupation by the United States and the former Soviet Union after World War II, and, in the early 1950s, a war that split the country between a communist north – which was backed by China and the Soviet Union until the 1980s – and a democratic south which, however, has been dominated by the military authorities.

For much of the period of rapid economic growth in the 30 years since the Korean War, the southern republic's politics were presided over by a trinity of strongmen, backed by the military: Syngnam Rhee (1948-1960), Park Chun-Hee (1963-1980) and Chun Doo-Hwan (1980-1987). The relative powers of the presidency and the national assembly have been a political issue since the creation of the Republic of Korea in 1948, and the country's economic growth took place in the context of an authoritarian presidential system. It was only in 1987, immediately before the country hosted the 1988 Summer Olympics in Seoul, that a modern democratic system can be said to have been genuinely implemented. The first truly civilian government for 36 years took power only in 1993, with the election of President Kim Young-Sam.

Historical introduction

Early history

Korea's history spans 43 centuries during which foreign influences, notably China, Russia and Japan, have been a recurrent theme. Koreans today are justifiably proud of the rich cultural heritage of their country over more than 4,000 years, and although it has been their modern history which has most directly shaped the institutions, attitudes and social norms of the Korean people, much is still owed to the past.

The original inhabitants of Korea arrived in approximately 3,000 BC and appear to have been allied to Tungusic tribes from Manchuria and Siberia. By the eighth century BC, bronzeware had developed and a movement towards forming tribal states was underway, and this pattern continued during the fourth century, as domestic animal husbandry and farming became established.

By the early years of the first millennium, the three powerful tribal states of Koguryo, Paekche and Silla had formed, so this era is often referred to as the Three Kingdoms period: Koguryo is said to have been founded in 37 BC, although its first king (T'aejo) ruled from

AD 53-146. Koguryo held sway over a huge area between the Yalu river in the north, down to a line south of the port of Inch'on outside Seoul and across to the Taebaek mountains in the east.

Paekche was mythically founded in 18 BC, and its first king, Koi, ruled between AD 234-286. The Paekche ruled over the south-west half of modern-day South Korea.

Silla was ostensibly founded in 57 BC, with King Naemul ruling it between AD 356-402. The kingdom was in the southeast of South Korea, around Kyongju, with the river Mektong forming part of its border.

The Three Kingdoms period was marked by greater centralisation of powers in the Koguryo, Paekche and Silla territories, and by the gradual emergence of Buddhism. Silla eventually overcame its rivals, conquering Paekche in AD 660 and then Koguryo in AD 668, with help from China. The Chinese were formally ousted in AD 676, but the new unified kingdom incorporated many aspects of Chinese culture including Chinese characters, laws and decrees, painting, and the religion of Confucianism. Buddhism also made a resurgence during this period, and an absolute monarchy developed under the Avatamsaka Buddhist system. Meanwhile, Confucianism became the religion of lower-grade aristocrats. The Hwabaek system, originally replaced by the absolute monarchy, was later restored when internal feuds within the Silla aristocracy weakened central authority.

As provincial aristocrats became more powerful, two of their leaders revived the Paekche and Koguryo kingdoms which, together with the Silla aristocrats, formed a unified kingdom in 935 – the Koryo kingdom. The country was administered by a Supreme Council, made up of the *Samsong* – the highest administrative body – and the *Chungch'uwon*, acting as the secretariat to the King.

The Koryo kingdom lasted until 1392, but was severely damaged by the Mongol invasion of 1231, which led to a peace treaty and big changes in landholdings. Buddhism, introduced from China, had been the dominant religion in the Three Kingdoms and Koryo periods.

The Yi Dynasty

The Yi Dynasty ruled Korea from 1392 until the Japanese annexation of 1910 and had its capital in Hanyang, or Seoul as it is now known. In this period, Confucianism became the dominant state religion. This period also saw the invention of moveable type printing in 1234 and of the Hangul script by King Sejong the Great. Attempts by Japan to invade Korea in 1592 and 1597 under Toyotomi Hideyoshi were thwarted, the former by the heroic Admiral Yi Sun-Shin, whose victories are still celebrated today, and are commemorated by several national monuments. Apart from incursions by the nomadic Manchu, who took Seoul in 1637, the seventeenth century was a period of economic expansion with great developments in agriculture, including the introduction of rice, tobacco and ginseng cultivation.

The mid-1600s also saw the first incursions by the European powers: the first western eye-witness account of Korea was written by Hendrik Hamel, captain of a Dutch merchant ship which grounded off the southerly island of Cheju in 1656. Meanwhile, Catholic missionaries and priests began to enter Korea, despite a lukewarm reception. Catholicism was suppressed periodically in the nineteenth century and the formation of the Tonghak religion around 1860 by Ch'oe Che-U was intended to stop the spread of western religions. The regent Taewon-Gun followed this up by declaring a policy of national isolation in 1864, and resisted all attempts by foreigners to establish links with the country. This self-imposed isolation was ended by the Kanghwa treaty of 1876 which ushered in the modern period and prepared the ground for Korea's occupation by the Japanese colonial powers.

Japanese rule

The Japanese ruled Korea from 1910 until their defeat in World War II. This recent colonial experience, followed by the bitterly opposed trusteeship of the country under the World War II allies, has encouraged strong feelings of nationalism among Koreans and even today patriotic pride remains intense. The resentment generated by the Japanese occupation is understandable: under Japanese colonial rule Korea was reduced to little more than a source of cheap agricultural labour and supplies, and an investment target for surplus Japanese capital. During World War II, the relationship became even more one-sided with Koreans being conscripted into the Army and forced to work in Japanese mines and quarries in virtually slave conditions. The issue of compensation for the victims of the colonial era affects relations between the two countries to this day.

The Japanese set up government in Seoul, with the generals and admirals appointed to govern Korea being endorsed by the Japanese emperor. There was little attempt to integrate into Korean society; rather, the colonial governors tried to impose a reverse cultural assimilation into Japanese ways by obliterating all traces of Korean culture. Protest against Japanese rule was made illegal, the freedom of the press was limited by heavy censorship, and dissident voices banned; and the freedom to assembly and right of free speech were limited. Meanwhile Japanese became the official national language in schools, and the teaching of Korean language and history was banned.

Land and property were acquired by the colonial power by subterfuge, and sold cheaply to Japanese citizens, notably by the setting up of a land survey ordinance under which Korean land owners were mandated to report their land holdings. This amounted to theft through bureaucracy: Koreans who failed to report had their land and property confiscated, and land held jointly by a group of people was also confiscated because no single individual could lay claim to it.

This repression was to become worse in the years prior to World War II: Koreans were forced to worship at Shinto temples, even though the religion was alien to them; newspapers and magazines in Korean were banned, and academic societies furthering the study of Korean culture were closed down; and Koreans were forced to take Japanese names.

Rapid industrialisation in Japan after the Meiji restoration left the country short of agricultural supplies, and Korea was used increasingly to fill the gap as the nutritional requirements of the growing Japanese military increased in the 1930s. The rice produced by farmers who had been forced to turn their fields into paddies was exported while the Koreans subsisted on cereals imported from Manchuria.

Japan's transformation from a semi-feudal to a capitalist country in the early 1900s left entrepreneurs looking for markets for their surplus production, and Korea provided a convenient outlet for Japanese goods and investment. The Japanese also developed Korea's transport network and set up a new monetary and financial system based on the more advanced Japanese model, but the economic benefits were largely in one direction.

This harsh regime sparked widespread popular protests, often brutally suppressed by the Japanese. In one of the most notorious incidents, on 1 March 1919, nationwide rallies and demonstrations erupted following the death of the Korean emperor Kojong. Thousands of mourners flocked into Seoul, a declaration of independence was read, and the movement was supported by peaceful rallies in which more than two million people took part. The protests brought a brutal response from the Japanese, however, with 47,000 Koreans being arrested, of which more than 10,000 were indicted and killed. The police, army and navy units sent to put down the protests wounded a further 23,000 people.

A brief period of relaxation in the 1920s saw the establishment of two Korean newspapers *Dong-a Ilbo* and *Chosun-Ilbo* and the growth of the New Cadre group of intellectuals, but repression intensified once more with Japan's entry into World War II.

The post-war split

After World War II, Koreans were ideologically and politically split between the American and Soviet occupation forces. The political parties in the South aimed for immediate self-government which conflicted with the US desire to set up a four-way trusteeship between itself, the USSR, China and Britain, which would lead to eventual independence.

Many of those in the resistance movement against Japanese rule had escaped abroad to continue their struggle, and as early as 1919 a provisional government had been formed in Shanghai, led by Syngman Rhee. The liberation army fought alongside the Allies in China against the Japanese between 1942 and 1945, having moved its base to Chungking when Shanghai fell to the Japanese in the early days of the war. The defeat of the Japanese fuelled demands for Korean independence, but the status of Korea had been left in doubt by the Allied victors, and growing tension between the Anglo-American alliance and the Soviet Union emerged.

At the Yalta Conference of February 1945 President Franklin D Roosevelt proposed the idea of a four-way trusteeship of Korea, but no formal agreement was reached with the USSR. Independence for Korea "in due course" had been proposed earlier during the war, under the Cairo Declaration of December 1943, but the terms of the transition to self-rule were never defined. The USSR entered the war against Japan in August 1945, having agreed to support Korean independence under the Potsdam Conference a year earlier. However, when the war ended, the outlook remained unclear. The Moscow conference of December 1945 set up the four-power trusteeship envisaged at the Yalta conference and a United States-Soviet joint commission was established to settle the question of a unified Korea.

The joint commission met in Seoul between March and May 1946 and between May and August 1947, and the question of Korean unification was debated by the United Nations in September 1946, but no agreement was reached. The division of Korea into 'spheres of influence' had been foreshadowed by the terms set by the United States for the Japanese surrender (General Order No 1, August 11) which had provided that Japanese forces north of the 38th parallel would surrender to the Soviet troops, who had entered Korea in August from the north via Manchuria. Troops south of the 38th parallel were to surrender to the United States, who entered the country on September 8. The USSR had quickly sealed off the 38th parallel, establishing two separate zones in Korea.

Disputes over the process of transition to self-rule quickly emerged between the US and the USSR. The setting up of the trusteeship had sparked violent protests in the southern sector of Korea. The Soviets argued that Korean political groups that had opposed the trusteeship should be barred from the talks on Korean unification; the United Nations, backed by the US, took the line that elections should be held as soon as possible as a prelude to the elected government negotiating the withdrawal of foreign troops from Korea. The United Nations declaration set up a UN Temporary Commission to oversee the elections, but the USSR prevented the commission from entering northern Korea. As a result, elections were held in the South on 10 May 1948 and the National Assembly was convened on 31 May. The Republic of Korea was declared on 15 August 1948, following the election of Syngman Rhee as President on July 20.

Meanwhile, the USSR proceeded with its own plans to set up a rival government in the north. A North Korean constitution was adopted in April 1948, and elections to the Supreme People's Assembly were held on August 25. The Assembly ratified the constitution on September 3 in Pyongyang, and the communist state of the Democratic People's Republic of Korea was declared in the north of the country, following the appointment of Kim Il-Sung as premier.

The UN General Assembly declared that the Republic of Korea was the only lawful government in the peninsula on 12 December 1948, after the USSR had recognised the Democratic People's Republic as the only lawful government on 12 October. The two World War II allies were on a collision course, and the fragile peace between the North and South was shattered in 1950.

The Korean war

On 25 June 1950, North Korea launched an attack on the South, triggering a war which raged until 1953. The war left almost four million dead, including soldiers and civilians, with about two-thirds of the casualties suffered by the communists. As wars go, little was achieved, but, arguably, much was avoided. The battle-lines remain drawn along the 38th parallel to the present day, reflecting almost exactly the pre-war spheres of influence.

The war divides neatly into four stages: the South lost almost the whole of the peninsula in the initial onslaught by the North Korean troops; the counterattack took the US-led coalition force of 16 nations to Pyongyang; a threat to continue the war into China led to Beijing's involvement, and the Southern forces were pushed back to south of Seoul; the sphere of fighting then narrowed, with the UN forces regaining the 38th parallel by March 1951, after which the war reached gridlock.

The initial North Korean successes were unsurprising. When the war broke out, the 100,000 South Korean forces were heavily outnumbered by the Northern troops, who also had tanks, unlike the badly-equipped Southern force. The US occupation forces had left Korea by June 1949, and although large-scale military aid had been approved by President Truman on the grounds that Korea had become a testing ground in the conflict between communism and democracy, the military equipment committed was still on its way when war broke out. The Soviet army, on the other hand had concluded a military aid agreement for heavy equipment before leaving the area and had also extended military training to thousands of Koreans. Meanwhile, China had transferred its own soldiers to the North Korean army in the two years before the war.

Seoul fell on 28 June, and the North Korean troops continued their advance. The United States reacted swiftly: the day after the invasion the UN passed a resolution condemning Pyongyang's aggression and the next day Truman gave the order for US forces to resist the communist aggression in Korea, and the UN approved the creation of a unified command in Korea. UN forces reached the peninsula from Japan on 4 July, under the leadership of General Douglas MacArthur.

North Korea came very close to taking over the whole peninsula. The US-led forces retreated until the only area they controlled was a small corner of Korea around the south-eastern city of Pusan, but the counterattack on 15 September was swift and successful. The Southern forces launched an amphibious attack on the North's flank at Inch'on harbour, west of Seoul and by the beginning of October the UN forces were back at the 38th parallel.

China had deployed forces along the Yalu River after the US counterattack on Inch'on. At the end of September 1950, Truman approved the advance of the US forces into North Korea, and the action was supported by the United Nations in early October. The US forces entered the North Korean capital of Pyongyang, reaching the Yalu River on 26 October. The US decision to carry their attack into North Korea, however, sparked a massive deployment of Chinese troops into its communist neighbour. The UN forces were forced to retreat, Seoul was evacuated in January 1951, and later that month the Chinese troops reached an area about 30 miles south of the Southern capital. However, the UN forces again counterattacked, and regained the 38th parallel by the end of March 1951.

For the next year and a half the frontline barely changed. General MacArthur was relieved of his command following his advocacy of extending the war into China, and the war degenerated into a long struggle over the 38th parallel, with an armistice being signed on 27 July 1953. Under the uneasy truce, a demilitarised zone was set up along the 38th parallel stretching 240 kilometres from the mouth of the Han River in the west, to just south of the town of Kosong on the east coast. The eerie "Peace Village" of Panmunjon lies along this border and remains the venue for inter-Korean talks.

Post-war political development

The Republic of Korea has been under the authoritarian rule of a series of military-backed presidents virtually since its inception in 1948. However, significant steps towards full democracy have been taken since 1987. There have been no less than six republics since independence, and nine changes in the constitution were made in the years between 1948 and 1987.

The first republic of 1948 saw the election of Syngman Rhee, who ruled Korea with an iron fist for 12 years until his authoritarian regime was undermined by student riots which brought the nation close to civil war. Rhee's long-standing quarrel with the National Assembly, which centred on the balance between the power of the president and that of the Assembly, was to become a recurrent problem in the years ahead. Rhee was re-elected president in August 1952, and in 1954 he passed a constitutional amendment making him president for life. He ran for a third term of office in May 1956 and then again in March 1960, but these elections were preceded by violence and Rhee was forced to resign and seek exile in Hawaii.

Under the second republic the presidential system was replaced by a parliamentary system, and power shifted to Prime Minister Chang Myon. Factional struggles weakened the government, however, and the military seized power nine months later, placing Korea under martial law and dissolving the National Assembly. During the ensuing period of confusion a referendum was held which approved the establishment of a weak National Assembly within a strong presidential system, and in late-1963, the leader of the military-backed Supreme Council for National Reconciliation, Major-General Park Chun-Hee, ran for president as head of the Democratic Republican Party successfully. Park was elected to a second term in May 1967 with his party winning a large majority in the National Assembly.

Under the fourth republic, Park moved to consolidate his term of power, arousing widespread opposition led by the current president, Kim Young-Sam. The existing constitution limited the president to two consecutive terms of office, but an amendment was proposed allowing a third term, and this was approved by a national referendum in October 1969. Park defeated the opposition leader Kim Dae-Jung in elections held on 27 April 1971, although Kim's New Democratic Party made gains in the National Assembly.

Park, however, was intent on holding onto power at all costs: he declared a state of national emergency in December 1971 and suspended the constitution in October 1972, promulgating a new constitution which allowed the president an unlimited number of six-year terms. He was elected again – without opposition – in December 1972 and December 1978. By this time his autocratic and undemocratic rule had raised widespread opposition, not only among his political enemies, but even within his own circle of ministers and advisors, and he was assassinated in October 1979 by his own intelligence chief.

Military rule was tightened following Park's assassination and in May 1980 the military extended martial law, and banned all political activity. Under these unpromising circumstances, Chun Doo-Hwan was appointed president in August 1980, promising free elections and a new constitution. The new constitution was approved on October 1980, with the presidential term extended to seven years, but with only one term allowed. Meanwhile, the powers of the president were reduced and those of the National Assembly strengthened. Martial law was lifted in January 1981 and Chun was elected with an overwhelming majority in February of the same year. During this period, the political climate grew more relaxed but popular dissatisfaction gained momentum, forcing the government to draw up a new constitution in 1987.

Under the sixth republic, the presidential term was reduced to five years and the president was elected by direct popular vote. The new constitution was approved by referendum in October, and Roh Tae-Woo was elected in December, taking office in February 1988, ahead of the Summer Olympic Games in Seoul.

The political system

The Republic of Korea, officially known as Tae-han in Korean, has nominally been a democracy since it was first created on 31 May 1948, but the Korean war and the military-led and military-backed regimes that followed during 1950-1988 centralised power in the president, who often acted in the name of democracy more in word than in deed. The activities of opposition parties were often severely limited, and human rights abuses common: "The constitutional forms and trappings of democracy had, in fact, often served as a meagre cloak for rule by the few who were able to draw power into their own hands."[1]

The election of President Kim Young-Sam in February 1993 marked a sea-change in the political realities in Korea. Kim had been a distinguished reformer in the years of the Park regime, suffering house arrest and hunger strikes in his fight for a truly democratic system. Kim's election marked him out as the first genuinely civilian president since 1956, following a fierce tussle between his own Democratic Liberal party, and the two key opposition parties; the Democratic Party of Kim Dae Jung, and the United People's Party, founded by the chairman of the Hyundai *Chaebol*, Chung Ju-Yung.

Since his election, Kim has acted rapidly to consolidate his power base, firing generals too close to the former regime, curbing the intelligence apparatus, forcing allegedly corrupt politicians out of office, and reprimanding many other political heavyweights. Kim's reputation for clean play has enhanced his public image, and he has appealed to public sentiment by distancing himself from the corrupt politics that characterised previous governments. In the early days of his government, he swore not to play golf for his entire five-year term in office, as a symbolic gesture in a country where land is in short supply and only the rich can afford to play. His habit of eating noodles, rather than expensive foreign foods has also added to his popularity. He has also proved a tough politician: in a bold bid to stem endemic corruption in the political system, he forced his fellow National Assembly members to reveal their assets, and over 1,000 officials have been charged with misdeeds. Kim has also launched a full-scale attack on corruption in the financial and commercial sectors by implementing the real name financial system. The popularity of the Kim government suffered a blow after it was forced to open the Korean rice market at the end of 1993 in order to achieve a successful conclusion of the Uruguay Round of the General Agreement on Tariffs and Trade (GATT), but this was also deftly handled, with the resignation of various cabinet members allowing the president to distance himself from the political fall out.

Kim's biggest test, however, remains in the economic sphere. He has promised to eliminate hundreds of regulations and to open up the economy to foreign investment, but his reforms have yet to show really significant results.

Political structure

Legislative power in Korea is vested in the unicameral National Assembly. Two-thirds of its 276 members are elected by popular vote with the remaining seats being allocated on a proportional basis to parties winning five seats or more in the elections. Members are elected for a four-year term, and the total number of Assembly members must be over 200. The National Assembly elects one speaker and two vice-speakers. The major activities of the National Assembly include its legislative functions, setting the national budget and ratifying treaties with foreign powers.

The presidency

The president heads the executive branch of the government and acts not only as head of state in domestic affairs, but also represents the state in foreign affairs. The president is elected by direct popular vote for a five-year term, and cannot be re-elected. Duties include safeguarding the country's independence and working for the peaceful reunification of the country. The president acts as head of the State Council – made up of between 15 and 30 members – through which he performs his executive functions. He also serves as commander-in-chief of the armed forces.

The State Council consists of the president, who chairs the council, the prime minister who acts as vice-chairman, two deputy prime ministers who double as heads of the Economic Planning Board and the National Unification Board, two ministers of state and 20 executive ministers. The prime minister acts as the principal executive assistant to the president and supervises the executive ministers on the State Council.

Several bodies act on behalf of the president and the State Council. These include the National Security Council, the Advisory Council on Democratic and Peaceful Unification, the National Economic Advisory Council, the Board of Audit and Inspection, and the Agency for National Security Planning.

The following ministries act on behalf of the president in their respective spheres:

- The Economic Planning Board (EPB): the Board acts as a kind of super-ministry and the EPB minister serves concurrently as deputy prime minister. The EPB is responsible for the development of economic policy, budget formulation, and overall coordination of the government's foreign and domestic economic plans.
- The National Unification Board (NUB): this is responsible for plans to bring about the reunification of the two Koreas, and also handles all forms of education and publicity related to this. The NUB minister has also acted as deputy prime minister since 1991, reflecting the increased importance attached by the government to planning for reunification following the collapse of the former Soviet Union.
- The Ministry of Foreign Affairs: the ministry handles foreign diplomacy, treaties and other agreements with foreign countries, and is also responsible for the protection of Korean nationals abroad.
- The Ministry of Home Affairs: has jurisdiction over local administration and elections and supervises internal security and the fire and police services.
- The Ministry of Finance: works with the EPB in the economic sphere, but its responsibilities are more specific. The Ministry of Finance handles all matters relating to the currency, national bonds, taxation and customs, and controls state-owned properties.
- The Ministry of Trade, Industry and Resources: this new ministry was established by the Kim government, which had promised to cut down the number of government ministries as part of its bid to trim state bureaucracy. It was formed by a merger of the former Ministry of Trade and Industry with the Ministry of Energy and Resources. The ministry handles commerce and foreign trade, patents and all aspects of industry.
- Several other ministries are empowered in specific areas, and these interact with other executive bodies in recommending and implementing state policy. These include the ministries of: Justice; National Defence; Education; Culture and Sports; Agriculture, Forestry and Fisheries; Construction; Health and Social Affairs; Labour; Transportation; Communications; Information; Government Administration; Science and Technology; Environment; Patriot's and Veteran's Affairs; and Legislation.

The judiciary

Judicial power is vested in the courts which are constitutionally independent. There are several types of court: the Supreme Court, district courts, family courts and appellate courts. Key members of the judiciary are appointed by the president following the model of the United States. The Supreme Court acts as the court of appeal on decisions made by the three appellate courts, which in turn hear appeals against verdicts handed down by the district courts in civil and criminal cases. The decisions of the Supreme Court are final and set judicial precedents.

The chief justice is appointed by the president for a six-year term, and the president's choice must be ratified by the National Assembly. The chief justice recommends the justices of the Supreme Court, and these are also appointed by the president. Judges at the lower courts are appointed by the chief justice, and his choices are ratified by the Conference of Supreme Court Justices.

District courts are established in major cities and deal with both civil and criminal cases. Matrimonial problems and juvenile cases are handled by the family court.

The constitution

The Constitution of the Republic of Korea was first adopted on 12 July 1948 based on the principal of liberal democracy. It provides for the independence of the three branches of government detailed above: the executive, the legislature and the judiciary.

The constitution guarantees a wide range of freedoms for the individual and establishes the basic principal that authority resides in the people, with state authority deriving solely from the people. Revisions in the constitution during more than 30 years of military rule, however, have seen this fundamental tenet honoured more often in the breach than the observance. Political and economic decision-making has largely rested in the hands of a strong president, and the National Assembly has often acted more as a rubber-stamp for the president than an independent policy-making organ.

Amendments to the constitution which heralded the birth of the sixth republic in October 1987, however, significantly reduced the powers of the president, stripping him of the power to introduce emergency measures and to dissolve the National Assembly.

Economic growth

Korea has been one of the star performers among the Asian Newly Industrialising Economies (NIEs), although growth rates have slowed in recent years. An outward-looking development strategy in which exports were pursued relentlessly, provided the engine for development, and although debt levels incurred in the course of Korea's leap into industrialisation were high, the government has always kept them within manageable limits.

GNP statistics provide a fair summary of the speed at which Korea is achieving its aim of advanced industrial status. In 1973, the country's GNP stood at just US$13.5 billion, by 1981 it had reached US$66.8 billion and by 1992 the size of the economy was just short of US$300 billion. Thus, the Hermit Kingdom has emerged as a major player on the international stage little more than a hundred years since it broke out of its self-imposed isolation: GNP in 1992 far exceeded that of the Asian dragons such as Taiwan, Hong Kong and Singapore, putting the country roughly on a par with medium-sized European economies such as Sweden, Switzerland and the Netherlands. However, the economy remains only about a twelfth of the size of that of Japan, on which Korea remains dependent for many technological imports.

The Korean growth record is even more impressive when compared with growth of GNP in the United States: in 1973, the Korean economy was just a hundredth of the size of that of the United States; in 1992, it had reached one-twentieth the size. Per capita GNP, however, remains low relative to first world countries: in 1990, it stood at US$5,659, ten times the 1974 level, but well short of that of Japan (US$29,794) and the other Asian tigers: Taiwan (US$10,140), Hong Kong (US$16,507) and Singapore (US$16,582).

What the economic growth figures do reflect is a country industrialising at a pace that has rarely been seen in either Latin America or Asia.

After a period of double-digit annual GNP growth in the late 1980s, growth slumped to about 4.5 per cent in 1992 and the government has had to revise down its 1993 growth estimate of 5.7 per cent. This slowdown was due to poor domestic demand and low capital investment, but by late 1993 the domestic economy was showing new signs of life: the beginnings of economic recovery in the United States combined with the strength of the Japanese yen in 1993 have helped to make Korean exports more competitive and have

Exhibit 1.1
Export and import price indices, 1982-1992 (1990=100)

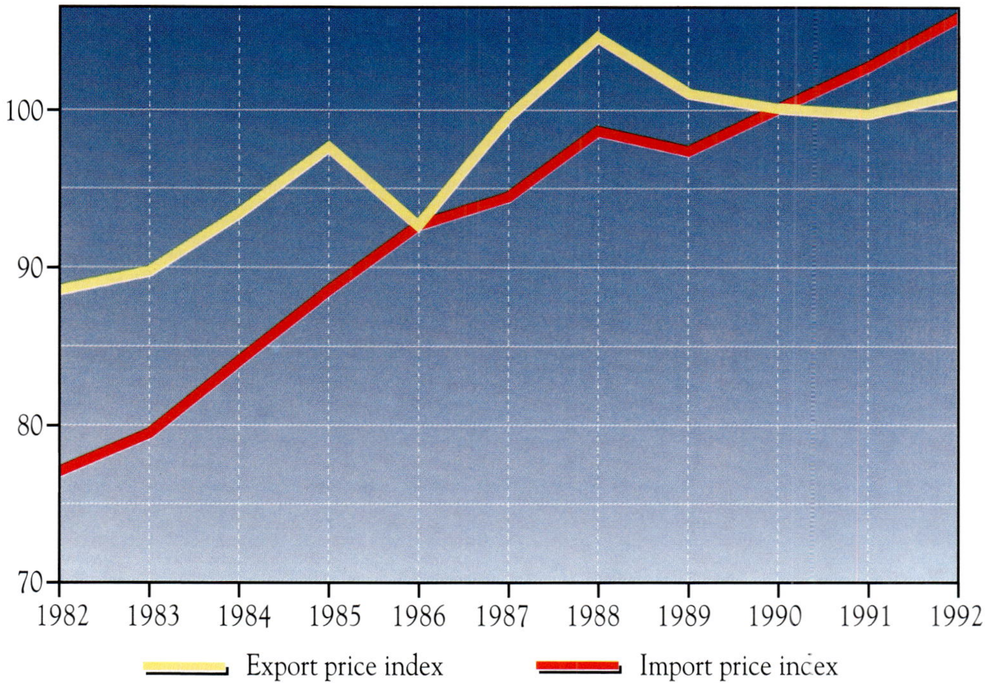

Exhibit 1.2
Current GNP, 1971-1992 (US$ billions)

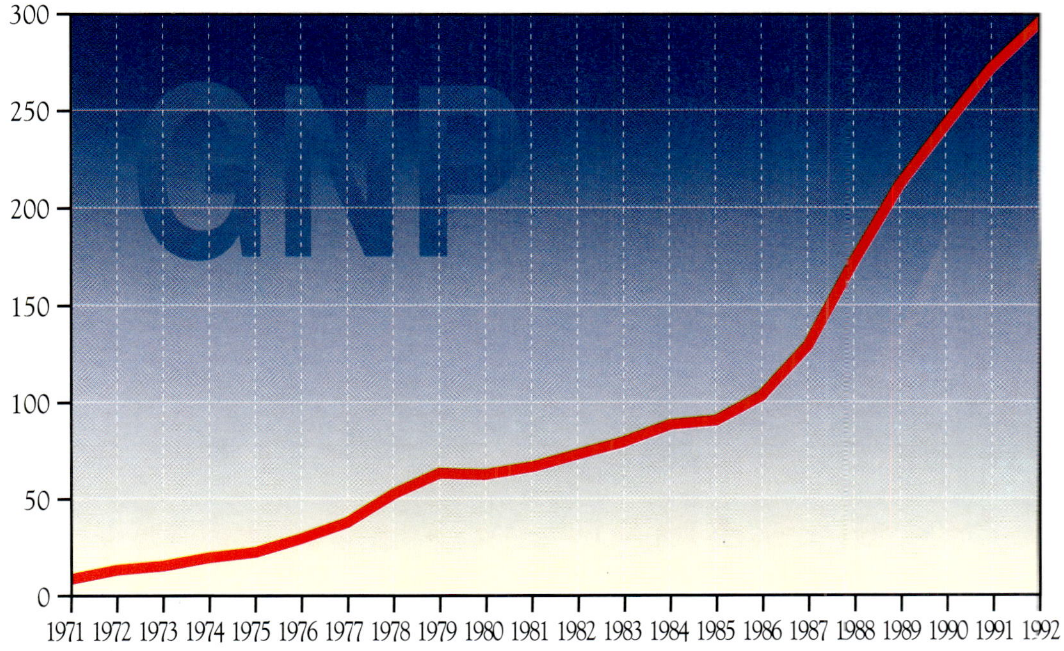

improved trade prospects. Even so, GNP growth for 1993 is unlikely to be much above 4.5 per cent, far short of the initial target.

Foreign trade remains central to Korea's success: trade accounts for 70-80 per cent of GNP, making the country vulnerable to external shocks such as trade friction and increases in commodity prices. Exports have surged from just US$4.46 billion in 1974 to US$76.6 billion in 1992, although imports grew commensurately – Korea's exports, particularly at the high value end, remain dependent on imported parts and components and licensed technology. Imports rose from just US$6.8 billion in 1974 to US$81.7 billion in 1992, leaving Korea with a trade deficit of more than US$5 billion for that year. Indeed, Korea's export success story has often obscured the fact that its economy is structurally skewed towards deficit, due to its low level of natural resources and, in particular, its high dependence on energy imports: apart from the boom years between 1986-1989, Korea has run trade deficits (which have reached up to US$6.9 billion) in most years since 1974.

The recurrent deficits are also partly due to the country's dependence on imports from Japan. The strength of the yen has often been cited as a key benefit for Korean exports in 1993, but in fact it is a mixed blessing for the country: although Japan remains Korea's major competitor in Asia, it is also the source of many intermediate imports, including parts and components, which become more expensive as the Japanese yen appreciates. As a result, the impact of the strong yen in 1993 on Korea's trade balance has been limited. Lower energy costs – because of the slump in world oil prices – have probably had a greater impact on trade figures, due to Korea's almost total dependence on imported energy: as a result, Korea was expected to register a small trade surplus of US$100-200 million in 1993.

Korea's currency, the won, could play a big part in the balance of trade pattern in the coming years, as the government moves towards full liberalisation of the foreign exchange market by 1996. Cost has always been a key factor in the success of Korean exports: exchange rate controls throughout the 1970s and 1980s, however, led to limited exchange rate risk for exporters and importers. The won was fixed at a rate of 484 to the dollar between 1974 and 1979, but by 1990 it had drifted down to around 716 to the dollar. In 1994, the won is expected to fluctuate between 791-810 per dollar[2], and significant weakness is likely to be counteracted by the inflow of funds into the Korean stock market in 1994, when limits on stock holding by foreigners are expected to be lifted.

The vulnerability of exports to cost increases means that the government will also seek to control wage increases, which were running at 9-10 per cent in early 1993. With unemployment rising from around 2.5 per cent in 1992 to 3 per cent in the first half of 1993, however, cost-push inflation is unlikely to become a major issue. A new industrial relations agreement in 1991 has also reduced the risk of significant disruption from labour disputes, although these continue in certain sectors.

Demand-pull inflation, however, remains a threat for Korea in the mid-1990s as better living standards feed the domestic demand for goods. Inflation had been a major problem in the mid-1970s, when the consumer price index (CPI) increased consistently at double digit rates (rising over 28 per cent in 1980 alone). Inflation rates have declined substantially since then, due to the government's efforts to cool the economy in the late-1980s, and to the issuing of Monetary Stabilisation Bonds (MSBs) to soak up liquidity in the financial system. The M2 money supply was expanding at the targeted rate of 18 per cent in 1993, but the aim of a 5 per cent rise in the CPI looked doubtful due to the implementation of the "real name" financial system, which compelled the government to loosen monetary policy. A poorly performing property market will continue to offset inflation rises, but despite this, consumer price inflation is expected to run at 6-7 per cent in 1994[3] and high capacity utilisation levels look set to allow little room for improvement in the short term.

Effects of recent economic policy

President Kim Young-Sam has moved quickly to stimulate and restructure the economy since February 1993. The speed with which the new government addressed its task astonished many observers, who had expected a much greater degree of continuity with the outgoing Roh regime.

In March 1993, Kim unveiled a 100-day plan to boost the economy and in July the new five-year plan was released. The main aims of the plan are to decentralise the decision making process at every level of the economy, and to give the private sector a far freer rein, moving away from the government-led development strategy of the previous 30 years: "the cornerstone of the economy lies in increasing productivity based on voluntary participation and private sector initiative."[4] The means of achieving a leaner government and a more competitive private sector are threefold: fiscal reform to make spending allocations more flexible, and to change the priorities of public investment; financial reform to boost the efficiency of the financial sector by promoting more competition; and administrative reorganisation aimed at reducing government intervention in local decision making, by delegating more to local government and lower-level organisations.

The government has been planning to deregulate the financial system since the early 1980s and the Kim administration looks set to speed up the pace of these reforms. So far, progress has been made in the freeing of interest rates on deposits, lending, and many financial instruments; the foreign exchange market is in the process of being deregulated with a view to freeing controls by 1996 when Korea aims to enter the OECD; and competition has been encouraged in the banking and financial sectors (see Chapters 5 and 6). The stock market has been opened to foreign investment up to a limit of 10 per cent of total capitalisation (discussed in Chapter 7) and moves are underway to internationalise the commercial sector by lowering barriers to imports and foreign investment.

In conjunction with the economic plans a clampdown on corruption was initiated. This has received widespread popular support and has been an essential ingredient in implementing the structural economic reforms. Within six months of the new government taking power, more than 1,000 officials had been arrested in a headline-grabbing purge that took many business leaders by surprise and left the public shocked and dismayed by the scale of corruption.

The real name system

Kim's most dramatic move so far has been in implementing the so-called real name financial system. Billed as "President Kim's Biggest Gamble" by the weekly *Business Korea* magazine, setting up a real name system had been on the government agenda for 12 years, but strong resistance from vested interests had previously prevented the plan from being implemented. Essentially, the system is another measure to fight corruption; all financial transactions involving false names have been banned and all those holding financial assets were required to register their real names by 12 October 1993. Real names must now be verified for all financial dealings, including those in stocks, bonds, certificates of deposit (CDs), and cheques, and the holding of anonymous accounts with banks has also been made illegal.

These were substantive changes. Previously, investors had been able to deposit money in anonymous or false name accounts, and were thus able to hide huge sums of money derived from illegal speculation in stocks and real estate. Politicians were no longer able to hide illegal contributions from big business and account holders were forced to reveal their assets for tax purposes.

Kim's boldness in getting rid of this system is all the more remarkable when one considers the size of the unofficial market. Estimates of the total money that had been tied up in false name accounts vary widely – but press reports suggest that between US$15-40 billion, accounting for 5-10 per cent of the entire deposit base, was withheld from the tax system as a result. The American business magazine *International Business Week* put holdings by anonymous investors at around 30 per cent of the total value of the stock market.

Low government-set savings rates had encouraged the development of this unofficial market, which became important as a funding source for small- and medium-sized businesses, including the many small firms supplying the big conglomerates or *Chaebol*. The smaller companies, lacking the clout of the *Chaebol*, have struggled to gain access to bank funding and have never enjoyed the influence which allowed the conglomerates to take advantage of subsidised credit from the government. As a result, the introduction of the new system aroused widespread trepidation. Of particular concern was the negative effect on Korea's GNP, although this has been partially offset by other factors such as an increase in export orders because of the strong yen.

The old adage that "nothing is ever as bad as you fear, and nothing ever as good as you hope", has been particularly apt in the case of the real name system. The immediate result of the introduction of the system was a 4.75 per cent drop in the Korean stock

Exhibit 1.3

Percentage growth in GNP, 1971-1992 (1985 prices)

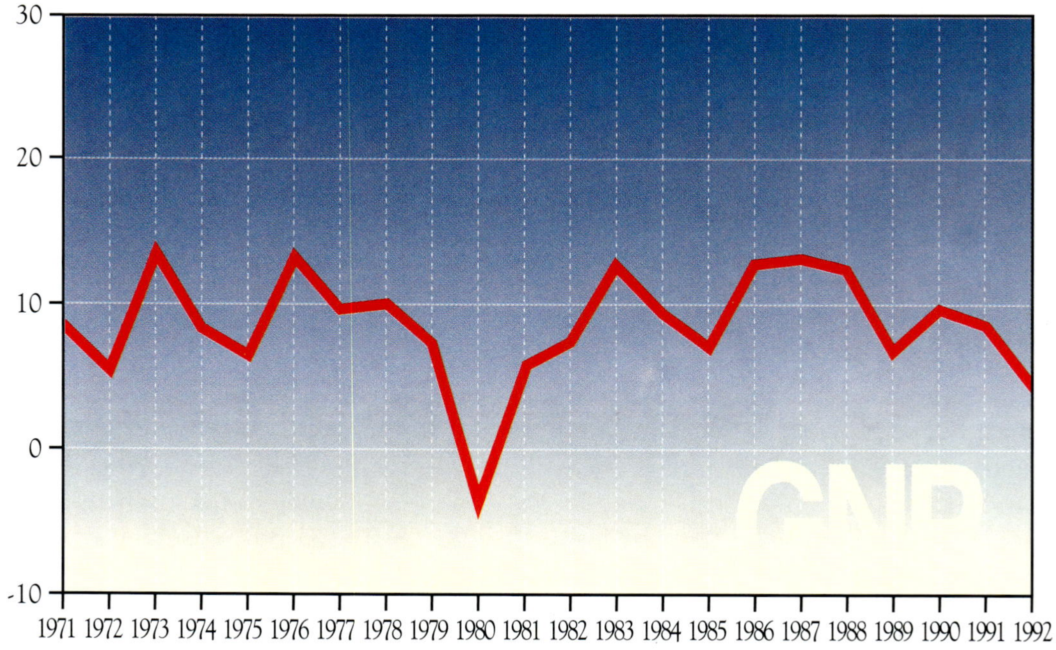

Exhibit 1.4

Money supply, 1982-1992 (end of period)

	M1	*M2*	*M3*
1982	5799.3	19904.2	31257.1
1983	6783.4	22938.1	38032.2
1984	6820.7	24705.6	45725.7
1985	7557.8	28565.2	55450.0
1986	8808.9	33833.1	-71594.2
1987	10107.3	40279.5	93637.7
1988	12151.4	48938.8	120358.6
1989	14329.0	58638.0	153831.2
1990	15905.3	68707.5	197847.0
1991	21752.4	83745.9	243955.9
1992	24596.3	96258.6	294843.7

exchange's key KOSPI index, the biggest ever loss in a single day, with bond trading, already at a low ebb, virtually grinding to a halt. It later became clear, however, that there was a net increase in the amount of money flowing into equities. Moreover, the massive number of corporate bankruptcies among the small- and medium-sized companies predicted by the Korean Federation of Small Businesses[5], never materialised – partly because the government pledged up to US$1 billion in loans and assistance to this sector.

Exhibit 1.5

Producer and consumer price indices, 1982-1992 (1990=100)

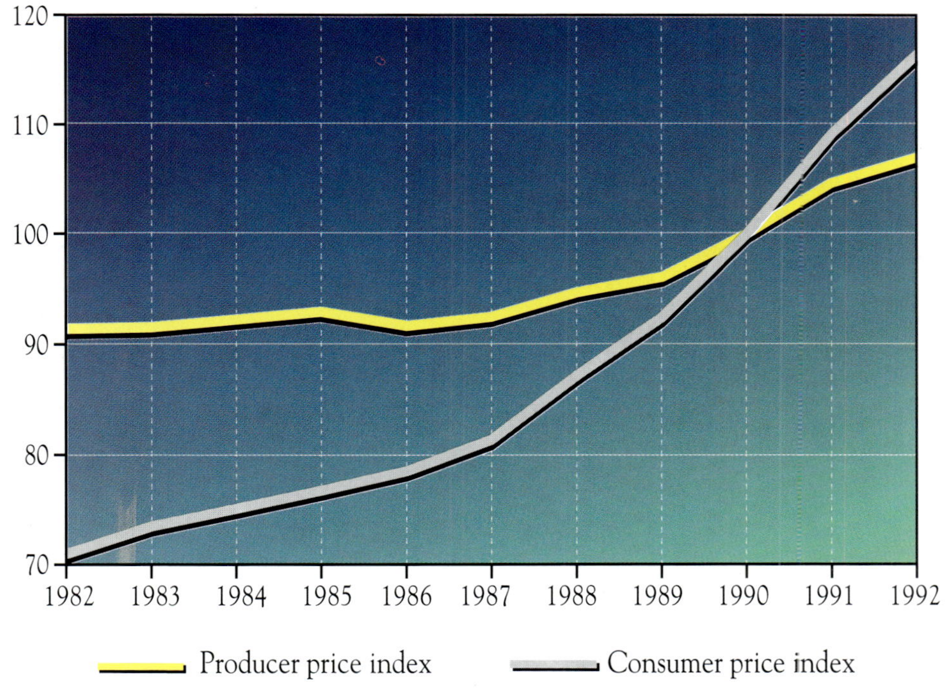

The longer-term benefits of the real name system have yet to filter through. Kim had described it as the "core and essence" of his reforms, and had argued that without it, no major restructuring of the economy would be possible. This could have been mere rhetoric to ease the passage of a measure that was less than popular in some quarters, but it is undeniable that the scale of corruption in Korea had become a serious structural problem, and that the relationship between big business and the government was increasingly anachronistic as Korea prepared to liberalise its economy in the 1990s.

During the rapid expansion of the last three decades, companies had looked primarily to expand their market share, and this was often achieved at the expense of the bottom line. The urge to expand at all costs was based, not on financial or commercial criteria, but on the knowledge that the government would give preferential treatment to those companies which met and then expanded their already ambitious export targets.

The pressure to clinch contracts without any reference to profitability was a reflection of the close links between the conglomerates and the government. Although the closed circle of mutual favours allowed the government to meet macroeconomic targets, it has been to the long-term detriment of an efficient commercial sector. The economic weekly *Far East Economic Review* estimated that, prior to Kim's accession, kickbacks had been running at 6-10 per cent of the value of contracts, a huge drain on corporate profitability. In this sense, Kim's contention that the real name system was "the reform of reforms" is accurate. The two-tier interest rate structure that emerged as a result of the previous system weakened the deposit base of financial institutions, and prevented government officials from effectively pursuing monetary policy. Inefficiency breeds inefficiency: the banks were reluctant to provide funding to small businesses, partly because of the risk and the sketchy credit profile of many ventures, but also because they knew that the government-backed *Chaebol* were a safer option since they were too big for the government to allow to fail. Thus, previous governments, together with the banks, had paid lip-service to the requirements of small firms, without setting up the structures to actually help them develop.

The result has been a highly asymmetric economic structure, characterised by a sprawling and powerful government sector, an inefficient financial sector, and a commercial sector skewed towards large business groups focused on growth rather than profit.

It is still unclear whether Kim's reforms will rectify these deep structural faults. Plans to tame the *Chaebol* have been shelved in the face of a slow down in business and a lack of investment in the early months of Kim's government; and the promotion of the small- and medium-sized business sector has long been an area that has attracted rhetoric rather than action. However, the bold moves taken so far have set up a positive framework for further action and the ministries will be expected to play a key role in the continued success of the Korean reforms.

Korean unification

Koreans have yearned for the reunification of their peninsula ever since the Cold War split between the North and South – a split which divided the peninsula not only ideologically, but which also tore apart thousands of families, and resulted in big differences in economic development between the Stalinist North and the democratic South.

The gap between the two countries is huge in economic terms. North Korean Gross National Product (GNP) in 1991 stood at just US$22.9 billion, less than a tenth of the size of the South; and per capita GNP was barely US$1,000, compared to US$5,618 in the South during the same year, according to South Korean government statistics. In this context, military expenditure remains a relatively heavy burden in the North, representing nearly one quarter of the country's GNP compared to just 3.8 per cent in the South.

The economic backwardness of the North is attributable mainly to its closed economy, reflected in the foreign trade statistics of the two nations. The South's foreign trade stood at just over US$153 billion in 1991, when exports reached US$71.8 billion; in the North, foreign trade languished at just US$2.7 billion, and exports were only a little over US$1 billion in the same year, according to South Korean data. Moreover, foreign trade in the North has been declining in recent years, dropping from US$5.24 billion in 1988, with exports declining commensurately, as the country lost influence with its ideological neighbours in China and the former Soviet Union.

The Stalinist political system in North Korea has suffocated any potential economic gains from its ample natural resources, and from the fact that it is less populous and has a wider land area than the South, with a population of just over 22 million in 1991 occupying 122,800 square kilometres, whereas the South had a population of nearly double that in an area of 99,300 square kilometres.

Infrastructure development in the North lags behind the South in almost all areas. Although the railway system is relatively well-developed, South Korea has more than double the length of roads than the North, and leads its Communist neighbour by factors of 10 and above in areas such as the number of aircraft, harbour capacity, and telephones.

These imbalances in development have made many South Korean planners fear the economic consequences of unification, even if emotionally the concept of a reunified peninsula strikes a chord in the heart of many citizens of the Republic. The example of Germany has contributed to the South's wariness, and many in the government now ask: "How much will it cost?" rather than just: "When will it happen?".

The bottom-line is extremely difficult to quantify because of gaps in knowledge about the development of the North, and also because the social cost of unification could well exceed the cost of developing the North's infrastructure to something on a par with the South.

As a result, the potential costs of reunification remain probably the single biggest unknown for the South, although some studies in this field have been hazarded, notably by the United Kingdom's Economist Intelligence Unit (EIU) and by bodies in South Korea such as the Korea Development Institute (KDI). Even so, these costs cannot be incorporated in the country's five-year plans, and as such, all the South Korean government projections could be thrown into disarray, if the Iron Curtain with the North was drawn back.

However, in early 1994, North Korea was reported to be making plans to reform its economy, based on the Chinese model of a gradual opening in which market forces would be allowed freer play. If this emerged, and given the South's misgivings about sudden reunification because of the huge costs involved, the likelihood is that North and South will deepen the existing tentative economic ties only gradually, and will slowly develop federal structures in the years ahead.

[1] *Korea Annual 1993*: Yonhap News Agency.

[2] Forecast by MMS International.

[3] Forecast by MMS International.

[4] *The Beginning of Korea's New Economy: the Kim Administration's 100 day Plan*: Korea Institute for International Economic Policy, May 1993.

[5] Lee Byung-Kyun, vice-chairman of Korean Federation of Small Business, quoted by international news agencies.

Chapter Two

Human and physical resources

Population and the labour force

Korea had a population of 44.0 million in 1993, a rise of over six million since the 1980 census. Two important demographic trends are clearly discernable:

- The population is slowly ageing, with life expectancy now reaching 70 years on average; and
- There is an increasing concentration of the population in the urban centres, despite active government campaigns to encourage people to settle in the less densely populated areas.

The problem of an ageing population is one which Korea has in common with several other East Asian (and many Western) countries, such as Japan, although this trend is more pronounced there due to the longer life expectancy of 79 years. Lower fertility rates and enhanced health care have helped to create a healthier and more long-lived population but will also lead to burgeoning medical, pension and welfare costs.

In 1993, 70.3 per cent of the population was in the 15-64 age bracket, with 5.4 per cent aged 65 and over (compared to 3.8 per cent in 1980). As a result, the average age of the population had risen to 29.5 years in 1990, compared to 26.1 in 1980. The Index of Ageing – a measure of the rate at which the population is ageing – issued by the National Statistical Office has risen from just 7.0 in 1965 to 21.1 in 1992, and the dependency ratio for the aged rose to 7.5 per cent compared to 5.8 per cent in 1965. Concurrently, the youth dependency ratio declined from 82.5 per cent in 1965 to just 35.5 per cent in 1992.[1] Demographic trends suggest that the proportion of the population aged over 65 will pass the three million mark by the year 2000, and that by 2020 this figure will have doubled, representing 13 per cent of the population.

This population is increasingly urban, which has helped to make the Korean capital one of the most populous cities in the world, with over 10 million people crammed into the Seoul metropolitan area. With almost a quarter of the country's population living in the capital, Seoul had a population density of 17,532 per square kilometre in 1990, but there is evidence that more people are now leaving Seoul than are moving in.[2] However, the spill-over from Seoul seems largely to have been absorbed in the nearby cities of Inch'on and Taejon. About three-quarters of the whole population now live in cities, mainly in the large centres of Pusan, Taegu, Inch'on, Kwangju and Taejon.

The concentration of population in Korea's six major cities has a huge social cost, and the physical demands put on the capital's inadequate infrastructure mean massive spending on SOC (social overhead capital) projects will be needed in the years ahead. With the population projected to reach 46.7 million by the end of the century and birth rates still outstripping death rates (although the gap is narrowing rapidly) the government would seem to have only two alternatives to reduce the chronic overcrowding in and around Seoul.

The first would be to continue providing incentives for people to move out of the capital: Korea's developed regions are centred around the northwest to southeast axis linking Seoul to Pusan, and the southwest and northeastern provinces are relatively underdeveloped. However, inadequate infrastructure in these regions will necessitate major building projects if the strategy is to succeed.

A second opportunity might result from the unification of the peninsula, as North Korea is less densely populated than the south, having less than half its population and a slightly larger land area. However, if the experience of East Germany is anything to go by, heavy migration from the impoverished north is more likely. Massive infrastructural improvements would also be needed if the south were to absorb this additional demand on its resources.

Culture and education

Korean culture is very homogeneous, which contributes to a high degree of literacy in the country. All Koreans speak the same language, which belongs to the Urals-Altaic group of central Asia. It shares characteristics with Finnish, Hungarian, Turkish, Mongolian, Japanese and Tibetan. Although there are different dialects, these are mutually intelligible, and the standard Korean is that spoken around Seoul.

The Korean script, or Hangul, was invented in the fifteenth century by King Sejong and a group of scholars under his partonage. The Hangul characters are extremely simple to learn. Korean newspapers also use Chinese characters, and indeed these were the only means of writing before the invention of Hangul.

Education is prized in Korea and, "Korea's greatest comparative advantage is in having a population educated at levels similar to those in the developed world, despite wage rates comparable to Newly Industrialised Countries."[3] At the end of the 1980s, expenditure for education as a percentage of GNP and of total government spending stood at 3.9 per cent and 26.6 per cent respectively.

The education system is administered by the Ministry of Education, which is responsible for formulating and implementing policies related to public education. Boards of education act as a second-tier form of administration in the provinces and the special cities. Under these boards, educational commissioners are responsible for the primary, middle and secondary schools in each province or city.

The school system consists of six-year primary schools, three-year middle schools and three-year secondary schools, the latter being divided into academic and vocational institutions. College or university degree courses generally last for four years, although this stretches to six for dental and medical colleges. There are also junior vocational colleges, teacher-training colleges and various specialist schools. Enrolment rates at the various levels of education are high: in 1992, 98.7 per cent of children of the appropriate age attended primary school, and 98.6 per cent of these progressed to secondary school. In 1992 Korea had 8,498 nursery schools, 6,122 primary schools, 2,539 middle schools, 1,058 general secondary schools and 677 vocational secondary schools. Higher education is also well-

Exhibit 2.1

Population statistics, 1981-1991

Year	*Total estimated mid-year population ('000s of people)*	*Per capita GNP (US$)*	*Per capita PDI (US$)*	*Ratio of national savings*	*Consumer price increase*
1981	38723	1734	1630	22.7	21.58
1982	39326	1824	1708	24.2	7.08
1983	39910	2002	1846	27.6	3.36
1984	40406	2158	1983	29.4	2.31
1985	40806	2194	2002	29.1	2.46
1986	41214	2505	2280	32.8	2.80
1987	41622	3110	2828	36.2	3.02
1988	42031	4127	3731	38.1	7.08
1989	42449	4994	4485	35.3	5.73
1990	42869	5659	5103	36.0	8.59
1991	43268	6498	5866	36.1	9.68

provisioned, with 121 colleges and universities catering for over a million students and a further half a million participating in other forms of further education.

Critics of the education system claim that the emphasis in schools is largely on rote learning rather than on developing skills and there appears to be some evidence to suggest that after children go through the "exam hell" of secondary school they tend to relax, with the result that their university years are less productive than they could be.

If this is the case, then the problem must be addressed: it is vital that innovative talents are nurtured as Korea moves from a phase of licensing foreign technology to an active programme of research and development aimed at inventing its own technology.

Employment and wages

Official unemployment in Korea is low, at just 2.3 per cent, but this figure does not reflect hidden unemployment such as that affecting transient workers, and underemployment. The unemployment rate tends to be higher in the cities than in the countryside (reaching 3.4 per cent in Seoul and 4.6 per cent in Kwangju) where family affiliation is stronger, and unemployed workers can be absorbed more readily by the family network into productive activity. Moreover, the trend of falling unemployment rates observed since 1980 seems to be in reverse. Throughout most of the 1980s Korea experienced a skills and labour shortage but in the 1990s it has been estimated that GNP growth will have to average 7 per cent annually, in order to absorb new workers coming onto the labour market.[4]

From this perspective, the sharp rise in wages is a worrying trait. Workers have increasingly demanded a bigger share of the economic rewards from Korea's development: between 1980-1985 productivity gains exceeded wage growth, as the government maintained export competitiveness by controlling wages, but full employment encouraged workers' demands, and it is estimated that real wages grew 79 per cent in the 1987-1991 period.[5] The Ministry of Labour's Nominal Wage Index reached 268.1 for all industries in 1992 (1985=100), while wages in the key manufacturing sector rose even further to 296.1.

On the same basis, the Real Wage Index for all industries rose to 163 in 1991 and that for the manufacturing sector rose to 179.

Unit labour costs have increased each year since 1986, at a time of stiff competition from China and newly industrialising countries in South East Asia where wages are significantly lower. Demands for wage increases led to labour unrest in the late 1980s, although this trend has waned since the government tightened the legislation on labour disputes in 1989, and took positive steps to improve labour relations.

As a result, the number of labour disputes has declined from a total of 3,749 in 1987 to just 235 in 1992; and the number of working days lost as a result of strikes dropped to 1,527612 in 1992 from a massive 6,946,935 in 1987.[6] However, the level of labour unrest is still well above the levels of 1975-1985, and disputes have increasingly been geared towards higher pay rather than political issues as was the case during the Park and the Chun regimes.

Geographical characteristics

The Korean peninsula extends south from the border of China and the former Soviet Union for approximately 950 kilometres, varying in width from 200 to 300 kilometres. The peninsula thus occupies about the same area as England and Scotland, with the West or Yellow Sea on one side and the Sea of Japan, known as the East Sea in Korea, on the other.

The peninsula has been divided along the 38th parallel into Communist North Korea (the Democratic People's Republic of Korea) and South Korea (the Republic of Korea) since 1948. The total area of the peninsula is just over 220,000 square kilometres, of which 98,445 square kilometres belong to South Korea. This area is about 1,000 kilometres long and on average about 270 kilometres wide.

Most of the country, about 70 per cent, is mountainous, and about two-thirds of the land area is forest, mostly broad-leaf and coniferous. Most of the arable plains are located in the west of the country.

The main rivers in the South are the Han (514 kilometres), which runs through the centre of Seoul, the Naktong (525 kilometres), the Kum (401 kilometres) and the Samjin (212 kilometres), and there are extensive lowlands around these which are farmed intensively and provide some of the most productive agricultural land in the country. Most of the rivers in the South have their source in the Taebaek mountains in the east of the country, and flow swiftly down from the mountains towards the west or southwest. These rivers provide an abundant water supply for agriculture, and have also allowed the large-scale development of a hydroelectric power industry (although dams have had to be built in order to ensure steady supply during the protracted wet and dry seasons).

The Taebaek mountains form the spine of the Korean peninsula, running the whole length of the east coast from Mount Paektu in North Korea southward, and falling away steeply into the East Sea. The coastal plain in the east is narrow. There are few harbours and islands off this coast, and the steep terrain discourages the development of agriculture. Most of the flat, arable land is in the southwest corner of the country.

Along the southern and western coastlines, there are more than 3,500 islands, the largest of which, Cheju, is home to Korea's highest mountain, Halla-san, and is a major tourist centre. The coastline is extremely irregular, with many bays and harbours, and the thousands of small islands that stud the sea are in fact the tops of submerged mountains.

Opposite:
Part of Korea's greatest comparative advantage

The sea around Korea has played a key role in its development. The Yellow or West Sea is a rich fishing ground and the seabed off the southwestern coast has been explored for petroleum deposits.

The Korean climate can be extreme, being influenced more by the Asian landmass than by the moderating effects of the surrounding seas. The temperature in Seoul ranges from -5°C to 26°C, with the average year-round temperature being approximately 13°C along the southern coast, and somewhat cooler in the north. Temperature differences can be considerable, depending on the area: the lowest temperature recorded on the peninsula is -45°C, but in summer maximum temperatures of 40°C are not uncommon.

Most of the annual rainfall, which ranges from 38 to 55 inches in the wetter regions, falls during the summer monsoon season in July and August. Korea is also subject to typhoons at the end of summer. The winter is dry, with long spells of clear skies and occasional snowfall.

Agriculture and mineral resources

Urban development largely lies along the axis linking Seoul and Pusan, while the southwestern and northeastern provinces have been relatively neglected by economic developments. The majority of the population lives in urban areas, but the declining rural population cultivates rice and other cereals such as barley and wheat, as well as fruits which include apples, pears, peaches and persimmon.

Mineral wealth is concentrated in North Korea, although the south has some metals including tungsten, low-grade anthracite coal deposits, and metallic ores such as aluminium, iron and copper. The much wider range of minerals to be found in the North could have economic consequences in the event of eventual reunification.

The cities and provinces

Administratively, South Korea is divided into nine provinces and six special cities. The provinces (*do*) are subdivided into cities or counties (*Gun*) and these are further subdivided into townships (*Myon* and *Up*). The nine provinces are: Kangwan-do, Kyonggi-do, Chungch'onbuk-do, Chungch'ongnam-do, Kyongsanbuk-do, Kyongsangnam-do, Chollabuk-do, Chollanam-do and the island province in the south, Cheju-do. *Buk* in Korean means north and *Nam* south; but the provinces are often referred to in guidebooks by their English equivalents, for instance, South Cholla province, rather than Chollanam-do. The six special cities are the capital, Seoul, and its nearby port, Inch'on; Pusan, the second biggest city, located at the opposite end of the peninsula; Taejon, southeast of Seoul, which hosted the Expo '93 world fair; Taegu, where many of Korea's top politicians have come from; and Kwangju in the south.

Kangwan-do, located in the remote northeast of the country, is Korea's most sparsely populated province, with the second largest land area at 16,898 square kilometres, but with the third lowest population at 1.58 million. Despite its isolation, the province has a low unemployment rate of just 1 per cent. The major cities are Ch'unch'on and Wonju. The province's northern border is formed by North Korea. Kangwan province has been an important logging centre because of its large stock of mainly coniferous trees.

Kyonggi-do is the province around Seoul, and as it acts as an overspill area for the Seoul workforce it is the most heavily populated province in Korea. A total of more than six million people are crammed into the 10,773 square kilometres, giving a population density of more than 571 per square kilometre. The province contains the major cities of Suwon and Inch'on, and the latter is also a key port.

Chungch'onbuk-do is situated in the heart of Korea, and has the lowest population of any province except the resort island of Cheju. The total population is just 1.39 million and the land area is also small, at just 7,435 square kilometres. The main town is Ch'ongju.

Just to the south of Chungch'onbuk-do lies Chungch'ongnam-do, containing the special city of Taejon. Other main cities in this province include Kongju and Ch'onan. The total land area is 8,318 square kilometres and population density a moderate 242 per square kilometre.

Kyongsanbuk-do is the largest province in Korea with a land area of 19,447 square kilometres, although it has the second lowest population density at 147 per square kilometre. The special city of Taegu is located in this province, as are the cultural centre of Kyongju and the industrial city of Pohang. The province is mountainous, and has therefore developed as a logging centre.

Kyongsangnam-do contains some of Korea's biggest industrial cities, including the port of Ulsan, the site of the country's biggest oil refinery, the population hub and major industrial port of Pusan, and the port of Masan, also a big industrial centre and free-trade zone. The total area is 11,776 square kilometres, and the population density is relatively high at 312 people per square kilometre, making it the second most densely populated province after Kyonggi-do.

Chollabuk-do is in the less developed southwestern corner of Korea, its main centres are Chonju and the port city of Kunsan located at the mouth of the Kum river. Chollabuk-do covers an area of just over 8,000 square kilometres, and has a population density of 257 per square kilometre.

Chollanam-do is the most southwesterly of the nine provinces and as a result, areas of it are among the least developed in Korea. The total population is approximately 2.5 million and the major port of Mokp'o is located in the southeastern tip of the province. The special city of Kwangju is located to the northeast of Mokp'o, further inland.

Cheju-do is located due south of Chollanam-do, and as a result of its isolated location and romantic tropical image, has become a popular tourist resort. This is the least populated of the nine provinces, with just over half a million people living on the island, which has an area of just 1,825 square kilometres.

[1] *Social Indicators in Korea, 1992;* Korean Statistical Association.

[2] *Ibid.*

[3] *The Case for Korea* stockbroker's report by W.I. Carr.

[4] Interview with KFTA official, November 1993.

[5] *The Case for Korea* stockbroker's report by W.I. Carr.

[6] Ministry of Labour: *Labour Unions and Labour Disputes*.

유공 YUKONG

Chapter Three

Infrastructure

Introduction

Korea's infrastructure is under increasing pressure due to a lack of investment in this sector during the 1980s. The country's roads are often choked with traffic, particularly within Seoul, and between the hubs of Seoul and Pusan. Foreign ships have refused to dock at some of the country's overstretched ports because of the heavy congestion and the rail and subway networks are all in need of, or in the process of undergoing, major overhauls, because of increasing passenger and freight burdens. A report by the Ministry of Construction estimated that congested Korean ports, cargo terminals and roads cost Korea won6.2 trillion in 1992.[1]

The freight sector has also suffered from excessive regulation although conditions for entering the various sectors of the cargo transport market will be simplified or abolished by 1995.

Roads

The huge growth in private vehicle use in the last five years – one of the side-effects of the country's rapid economic growth – is now threatening to stifle further economic growth.

The number of passenger cars on the road rose from just over 80,000 in 1975 to more than two million in 1990. This has led to environmental problems and is also a huge drain on the nation's resources: according to the Korea Transport Institute[2], more than won13 billion is wasted daily throughout Korea due to traffic jams, with 61.3 per cent of that sum accounted for by Seoul and its environs. The same report estimated that losses due to the waste of time and fuel resulting from motorists being unable to travel at 50-60 kilometres an hour amounted to won7.96 billion daily in and around the six largest cities, of which Seoul was responsible for won3.75 billion.

The extension of the Seoul subway system has made the problem temporarily worse, leading to traffic bottlenecks, although its completion should make commuting easier and reduce the number of cars on the roads. As a result of traffic, the 18-kilometre journey from the main Kimpo airport outside Seoul to the City Hall now takes a minimum of 30 minutes, and at times of maximum congestion it is not uncommon to grind along in a taxi for up to two hours, at an average speed of less than 10 kilometres an hour.

Expressways

The development of expressways has been an attempt to remedy this situation. These cross the country mainly along the north-west to south-east axis linking Seoul and Pusan,

Opposite: The road network is extensive but heavily used

although spurs have been extended to the remoter areas in the southwest and east of the country. The Chungbu expressway links Inch'on port outside Seoul with Taejon, one of the special cities and the host of the Expo' 1993 exhibition. A second expressway runs through Suwon and links up with the Chungbu expressway outside Ch'ongju. From here, the road splits into the Kyongbu and Honam expressways. The Kyongbu road passes through the cities of Taegu and Kyongju on its way to Pusan, with a spur to the industrial centre of Ulsan. The Honam expressway links the cities of Nonsan and Ch'ongju and ends up at Kwangju.

Apart from this primarily north-south grid, three expressways run on a west-east axis: the Namhae expressway linking Kwangju and Pusan through the cities of Sunchon and Masan; the 88 Olympic expressway running north of that and linking Kwangju with Taegu; and in the north, the Yongdong expressway, linking Suwon and Tonghae via the cities of Wonju and Kangnung. In total there 10 major expressways with a total length of 1,390 kilometres; the total length of roads stood at 58,088 kilometres in 1991.

Although the road network covers a wide area, many of these roads suffer from an excess of traffic. The road from Seoul to Pusan, built during the late 1960s, remains the only direct link between the key industrial and financial centre and the main port: the heavy volume of freight and passenger traffic means that the road is congested for much of the year.

Railways and subways

Compared to the road network, the rail system is relatively well-developed, although passenger travel on trains other than the super-express *Saemaul-ho* can be uncomfortable. Rail fares are inexpensive, and on the *Saemaul-ho*, the journey from Seoul to Pusan can be made in just over four hours. There are three additional classes of train, the *Mugunghwa-ho*, the *T'ongil-ho*, both express services, and the ordinary *Bidulgi-ho* trains.

There is a need for new investment in the railways as the stock is ageing (the last phase of major investment was in the early-1980s), and the volume of traffic on the railroads has actually declined in the last 10 years as a percentage of all traffic moved. This has aggravated the problems on the roads and at the country's seaports, and revitalising the rail network must be a priority for the government.

There are two subway systems in Korea, one in Seoul and the other in Pusan. The four Seoul subway lines serve the whole city and its suburbs, and Line 1 merges into the national rail network linking Seoul with its major satellite cities of Inch'on, Suwon and Uijongbu. The network was constructed between 1971 and 1990, and another four lines are currently being added now that over four million passengers use it every day. A further route out to Kimpo Airport is due to begin operation in 1994.

There is also a smaller subway network in Pusan, begun in 1981 and completed in 1990. Its total length is 26.7 kilometres, it has 28 stations and carries over half a million passengers daily.

Airports

The country's three international airports are Kimpo in Seoul, Kimhae in Pusan and the tourist-oriented airport at Cheju Island. Korean Airlines, the national airline, flies to Seoul daily from a wide variety of cities, including Tokyo, Osaka, Hong Kong, Bangkok and Taipei; Asiana, its rival, flies nine routes to Japan as well as to other Asian and North American destinations.

Both airlines also operate an extensive network of domestic flights linking Seoul with 13 of Korea's major cities. From Seoul, it is possible to fly direct to the cities of Sokch'o, Kangnung, Yech'on, Taegu, Pohang, Ulsan, Pusan, Chinju, Yosu, Kwangju, Kunsan, Mokp'o and Cheju. Kwangju functions as a minor hub, with flights available to Cheju and Pusan. Several other airports serve the island resort of Cheju. All these flights take no longer than an hour, providing the most comfortable and time-effective method of passenger transport. However, the airports are largely associated with military bases, and their facilities fall short of those required for the larger commercial airplanes.

All of the airports are operating at close to their full capacity and headline-grabbing accidents such as the crash of an Asiana airplane south of Seoul in 1993, with the loss of more than 40 lives, have lent strength to calls for the upgrading and modernisation of the existing facilities.

Added to the infrastructural problems, government regulation of the domestic airline business also limits the development of this sector. Ticket prices are kept low and the frequency of flights is also controlled, limiting the potential for this means of transport to take pressure off the roads.

Ports

The major ports in Korea are at Inch'on, Pusan, Ulsan, Kwangyang and Pohang, with additional capacity at P'youngtaek, Kunsan, Daesan, Mokp'o, Yosu, Ch'ungmu, Samch'onp'o, Chinhae, Mukho, Okgye, Sokch'o, Tonghae and Cheju. However, foreign shippers have to rely almost entirely on just the three main ports of Inch'on, Masan and Pusan.

Within Korea, both coastal freight and passenger traffic is considerable. In 1992, a total of more than 8.7 million passengers travelled, and coastal freight traffic amounted to more than 85 million tons. Of the freight total, the bulk of the traffic was in raw materials: internal movements of oil accounted for 41.6 per cent of the total, cement 14.3 per cent, ore 1.9 per cent and coal for 1.3 per cent.[3]

Ocean-going freight totalled 285.5 million tonnes in 1992, with the lion's share being transported to South East Asia (29.8 per cent); 22.1 per cent went to the Americas, with North America taking 16.2 per cent; the Middle East accounted for 22.5 per cent; Japan 9.7 per cent; and Europe 3.3 per cent.

Congestion at the major seaports has become a key source of concern, however, and international shippers often avoid Korean ports as a result: the waiting periods at Pusan container port were estimated at 45 hours in 1992, and those at Inch'on around 74 hours.[4] These long delays disrupt trade flows and have led to extra costs for distribution by alternative means and routes. This is a particularly serious problem when one considers Korea's heavy reliance on exports.

Sea-going freight traffic is also extremely concentrated (Pusan handles over 90 per cent of all container traffic) and this leads to higher overall costs because of the need to link sea-freight with inland freight by road or rail.

Passenger ferries travel daily between Pusan and Shimonoseki in Japan, and twice-weekly between Osaka and Pusan. A ferry also services Pusan from Weihai on the Chinese coast.

CALTEX

New projects for the 1990s

Korea has launched an ambitious 10-year, US$120 billion, plan to develop its overworked and ageing infrastructure, not only in the crucial transportation sector, but also in areas such as sewerage facilities and electrical power supply. The government plans to raise spending on these so-called "social overhead capital investments" (SOC) to 5 per cent of GNP during the 1992-1996 period (won62 trillion), compared to just 3.5 per cent of GNP in the 1987-1991 period (won26 trillion), and less than 2.0 per cent in the five years prior to that. With the pace of economic growth declining in recent years, work on these projects is likely to be speeded up to give a kick-start to the economy and provide the right conditions for longer-term growth.

The government has outlined four key sources of funding for the projects:

- Indirect taxation: primarily by increasing the tax rate on oil products such as petrol, the price of which is below that found in other oil-importing countries. The tax on petrol is currently being used in part to fund provincial and educational activities, but in the future it is likely to be devoted almost entirely to transportation projects. These include the building or upgrading of highways and subways, the high-speed railway and the new Seoul airport.
- Raising user fees: the seventh five-year plan envisages raising electricity rates, airport fees and water charges to a "more realistic level". Details of these politically sensitive increases have yet to be announced.
- A regional development tax: this would be introduced to help local governments improve facilities such as city roads. This is in line with the government's aim to devolve some of its powers to the provincial governments, giving them both financial and management responsibility for local infrastructure projects.
- Increased borrowing and the stimulation of investment: the latest five-year plan mooted the possibility of measures designed to increase bond issuance by local authorities and government-supported enterprises, as well as encouraging private investment in road and harbour projects.

In the meantime, the government plans to purchase the necessary land for these projects, although construction will not begin for some time: the aim of this strategy is to offset speculation and to spread the huge costs which these projects entail.

Apart from developing new infrastructure, there are also plans to increase the efficiency of the existing infrastructure. Priority is also being given to providing links between different types of transport.[5] Private sector investment is expected to play a crucial role in the whole strategy.

Transportation

The Korean government, faced with a surge in the volume of freight within the country, and the number of motor vehicles on the road, has developed a multi-pronged attack on congestion on the roads and railways and in the harbours.

In its original seventh five-year plan, covering the period 1992-1996, the government had estimated that domestic passenger traffic would rise at 3.7 per cent each year and freight traffic at 4 per cent a year. International passengers and freight are expected to rise 11.1 per cent in the same period.

Opposite: Further enhancement of rail infrastructure is underway

Roads

Seoul's roads are a traffic planner's nightmare and pollution from older cars is a major problem. By 1996, the number of private passenger cars on the road is projected to be 3.4 times the 1990 level. By the year 2001, an estimated 14 million cars are expected to be on the road.

To alleviate the problem, several major road projects were outlined in the 1992-1996 five-year plan. Two projects are underway in the Seoul metropolitan area: a ring-road around the capital, and a second expressway between Seoul and the main port of Inch'on.

The inter-regional expressway network is also due for a major overhaul, with priority being given to upgrading the network in the relatively underdeveloped west and southwest of the country. Expansion work on the Seoul to Pusan expressway (Hannam-Hoedeok) and on the Yeongdong (Singal-Saemal) expressway is to be speeded up, and the Jungang expressway linking Taegu and Ch'unch'on will be constructed.

A programme of road-widening and paving is also underway, the latter due to have been completed by end-1993. Roads near major industrial complexes are also targeted for widening, and a greater degree of linkage between the road and rail networks is planned.[6]

Railways

The building of the new high-speed rail link between Seoul and the southeastern port of Pusan is expected to raise productivity by won15.5 trillion (US$18.20 billion by the end of the decade), and will also create almost 900,000 jobs.[7] By 2001, the high-speed train will travel the 410 kilometres between the capital and the southern port of Pusan in about 100 minutes, saving the country some US$3 billion a year in other transportation costs. In order to link up with the high-speed railway, the Korean National Railroad plans to spend US$1.45 billion on building 1,015 kilometres of electrified railway track between the mid-1990s and the year 2010.

In August 1993 the government announced the selection of GEC Alsthom as priority bidder to supply equipment for the high-speed rail link. The project is expected to cost more than US$13 billion in total. The government postponed the original completion date of the project by three years to 2001 because of a rise in the project's total construction cost due to the need to purchase land along the route and build the railbed.

The government decision to negotiate a final deal by the end of the year with GEC Alsthom has virtually eliminated German rival Siemens AG, manufacturer of the Inter-City Express. A consortium led by Japan's Mitsubishi Corporation, which included Mitsubishi Heavy Industries, Hitachi Ltd and Marubeni Corp., was eliminated in June 1993. Korea's persistent trade deficit with Japan and Japan's reluctance to transfer technology were seen as important factors mitigating against their bid.

GEC Alsthom is a joint corporation established in 1989 by Britain's General Electric Company and France's Alcatel Alsthom, the builders of the famous Train à Grande-Vitesse (TGV). The TGV holds several records, including one for speed and one for the most advanced technology and has a commercial speed of 300 kilometres an hour.

GEC Alsthom, which has already exported its TGVs to Spain and has contracts pending in several other countries, won the right to negotiate a final deal by coming in with a US$2.3 billion bid to provide 46 trains (each consisting of two engines and 18 coaches with 1,038 seats), suspension wires and signal equipment. The company has agreed to allow 50 per cent local input in the manufacture of the trainsets and to transfer its technology to Korea once the contract is finally concluded; this means that Korea should be able to produce and export its own TGVs within 10 years.

France's state-owned railway company Société Nationale de Chemins de Fer (SNCF) is expected to play an important role in providing consultancy services and technical assistance to its Korean counterpart.

The new Seoul-Pusan line is expected to carry about 120 million people a year by 2011, a decade after going into service. The idea for the link dates back to 1979 when it was suggested by President Park Chung-Hee. After his assassination, the project was shelved until March 1983 when Chun's government launched a feasibility study. Seven years later, in May 1990, a special committee headed by the deputy prime minister was formed to promote the railway project. In June 1992, ground was broken for the construction of a test track between central Ch'onan and Taejon and the train is expected to be in operation 20 years after it was first proposed.

The Korea High Speed Railway Construction Authority (KHRC) has selected Bechtel International of the United States and Korea Power Engineering Corporation to conduct a study scheduling the design, land purchase and construction of the US$13.2 billion railway. Construction of the railbed for the high-speed train will be divided into 42 sections, each of which will measure approximately 10 kilometres and will take about five years to complete. The construction will start as soon as Bechtel and KEPCO complete the design work, with the construction of the track and electric and signal systems by Korean firms to follow.

Work on the test section between Ch'onan and Taejon began in 1992 and should be completed by 1997, with the Seoul-Taejon section finished by 1999 and the complete Seoul-Pusan line completed by 2001.

GEC Alsthom sees its partnership with Korean firms over the next 10 years as providing a base from which it can make inroads into the potentially lucrative Asian rail market in the 21st century. However, some experts believe that Korea may be capable of servicing these markets on its own: the deal with GEC Alsthom will make Korea Japan's leading competitor in rail technology, with the right to export the TGV worldwide except within Europe.

A second TGV train

President Kim Young-Sam announced in August 1993 that a feasibility study for the building of a second high-speed railway line between the capital and the southwestern provinces of North and South Cholla would be launched.[8] The move reflects Kim's recognition of the need to improve links to the relatively depressed southwestern provinces in order to attain balanced regional development. The government is likely to include the cost of the second line in the 1994-1995 budget. Related ministries have been instructed to hold working-level discussions on ways to finance the second line. The decision is likely to defuse criticism of the Seoul-Pusan line by the opposition Democratic Party, whose power base has traditionally been the Cholla region.

The government is considering three ways in which to link Seoul with the southwestern port of Mokp'o, some 350 kilometres south of Seoul, by high-speed train. One option is to lay a completely new line from Seoul to Mokp'o at a cost of some US$8.75 billion, while the other two options involve using sections of the Seoul-Pusan TGV line. Financing details have yet to be decided.

Airports

President Kim Young-Sam vowed in August 1993 to re-start work on a huge international airport, Youngjong-do, being built to the west of Seoul near Inch'on Harbour, in order

GIANNI VERSA
istante

to help overcome an expected slowdown caused by government anti-corruption measures. Work on the airport had started in November 1992, but lack of funds led to a swift winding down of the initial construction work. The total cost of the project is estimated at about won4 trillion (about US$5 billion). The target date for completion is 1997. The new airport is facing opposition from environmental groups who claim that it could devastate the bird population that migrates there each year.

Ports

The government also plans to upgrade the country's main ports, although progress in this area has been rather slow. The key section that has been completed so far involved upgrading the main Inch'on Port outside Seoul. A new won430 billion container terminal project at Kwangyang Bay is also underway.

Electricity

The development of the power sector in Korea is being led by the state-owned Korea Electric Power Corporation, which has launched a plan to boost generating capacity to 25,832 megawatts by 2001. Nuclear energy will play a large part in this US$40 billion project, with nine units to be built by 2001 and a further nine between 2002 and 2006.[9]

[1] *Business Korea*.
[2] Ministry of Construction Report, November 1993.
[3] Transportation Yearbook 1993.
[4] *Business Korea*.
[5] Government Five-year Plan, pp. 53-62.
[6] Government Five-year Plan, pp. 55-56.
[7] Korea Development Institute (KDI) quoted by news agency sources.
[8] Government Five-year Plan, p. 56.
[9] *Business Korea Yearbook* 1993/4, p. 648.

Chapter Four

Trade, industry and resources

Export strategy

The huge surge in Korea's economic growth since the 1960s has been led by an outward-looking development strategy in which exports were pursued relentlessly, often at the expense of the domestic market and of developing domestic infrastructure. Korea has followed the pattern established by post-war Japan and other resource-poor NIEs.

In the 1950s and 1960s, exports were supplied by the labour-intensive industries such as textiles, taking advantage of Korea's abundant reserves of hard-working labour. The first stage of import substitution was completed in the 1950s under the government of Rhee, and the export drive was speeded up during the early years of Park's military government.

In the early 1970s, the government launched its heavy and chemical industries (HCI) promotion to boost the industrial export capacity of the nation. This drive, which reached its peak in 1973-1979, was highly controversial. An interventionist strategy was adopted through which specific sectors were targeted, with funds being channelled to the large *Chaebol* on preferential terms. These companies, under government pressure to increase exports, took on huge bank loans which resulted in Korea becoming the fourth most-indebted country in the world in the 1970s.

The strategic industries included metals, machinery, shipbuilding, electronics, and chemicals. A variety of tax incentives were offered to companies investing in these areas. The average cost of borrowing in these sectors was much lower than that in the light manufacturing sector, in which small- and medium-sized companies were predominant, leading to a system of credit allocation that benefited the large conglomerates. It is estimated that almost 60 per cent of total loans from 1975 to 1977 were directed towards HCI projects.[1]

The strategy appears to have helped Korean firms to enter the key areas in which they made their names in the 1980s: automobiles, shipbuilding, manufacturing domestic consumer durables, and increasingly in the 1990s, high-technology. However, in certain sectors optimisation of plant-scale was made the priority rather than realistic demand-side projections, resulting in over-investment and overcapacity that remain a problem in industries such as petrochemicals.

Korea faces a challenge if it is to sustain the phenomenal export growth it showed in the 1970s and 1980s. Although many Korean exports have become household names in the West, many of their components depend on "borrowed" technology from abroad, and Korea is heavily dependent on imported components from Japan, a key business rival.

Thus, while Korea runs a huge trade surplus with the United States, it also runs a large deficit with Japan, creating a triangular relationship, within which Korea acts as a kind of assembly plant for Japanese exports. This leaves Korea highly exposed not only to exchange rate fluctuations, but also to its dependency on licensing or buying in the technology it needs for its exports.

Korea's relationship with Japan and the United States has been the subject of various studies in the last few years, the most pessimistic of which foresees a situation in which Korea – its agricultural base neglected as a result of the focus on exports – fails to close the technological gap with its wholly-industrialised competitors, who remain always one step ahead in the sophisticated technology fields.

The situation is demonstrated most clearly in the high-technology areas of computers and consumer electronics, which reflect the uphill struggle that Korea faces in moving up the value chain from heavy industry exports to capital- and technology-intensive products. Most of the pioneering work in the higher value-added fields has been done by the *Chaebol*, and the smaller firms which make up the bulk of electronics companies have little presence in the export market: "Some 80 to 85 per cent of Korea's roughly 1,300 electronics companies are small- or medium-sized enterprises, yet production is dominated by a few *Chaebol*."[2]

The push into electronics began when Goldstar produced its first radio in 1958. Since then, and particularly during the 1960s and 1970s, foreign companies relocated their assembly operations to Korea because of its low-cost, disciplined labour force. Most of these relocations took the form of joint ventures with Korean companies, who derived the benefit of technology transfers. In fields as diverse as microwave ovens and computers, US and Japanese firms tied up with Korean companies, with an increasing trend towards forming supplier relationships such as those between Samsung and General Electric, or Daewoo and IBM.

Exhibit 4.1

South Korean exports and imports – SITC classification, 1982-1992 (US$ millions)

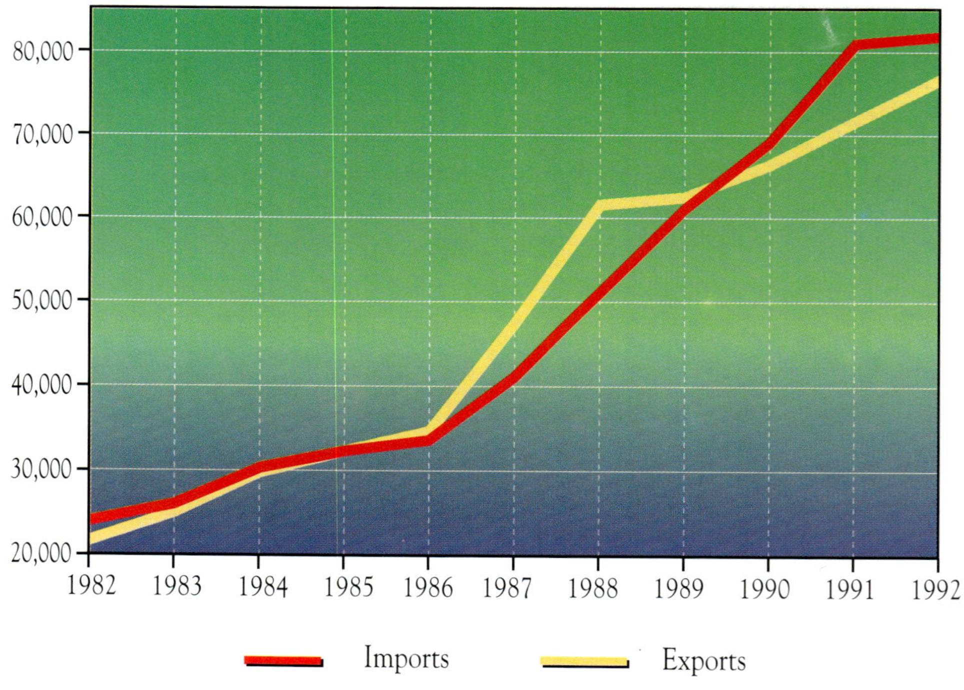

The success of the Korean high technology drive has surprised many competitors. Since 1975, when Korea began producing colour televisions with an output of just 43,095, production has risen to just short of 15 million sets in 1992. The same pattern can be seen for both video tape recorders and microwave ovens.

However, it is at the more specialised end of the market that Korean companies have scored their biggest successes in recent years, notably in the manufacture of semiconductors, the building block for making computers. Korean chipmakers have now surpassed their Japanese competitors in terms of volume for the 1-megabyte and 4-megabyte DRAMs (dynamic random access memory), and are rapidly developing the technology for 16- and 32-bit chips.

The export value of semiconductors has grown rapidly, from US$1.4 billion in 1986 to more than US$4.5 billion in 1990, with an average annual growth of 34.2 per cent during that period. The 1990s saw Korea seeking more diversified markets for its semiconductors and recent years have seen an increasing volume of exports to Japan, at the expense of the US market. Production is largely of integrated circuits: Korea manufactured 4.11 billion of these in 1992, about four times the number it had made 10 years previously.

Imports of semiconductors in specific fields have also increased substantially, however, rising 29.3 per cent in the period 1986-1990.[3] The need to import results from technology deficiency in high value-added products such as micro-devices, high grade linear integrated circuits (IC), and application specific integrated circuits (ASIC). The Koreans are heavily dependent on the United States and Japan in these fields, with about 75 per cent of imports coming from these two countries in 1990. "Korean manufacturers are severely dependent on foreign technology; they continue to depend on Japanese suppliers for crucial parts and components; and they are stuck at the low, unprofitable end of the market for popular consumer commodities."[4]

Sectoral analysis of the economy

Agriculture

Korea's agricultural sector has a political importance far beyond its actual contribution to the country's GDP: provisional data for 1992 suggest that the agriculture, forestry and fisheries sectors contributed won17,682 billion to Korea's GDP, equivalent to just 7.5 per cent of the total. However, about three million people are employed in this sector, about 15 per cent of the total working population. The speed of industrialisation in Korea in the last three decades means that a generation ago most people lived on the land; those that still do, earn the larger share of their income from agricultural rather than non-agricultural activities as is the case in both Japan and Taiwan. It is estimated that 50-60 per cent of rural household income derives from agriculture, whereas in Taiwan, over 80 per cent comes from other activities. Even though only 15 per cent of the population is rural, it is estimated that 75 per cent of the population have immediate family connections in rural areas.[5] Most Korean farming households have very small landholdings, averaging 1.27 hectares. Farmers have been attracted to the large cities by higher wages and a better lifestyle and education for their children, but despite migration the farming population still numbers 6.6 million.[6]

As a result, the opening of the rice market under the Uruguay Round of GATT in late-1993 had a huge emotional significance for Koreans, sparking riots in Seoul and the resignation of most of the cabinet. The opening of the Korean agriculture market, still much more heavily protected than the manufacturing sector, is likely to force a rapid change in work practices. Korea has embarked on a major reform plan for the agricultural sector to allow farmers to achieve economies of scale in order to become more competitive. The government has earmarked US$52 billion in 1992-2001 for restructuring agriculture, which will include the establishment of processing plants. In 1993 the government announced measures allowing larger private landholdings to make farming more competitive in preparation for the expected market liberalisation. Under the new law, due to take effect in mid-1994, Korea's traditional family farms are expected to make way for larger farming corporations. These will be able to cultivate up to 100 hectares of land. Only established farmers will be allowed to form these corporations, following strong opposition from farmers to the idea of allowing business firms to join in. The new law doubles the ceiling on farmland ownership from 10 hectares per family to 20 hectares and will make it easier to use farmland for other purposes, which could include the building of industrial plants.

Automobiles

The growth of the Korean automobile market has been rapid, and a number of best-selling models, notably the Hyundai Excel in the United States, have carved a niche for Korean manufacturers in the low-cost family saloon market. Production of cars has expanded rapidly as the domestic economy has grown: in 1992, Korean factories made 1.25 million passenger cars, 113,500 trucks and 321,780 motorcycles; the total number of cars produced was 60 per cent higher than the figure for 1987, and compares with a 1980 total of just 57,000 vehicles. Passenger car exports have also risen rapidly, and were valued at US$2.5 billion in 1992, compared to just under US$50 million 10 years previously. The price differential between similar Korean and Japanese-made cars is estimated to have widened from the previous US$1,500 to more than US$2,000 in 1993, boosting demand for Korean cars in the Middle East, South East Asia and Latin America.

Exports are expected to hold up until at least the mid-1990s, but the strong yen is likely to encourage the Japanese to increase production in low-wage countries. Meanwhile, domestic demand in Korea is set to slow down as the government tackles the problem of overcrowding on the roads and Korean manufacturers face a widening technology gap with competitors in more advanced countries. Developing technology and upgrading the role of the small parts suppliers are seen as key areas in which Korea's competitive edge can be improved. Cut-throat competition has led to low profit margins, and ambitious investment plans announced by the country's car manufacturers threaten potential overcapacity in this industry in the longer term. Profits as a percentage of sales were estimated to be as low as 0.07 per cent in 1993.

The industry plans to invest a total of US$9.8 billion by 2000 to double its total annual production capacity to more than five million automobiles, most of them passenger cars. This would push Korea up to fifth place in the world rankings, after Japan, the United States, Germany and France.

The five major manufacturers are Hyundai, Daewoo, Kia, Asia and Ssangyong. Hyundai Motors Co is Korea's largest car manufacturer. It plans to invest up to US$3.7 billion to build a new plant to increase capacity from 1.15 million units to 2 million units by 2000. Daewoo Motors is the second-ranked manufacturer and it also has plans to increase investment (by US$2.1 billion) in order to increase capacity from 740,000 to 1.2 million units. The other major players are all planning similar levels of expansion and the Samsung business group plans an initial investment of US$2.5 billion before 2000 to break into the industry.

These levels of investment have been prompted by surging domestic demand and a buoyant export market which raised its projections for car exports in 1993 to around 620,000 vehicles, compared to just 456,000 in 1992. However, the *Chaebol*'s concern to expand market share in existing growth markets could lead to further investment, and the prospect of over-capacity in the longer term.

Cement

Korean cement production lagged behind domestic demand in the late 1980s and early 1990s, despite increases in production capacity, which totalled 38.5 million tonnes in 1990. This has largely been as a result of strong domestic demand from the building industry during the boom years of the late 1980s, particularly around the time of the 1988 Olympic Games. Korean cement makers have traditionally depended more on the domestic market than on exports: the value of cement exports declined to just US$75 million in 1992 compared to annual levels of more than US$300 million in 1981-1982, when Korea supplied the expanding Middle East market. In the past, Korean manufacturers have depended on Japan for markets, but economic growth in the South East Asian NIEs has encouraged a shift in strategy. As a result, shipments of cement to Japan have dropped substantially, accounting for only 21 per cent of exports in the first eight months of 1993, compared to more than 50 per cent the year before. This trend looks set to continue in the near-term as falling property prices in Japan and the continued economic slowdown will lead Korea to focus primarily on the NIEs for markets.

Computers

Korea has emerged as a world leader in semiconductor production, with quality and quantity levels on a par with those of Japan, and an excellent reputation in the production of DRAMs. Semiconductors with a capacity of 4-megabyte DRAM and over have emerged as the chief force behind Korea's semiconductor exports, after a massive investment programme launched in the late 1980s and early 1990s. Korean companies aim to start large-scale production of 16-megabyte DRAMs in 1994, and look well placed to take advantage of rising global demand for superchips.

The big three manufacturers in this high-technology sphere are: Samsung Electronics, which can make eight million 4-megabyte chips a month, more than any other company in the world; Hyundai Electronics Industries, which produces 4.5 million chips a month; and Goldstar Electronics, producing 3.5 million of these chips monthly.

However, the Koreans have lagged behind in certain areas such as chip-design technology, application specific integrated circuits (ASICs), non-memory chips and liquid crystal panels. They also suffer from their dependency on foreign sources for semiconductor-making equipment: "A big disparity exists between Korean companies and their Japanese and Taiwanese competitors in base technologies – in materials and manufacturing equipment – that support the higher DRAM technology. Both Japanese and Taiwanese producers have broad-base technologies, while the technology structure of the Korean company is narrow and top-heavy."[7] As a result, further tie-ups between Korean and Japanese companies are likely in the years ahead, following the agreement between Toshiba and Samsung Electronics reached in late-1992.

Consumer electronics

The big three producers of electronic goods in Korea are Samsung Electronics, Goldstar and Daewoo Electronics. The three have evolved sophisticated manufacturing processes in all areas, starting from virtually nothing in the mid-1970s and early 1980s. However, as is the case for many high-technology products, Korea remains dependent on imported technology, parts and components for the production of consumer electronics.

Korean exports of electric and electronic products totalled US$21.5 billion in 1992, with electronic home appliances such as colour televisions, video tape recorders, radio cassettes, component stereos, refrigerators and microwave ovens making up over a quarter of that total. Total exports of electrical and electronic items, including high-technology products such as semiconductors, were responsible for more than a quarter of Korea's exports in 1992.

As the Korean domestic market grows, production is likely to be boosted by the increasing affluence of the population. Already the growth has been dramatic: production of colour televisions, for example, reached almost 15 million in 1992, more than 15 times the 1980 total.

Metals

The metals industry in Korea has expanded faster than the overall economy, with demand for machinery and parts fuelling the rise. However, the country is relatively resource poor and the production of key metals such as zinc, copper and lead ore has been declining since the 1970s. Although the production of iron ore has been steady in recent years at 560-580 tonnes a year, the Korean steel industry is almost totally dependent on imported raw materials: in 1990, raw material imports were worth US$2.2 billion, of which iron ore accounted for 25 per cent and coking coal 29.8 per cent. This dependence is likely to increase even further if growth in the steel industry continues at the rate seen in the 1980s: steel production in Korea increased at double-digit rates in the late 1980s, and steel consumption increased twice as fast as the GNP growth rate.

The ferrous metals industry is dominated by Pohang Iron and Steel Co (POSCO), which ranked third behind Nippon Steel of Japan and Usinor Sacilor of France in terms of 1990 production capacity. Korea's annual steel production at the time was ranked eighth worldwide with annual production capacity of 25.5 million tonnes; POSCO was responsible for more than two-thirds of this total. The steel industry comprises about 200 companies in total but few have integrated production facilities.

Non-ferrous metal production, which includes metals such as zinc, lead, nickel, copper, aluminium, magnesium, titanium and precious metals such as gold and silver, consistently fell short of domestic demand in the late 1980s, and the poor availability and grade of domestic ore deposits has made the industry heavily dependent on imports of raw materials, except for lead ores. Growth in the 1990s is likely to be slower than that seen in the previous decade, but domestic demand for speciality alloys is likely to increase. Substantial new investment in this field will have to be made to meet the country's needs.

Petrochemicals

Korea's petrochemical industry was established in the 1970s and 1980s under the government's HCI initiative. Huge investments reversed the acute shortages suffered until

Exhibit 4.2

Primary energy consumption, 1992 (percentage of total)

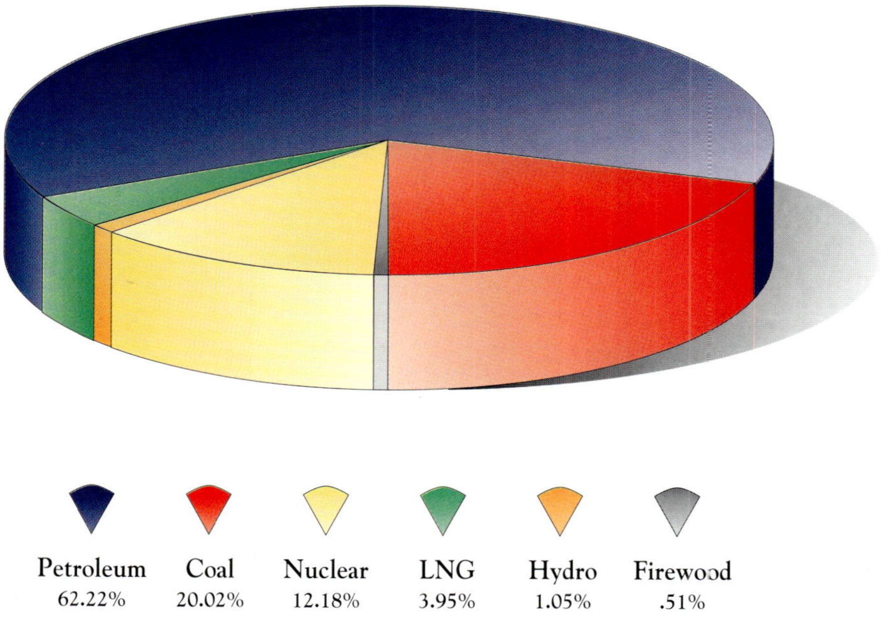

the late-1980s, but left the country with serious overcapacity problems in all areas except in the production of some fibre intermediates. In the 1970s, petrochemicals production grew, on average, 20 per cent a year, falling to 13 per cent by the 1980s. A slowdown in domestic demand in the 1990s has led to Korea becoming a major exporter of petrochemical products, notably of synthetic resins. Korea's aggressive export push has been mainly aimed at allowing a stable level of operation at its petrochemical plants, in order to pay off the investments of the previous decade. Declining prices have eroded the profitability of the petrochemical firms, however, pushing some of them to the verge of bankruptcy.

At the end of the 1970s, Korea's petrochemical facilities were limited to one naphtha cracker with a capacity of 155,000 tonnes/year. Since then, petrochemical plants have been developed at the three key centres of Daesan, south of Seoul, Yeochon in the southwest and Ulsan, north of the city of Pusan. Korea is now a major petrochemical producer, with an annual ethylene capacity of 3.5 million tonnes and significant further capacity in downstream derivatives. Ulsan has three naphtha crackers with a total capacity of 855,000 tonnes per year; in Yeochon, there are five naphtha crackers with an annual capacity of 1.85 million tonnes; and the two naphtha crackers at Daesan have a capacity of 800,000 tonnes a year.

Petroleum

Korea's oil industry faces the twin challenges of a rapidly expanding domestic demand and increasingly stringent environmental standards. The country's five oil refineries have a combined capacity of around 1.675 million barrels per day (b/d) but Korea is still heavily dependent on Middle Eastern oil, and has intentions to diversify its sources of energy supply, notably by developing the nuclear sector.

Yukong Ltd is the largest refiner, with a 585,000 b/d plant located at the Ulsan Petrochemical Complex. This was the country's first oil refinery, built as a joint-venture with Gulf Oil in 1964, with the American company withdrawing in 1980. Honam Oil, part of the Lucky Goldstar group, has a 380,000 b/d refinery at Yochon, with plans to expand capacity by 220,000 b/d. The refinery began operating in 1969 and is a joint venture between the Lucky group and Caltex Petroleum. Kyung-In has a 275,000 b/d plant at Inch'on, started in 1971. Ssangyong has its 325,000 b/d refinery at Onsan; Ssangyong Oil Refining Co is a subsidiary of Korea's Ssangyong Group and the refining company is now 35 per cent owned by Saudi Arabia. Kukdong Oil's 110,000 b/d refinery at Daesan has been in financial trouble since the 1990s, and was recently taken over by the Hyundai group after a complex restructuring deal. The company was founded in 1966, and was formerly a joint venture with Shell, who withdrew in 1977.[8]

Pulp and paper

A high level of literacy and the wide distribution of newspapers and magazines have led to strong annual growth in pulp production. Paper production stood at around 4.5 million tonnes in 1990. Korea is well-forested with almost 6.5 million hectares of forests out of a total land area of 9.9 million hectares but a lack of suitable timber and the capital-intensive nature of the pulp industry has led to a concentration of production in newsprint paper, printing and writing paper for the domestic market.

Shipping

Korean shipyards experienced a boom in 1993 due to low costs, which were a result of the won's slide against the dollar, and the strong yen which attracted business away from Japan. Moreover, the ruling by the International Maritime Organisation (IMO) that all very large crude carriers (VLCCs) built after July 1993 were to be equipped with double hulls led to a rush of orders in the first part of that year. Korean shipbuilding capacity now stands at 4.5 million tonnes annually, although lack of investment in R&D has led to low productivity from the existing yards.

Prior to the yen windfall, Korean shipbuilders had been suffering from a slump in business. New orders in 1993 totalled 6.66 million gross registered tonnes against just 1.64 million gross registered tonnes in the whole of 1992. The decline in orders in 1992 led shipyards in Korea to cut prices by as much as 20 per cent, and profits are likely to be squeezed as a result. The strong yen, however, also has a downside: Korean yards import about 15 per cent of their parts from Japan.

Telecommunications

Korea's telecommunications market is well-developed, and heavy investment by the recently privatised Korea Telecoms (formerly the Korea Telecommunications Authority) has gradually enhanced the availability of telephones in the country.

In 1993, the penetration ratio for telephones had reached 35.7:100 according to Datapro (Korean government data suggest that a figure of 36.7 per 100 population had been reached in 1990), and the number of telephone subscribers had risen to 17.5 million in 1991, compared to just 2.4 million as recently as 1979, according to government data. Korea Telecoms has plans to add 5.8 million telephones over five years, and has invested over US$1.5 billion annually in providing one million circuit lines per year.

Datapro estimate that at the end of 1992, the country had just over 19 million telephone lines in operation. By end 1993, government projections suggest that the total will have risen to 20 million.

Korea has developed its own digital switching system (TDX) through a collaborative effort by the state-run Electronics and Telecommunications Research Institute and private sector companies.

Korea Telecoms enjoys a monopoly on providing telephone services. Originally state controlled, the Telecommunications Business Act was revised to allow for the deregulation of the industry, allowing the telecommunications company to double its paid-up capital. The planned share offering of 49 per cent of the government's stake in the company was put off as the stock market declined in 1991 and 1992, and there is still disagreement over plans for the sale of this stake. The 1993 government budget projected revenues of around US$738 million from the sale of telecom shares.[9]

Textiles

Textiles were a major source of export revenue for Korea in the 1970s, but the importance of this labour-intensive industry has declined as wage costs rise and pressure from lower cost NIEs, including China, increase. In 1992, textile exports were worth US$15.7 billion, much the same figure as was recorded in 1989-1991. Although exports of textiles have expanded five-fold since 1977, their share of total exports has declined from almost a third to just 20 per cent in the same period. Production has also declined in recent years, particularly for silk and cotton fabrics, although synthetic fibre output grew steadily until 1991, partly because of the petrochemical industry which has produced a surplus of the chemicals used for their manufacture. Without the advantage of low wage costs, the textile industry is increasingly moving towards the manufacture of quality goods rather than focusing on low-cost production; a significant investment in automated machinery will be needed if this sector is to retain its profitability.

Trade patterns

Korean exports grew more slowly than imports in 1987-1992 with export growth measuring 10.5 per cent in 1991 and only 6.6 per cent in 1992, compared to double-digit import growth rates.

Export growth rates of 36 and 28 per cent had been recorded in 1987 and 1988. The value of imports has risen from US$31 billion in 1985 to more than US$80 billion in 1992, whereas export growth has lagged behind, reaching just US$76.6 billion in 1992. This has resulted in three consecutive years of trade deficits between 1990-1992, although it is likely that there will be a small trade surplus in 1993, due to the increased competitiveness of Korean exports.

Korea's top 10 export destinations in 1992 were the United States, Japan, Hong Kong, Singapore, Germany, China, Taiwan, Indonesia, Panama and the United Kingdom. The top 10 import sources in 1992 were Japan, the United States, Saudi Arabia, Germany,

China, Australia, Indonesia, Singapore, Malaysia and Canada. However, Korean trade is not nearly as diverse as this might imply.

The United States and Japan

The United States and Japan account for a large part of Korea's foreign trade although overall trade dependence on these two markets is declining. In 1987 they accounted for 74.6 per cent of Korea's total trade, absorbing 56.6 per cent of Korea's exports and supplying 41.9 per cent of its imports: they now account for less than half of Korea's total trade with the outside world.

Traditionally, Korea has run a trade surplus with the United States, and a deficit with the Japanese. This trend appears to be changing gradually, with the surplus with the United States turning into a deficit. Korean exports to the United States have declined in dollar terms every year since 1988, reflecting keen competition in the US market from low-cost competitors in Latin America and in Asia, notably ASEAN and China.

Exports to the United States totalled US$18.1 billion in 1992, or about 23.6 per cent of total exports, while imports were valued at just below US$18.3 billion, about 22.3 per cent of the total. This led to a net deficit with the United States of US$181 million. In 1988, in comparison, Korea's trade surplus with the United States had been over US$8.6 billion, which had provoked bilateral pressure from Washington to cure structural trade imbalances.

Korea remains a huge net importer from Japan: in 1992, exports to Japan reached US$11.6 billion (15 per cent of the total), compared to imports of US$19.5 billion (23.7 per cent of total imports). Although imports from Japan have declined as a percentage of total Korean imports, Japan's share of Korea's export market has also declined: in 1988, Korean exports to Japan amounted to over US$12 billion, or 19.7 per cent of the total, whereas imports from Japan were US$15.9 billion, or 30.7 per cent of the total import bill.

Asia

The highly skewed trade relationship with the United States and Japan is of considerable concern to Korean planners since trade accounts for 70-80 per cent of the GNP[10], and the country is actively seeking new markets, as far afield as Hungary and China. However, none of these promise to break Korea's dependence on its two largest trading partners. Korean trade with Asia, in particular, has expanded in recent years, with exports reaching US$32.9 billion in 1992 against imports of US$33.1 billion. Japan accounts for 35 per cent of the export total and 58 per cent of imports, but this is a considerable improvement from 1988 when the figures were 57 per cent and 70 per cent respectively.

The negative trade balance with Japan has resulted in overall Korean trade deficits with its Asian neighbours throughout the last decade. These narrowed substantially in 1992, however, to just US$0.25 billion from US$5.3 billion in 1991, largely because of an improving trade position with the member countries of ASEAN. Exports to ASEAN countries have risen 181 per cent since 1988 to reach US$8.5 billion in 1992. Future trends remain uncertain, however, as Korea is both a natural resource importer from such mineral-rich nations as Indonesia and Malaysia, and a supplier of finished and intermediate products to the rapidly-industrialising economies of Singapore and Hong Kong, with both of which runs a consistent trade surplus.

Exhibit 4.3

Korea's exports to and imports from the EC and ASEAN, 1982 and 1992 (US$ millions)

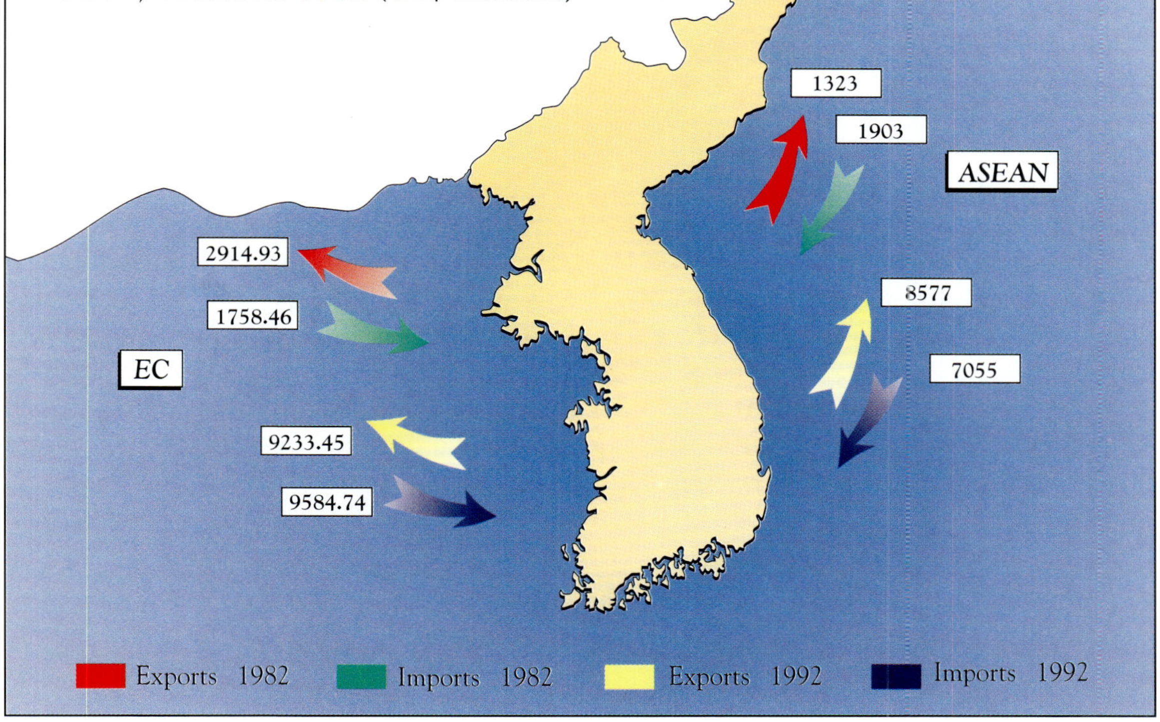

Europe

The picture is also fairly balanced as far as Europe and the European Community (EC) is concerned although imbalances in specific sectors have been the source of periodic trade friction. Korean exports to Europe totalled US$11.8 billion in 1992, compared to just US$3.1 billion in 1980, but rising imports meant that, in 1992, Korea ran a small trade deficit with Europe for the first time in years. Exports to the EC declined 5.1 per cent in 1992 from 1991, following a sharp rise of 17.3 per cent between 1990 and 1991. Between 1991 and 1992, Korean exports lost ground in key markets such as Germany, the Netherlands and France, although increasing volumes of exports to the United Kingdom, Italy, Spain, and Greece partially compensated for this. Deliveries in textiles, footwear and ships were the key areas that suffered. The EC remains a stable partner in terms of two-way trade with Korea: trade in 1992 amounted to US$24.2 billion, or 15 per cent of Korea's total.

The Middle East

Korea's reliance on imports of Middle Eastern oil is another structural imbalance the government is trying to reduce, with limited success. In 1992 Korea ran a US$5.1 billion overall trade deficit with its Middle Eastern suppliers who account for 70 per cent of the country's energy imports. Korea has addressed these imbalances through a three-pronged strategy: to invest abroad in oil exploration, which it has done with notable success in the Yemen; to encourage conservation policies domestically; and to engage in an active programme to develop nuclear energy. These programmes are unlikely to have a significant effect on the problem until 2000 at the earliest, but the downward trend in oil prices should go some way to reducing the seriousness of the problem.

The *Chaebol*

Korea's *Chaebol* are the massive, usually family-run, business conglomerates which have spearheaded the country's export drive and been the engine of economic growth since independence. The *Chaebol* have transformed Korea from an agricultural society into a highly industrialised economy. In the 1970s, they were the darlings of the government and the recipients of significant incentives in order to increase exports, but many feel that they have become too powerful and the government itself now favours smaller-scale companies.

There is no strict definition of a *Chaebol*. Reminiscent of the pre-war *Zaibatsu* in Japan, they differ in management structure, orientation and decision-making characteristics. The top 30 *Chaebol* are generally reckoned to account for 70 per cent of Korean exports,

Exhibit 4.4

South Korean exports by commodity – MTI classification, 1982-1992 (US$ millions)

Year	*Agriculture*	*Forestry*	*Marine*	*Minerals*	*Chemicals*
1982	463.117	360.774	829.196	83.556	650.696
1983	485.312	302.366	792.862	83.442	651.527
1984	505.830	262.377	853.752	70.666	804.432
1985	434.696	226.332	869.258	58.741	895.167
1986	520.041	289.529	1246.828	66.398	1020.318
1987	587.515	419.488	1626.285	129.382	1212.107
1988	737.687	558.203	1911.116	158.562	1637.496
1989	840.003	660.646	1690.467	195.443	1824.073
1990	842.837	610.302	1515.258	277.615	2348.211
1991	805.776	586.794	1642.708	290.785	2889.007
1992	857.205	569.815	1518.129	332.620	4242.178

Year	*Textiles*	*Iron & steel or metal*	*Electrics & electronics*	*Machinery & transport equipment*	*Miscellaneous*
1982	5975.510	2945.101	2296.430	3615.483	727.932
1983	6117.153	3098.718	3001.763	4620.963	1026.792
1984	7162.144	3548.783	4717.959	5952.245	603.036
1985	7078.736	3326.369	4853.172	6897.742	581.837
1986	8794.844	3400.647	7575.733	4853.569	624.472
1987	11822.864	4125.465	11563.823	6209.698	833.173
1988	14111.272	6043.445	16313.966	8160.833	548.425
1989	15140.475	6675.066	17138.492	7301.411	525.930
1990	14669.669	6444.696	17869.538	8561.087	739.165
1991	15477.919	6644.760	20157.224	10986.549	635.529
1992	15709.504	7852.662	21573.436	11872.397	601.149

representing about 43 per cent of its GNP. "Among the more salient characteristics of the typical *Chaebol* are: family control and management; paternalistic leadership; centralised planning and coordination; an entrepreneurial orientation; close business-government relations; and strong school ties in hiring," according to one recent book.[11] The government estimates that almost two-thirds of the shares of the major *Chaebol* are held or controlled by the founder or his family members. The Fair Trade Commission designated 61 conglomerates (controlling 915 subsidiaries) as *Chaebol* in 1991.[12] The share of these conglomerates in the economy has expanded enormously in the last 30 years, although exact statistics are unavailable due to cross-shareholdings between the multitude of subsidiaries.

The *Chaebol* also tend to have high debt ratios, reflecting the ease with which they have been able to receive credit, both from the private sector banks and the from the state sector, something denied to many of the smaller companies. Another defining characteristic is the range of their businesses: these groups are highly diversified, and defining their core business (among the government's methods for controlling the *Chaebol* is to get them to focus on their core businesses) is often none too easy. A single group may have 20 or 30 subsidiaries (with a few having over 50), in fields as diverse as electronics,

Exhibit 4.5

South Korean imports by commodity – MTI classification, 1982-1992 (US$ millions)

Year	Agriculture	Forestry	Marine	Minerals	Chemicals
1982	2938.020	691.454	59.180	7639.078	3773.797
1983	3204.655	688.526	59.269	6983.698	4106.306
1984	3477.543	695.497	70.261	7318.060	4971.320
1985	3108.756	614.580	92.403	7504.638	4943.900
1986	3301.212	632.918	118.257	5324.597	5894.644
1987	4114.879	845.985	218.111	6043.700	8170.183
1988	5469.163	1295.494	318.204	6408.829	10159.667
1989	6408.456	1519.073	321.878	8235.503	11691.215
1990	6528.107	1677.162	369.827	9747.269	14380.966
1991	7071.464	1947.989	577.079	12126.850	15362.837
1992	7136.930	1872.736	506.516	13579.335	15118.363

Year	Textiles	Iron & steel or metal	Electrics & electronics	Machinery & transport equipment	Miscellaneous
1982	525.168	1349.514	2216.490	3997.270	212.147
1983	565.624	1574.050	2785.083	4969.168	250.697
1984	656.098	2491.632	3823.181	6644.097	309.889
1985	708.956	2278.793	3668.638	7757.161	325.035
1986	1027.201	2805.388	5396.251	6546.294	402.331
1987	1536.835	3790.725	6946.928	8650.058	519.616
1988	1710.648	5285.079	9393.652	11068.100	612.915
1989	2047.761	6514.066	10227.527	13631.249	740.328
1990	2266.378	6691.309	11222.210	15938.948	909.069
1991	2713.160	8389.860	13017.791	19093.395	1101.401
1992	2849.648	6699.973	13471.634	19216.168	1231.078

shipbuilding, and automobiles. The nature of these groups allows significant degrees of synergy between the various business areas, notably in finance, insurance and shipping, and also in technology sharing. The problem of duplicated investment between the *Chaebol* has led to cut-throat competition and the criticism that the conglomerates are overdiversified: Korean government figures show that the top 10 *Chaebol* in Korea are engaged in an average of nine industrial sectors each, while Japan's 40 largest companies specialise in a maximum of three industrial sectors.

As a result of the widespread perception that the *Chaebol*'s iron grip on the economy is actually against the public interest, Kim Young-Sam's government had planned to break them up into smaller units. In the late 1980s, in particular, the *Chaebol* attracted public and government criticism for their hunger to expand and their participation in property speculation. There is concern that their profits increasingly come, not from production, but from rental activities. The conglomerates have proved difficult to control, partly due to their huge contribution to the economy, and the Kim government has discovered, like its predecessors, that there is a fine line between controlling the *Chaebol* and crippling the economy.

Kim took office with the explicit promise of boosting small- and medium-scale industries, and in his first days in office, announced that he would not receive any form of political funds during his term. This was a bold move, considering that previous governments had routinely received funds from big business implicitly in return for favours. Kim pressurised the *Chaebol* to tighten the repayment period on promissory notes to suppliers; charged Hyundai founder, Chung Ju-Yung, who ran against him for the presidency during the 1992 elections, with diverting funds from his company to the United People's Party; and presented the *Chaebol* leaders with a *fait accompli* in terms of his economic reforms.

In fact, Kim's widely-publicised poker game with the *Chaebol* has led to few substantive changes: the conglomerates, backed by the Federation of Korean Industries, simply stonewalled the government, by postponing their investment plans in such a way as to hold the Kim administration to ransom given its own need to deliver on the economic front. The sluggish economy in mid-1993 discouraged confrontation between the government and the large *Chaebol*, which are widely regarded in business circles as being the only entities big enough – and possessing the relevant expertise – to lead an economic recovery by competing in the international arena.

Plans to use anti-trust laws to restrict cross-ownership between the *Chaebol* subsidiaries have been put on hold, at least for the time being. However, as a result of the concentration of power in the hands of the top 30 conglomerates, the government is still trying to exert pressure on the *Chaebol* to specialise in core business sectors, to allow them to compete more effectively in international markets.

Under a proposal of October 1993, and in fulfilment of a pledge in the five-year plan to boost the international competitiveness of Korean industry, the government urged the 10 largest *Chaebol* to choose three core sectors (defined as those sectors that account for more than 10 per cent of the group's total sales) in which they would concentrate their business, with the next 20 largest companies urged to specialise in a maximum of two core sectors. The plan, due to take effect in 1994, provides for loans at preferential rates to be made available only for investment in the selected "core sectors". The aim of the proposal is to help make the *Chaebol*'s business strategies more specific but similar measures have failed in the past as the *Chaebol* have simply used the core companies to channel money into other subsidiaries.

The plan is, moreover, bitterly opposed by the very companies it is intended to benefit. The *Chaebol* argue that the Korean economy is too sophisticated for such government-led restructuring, that the proposal would disrupt investment plans, and that the government's aims would be better served by providing positive incentives to develop the country's infrastructure instead.

Confrontations between the government and the *Chaebol* are nothing new in Korea, and the government has almost invariably lost: there is just too much at stake. The government's most realistic option at this stage would appear to be for it to encourage a process whereby the *Chaebol* undertake to reform themselves, and to withhold incentives if this does not take place. It is clear that there is a real need for some process of restructuring to take place, if only to improve the profit margins of the *Chaebol*, which have been eroded by competition for market share and debt servicing. The return on sales for the major *Chaebol* was estimated to be only 1.27 per cent in the late 1980s.[13]

In 1993, the Fair Trade Commission listed the top four conglomerates as Hyundai, Samsung, Daewoo and Lucky Goldstar (discussed in more detail below). The second-tier conglomerates, with assets of more than won5,000 billion include Sunkyong, Hanjin, Ssangyong, Kia, Han Wha and Lotte. Included in the top 30 are Kumho, Daelim, Doosan, Dong Ah, Hanil, Hyosung, Dongkuk, Sammi, Halla, Hanyang, Tongyang, Kolon, Jinro, Dongbu, Kohap, Kukdong, Woosung, Haitai, Byucksan and Miwon.

Hyundai group

The Hyundai group is Korea's largest conglomerate. Its subsidiary, Hyundai Heavy Industries, is the nation's biggest car producer and the group is renowned internationally for its shipbuilding activities. Recently, its founder Chung Ju-Yung hit the headlines by running, on behalf of the United People's Party (UPP) against President Kim Young-Sam in the 1992 general election, a move which has brought controversy to the group. Hyundai Corporation, the trading arm of the Hyundai group, is the second largest general trading company in Korea, and accounts for 11 per cent of Korean exports, largely comprising heavy industrial products. Exports are supported by a network of around 50 overseas offices.

The Hyundai group was founded in 1947, and it is now involved in fields as diverse as engineering, construction, steel, finance, trade, electronics, robotics and petrochemicals. Over 90 per cent of its products are marketed through the general trading company, which also handles business for companies outside the Hyundai group. Imports have been a growing part of the company's business, increasing to 34.5 per cent of turnover in the 1991-1992 financial year.

Heavy industry makes up the mainstay of the group's exports but it is also moving into new areas: in November 1993 Hyundai Precision and Industry Co set up a joint venture with Russian aircraft maker Yakovlev to develop passenger jets, aiming to develop 150- and 30-seater airplanes to be sold in the United States, Europe and South East Asia.

Hyundai group subsidiaries include: Hyundai Corporation (trading); Hyundai Engineering & Construction Co Ltd, Hyundai Engineering Co Ltd, Hyundai Housing & Industrial Development Co Ltd, Koryeo Industrial Development Co Ltd (construction and engineering; Hyundai Heavy Industries Co Ltd, Hyundai Mipo Dockyard Co Ltd (shipbuilding and plants); Hyundai Motor Co, Hyundai Motor Service Co (automobiles); Hyundai Electronics Industries Co Ltd, Hyundai Precision and Industry Co Ltd, Hyundai Robot Industry Co Ltd, Hyundai Construction Equipment Industries Co Ltd, Hyundai Electrical Engineering Co Ltd, Hyundai Elevator Co Ltd, Hyundai Steel Tower Industries

Co Ltd (machinery and equipment); Inchon Iron & Steel Co Ltd, Hyundai Pipe Co Ltd, Aluminium of Korea, Hyundai Aluminium Industry Co Ltd (steel & metals); Hyundai Wood Industries Co Ltd, Dongsu Industrial Co Ltd, Keumkang Development Industrial Co Ltd (light manufacturing); Hyundai Merchant Marine Co Ltd (shipping); Hyundai Marine & Fire Insurance Co Ltd, Hyundai Securities Co Ltd, and KKBC International Ltd (financing and securities).

Samsung group

Samsung Co, the trading arm of the Samsung group, was listed in 1975 and is now the largest general trading company in Korea, with 45 offices worldwide. The Samsung group now has 200,000 employees, with 272 sales offices around the world, 37 factories and 13 research and development centres overseas. Samsung Electronics now ranks among the world's leading semiconductor manufacturers.

The Samsung Group was founded in 1938 in Taegu, home to many of Korea's political elite, by Lee Byung-Chull. The company was started with capital of US$2,000 and a workforce of 40, and trading partners in Manchuria and Beijing. The company moved its headquarters to Seoul in 1948, and began to trade internationally with South East Asian nations and the US. Samsung moved into manufacturing in earnest after the end of the Korean war. In 1953, it built a sugar refinery, and in 1954 moved into wool processing. In the late 1950s it branched out into banking. The key period of expansion was in the 1960s: Samsung built a paper plant in 1965; in 1967 it completed a 330,000 tonnes/year fertiliser plant, laying the foundation for its expansion into the heavy and chemical industries; and in 1969 it began to move into electronics.

In the 1970s, Samsung consolidated its activities in trading, electronics, engineering and chemicals. Samsung Heavy Industries was founded in 1974, and from this base the company formed subsidiaries in shipbuilding, petrochemicals, aerospace, and precision industries. In 1974, Samsung started manufacturing silicon wafers, and in 1975 it started producing electro-guns for cathode ray tubes. By the end of the decade, it was making video cassette recorders, integrated circuits for televisions, and telephone exchanges. The early 1980s saw further developments in high-technology fields, as Samsung moved into industrial robots, and opened a consumer electronics factory in Portugal. In 1989, Samsung developed a four-megabyte DRAM semiconductor chip, and in 1990 a 16-megabyte DRAM. Samsung is now working on a 64-megabyte DRAM. Samsung's chemicals division opened a two million tonnes/year petrochemical complex in 1991.

Key developments for the 1990s are planned in the fields of electronics, engineering and chemicals, with an intensifying involvement in commercial vehicles, material handling systems, and high-precision machinery.

Subsidiaries and affiliates include: Samsung Electronics Co Ltd, Samsung Electron Devices Co Ltd, Samsung Electro-Mechanics Co Ltd, Samsung Corning Co Ltd, Samsung Medical Systems Co Ltd, Samsung Data Systems Co Ltd, Samsung Hewlett-Packard Co Ltd (electronics); Samsung Heavy Industries, Samsung Engineering & Construction Co Ltd, Samsung Engineering Co Ltd, Samsung Aerospace Industries Co Ltd, Samsung Watch Co Ltd (engineering); Samsung Petrochemical Co Ltd, Samsung General Chemicals Co Ltd, Samsung-BP Chemicals Co Ltd (petrochemicals); Samsung Co Ltd, Samsung Life Insurance Co Ltd, Ankuk Fire & Marine Insurance Co Ltd, Samsung Winners Card Co Ltd (financial and information services); Cheil Foods & Chemicals Inc, Cheil Industries Inc, Cheil Synthetics Inc (food); Hotel Shilla Co Ltd, The Joong-Ang Daily News Joong-

Ang Development Co Ltd, Cheil Communications Inc, Korea Secom Co Ltd, Samsung Advanced Institute of Technology, Samsung Economic Research Institute, Samsung Foundation of Art & Culture, and the Samsung Welfare Foundation (services).

Daewoo group

Daewoo was founded in 1967 by its current chairman Kim Woo-Chong. It has followed the same pattern as the other main *Chaebol*, moving from light industry to heavy and chemical industries, including automobiles, and more recently into the high-tech industries. The company is structured through its holding company Daewoo Corporation, which was listed on the Korea Stock Exchange in June 1973. The group has subsidiaries in trading, construction, machinery, electronics, telecommunications, automotive manufacturing and parts, shipbuilding, finance, research, hotels, textiles and other light industries. Daewoo is Korea's third largest general trading company and accounts for 8 per cent of Korean exports. It has 80 branch offices and subsidiaries, and operates in 120 countries worldwide. The major shareholder is the Daewoo Foundation with 9.2 per cent of shares. Total assets in June 1993 amounted to won6,661 billion, and sales were up 12 per cent in the six months prior to that period. Overseas construction is expected to be a key growth area for the company. The group also owns two Hilton hotels in Korea, the Seoul Hilton Hotel and the Kyongju Hilton.

Daewoo Group companies include: Daewoo Corporation, Keangnam Enterprises Ltd, Kyungnam Metals Co Ltd (trading/construction); Daewoo Heavy Industries Ltd, Daewoo Precision Industries Ltd (machinery); Daewoo Electronics Co Ltd, Orion Electric Co Ltd, Daewoo Electronic Components Co Ltd, Daewoo Electric Motor Industries Ltd, Orion Electric Components Co Ltd (electronics); Daewoo Telecom Ltd, Daewoo Information Systems Co Ltd (telecommunications), Daewoo Motor Co Ltd (automobile manufacturing); Daewoo Precision Industries Ltd (parts and components); Daewoo Automotive Components Ltd, Koram Plastics Co Ltd (automotive parts and components); Daewoo Shipbuilding and Heavy Machinery Ltd (shipbuilding); Daewoo Securities Co Ltd, Daewoo Research Institute, Daewoo Capital Management Co Ltd (finance); and Dongwoo Development Co Ltd (hotels).

Lucky Goldstar

The Lucky Goldstar group is Korea's third largest manufacturing group, headquartered in the impressive Twin Towers building on the island of Youido on the Han River in Seoul. Electronic and chemical products are the group's mainstays. Lucky Ltd is the flagship company of the group, and is Korea's largest integrated general chemical firm, making 8,000 products from cosmetics to advanced materials. The Lucky group's trading arm, Lucky Goldstar International Corporation, operates 38 offices worldwide, marketing a wide range of products. The group significantly reorganised its management structure in 1988 in a bid to give more autonomy to lower-level executives, and to decentralise management in order to enhance flexibility.

The Lucky Goldstar group developed out of the Lucky Chemical Co founded in 1947 by Koo In-Hwoi. Initially manufacturing cosmetic creams for women, the company was making Korea's first plastic products by 1952, and soon expanded into manufacturing daily necessities such as toothpaste. In 1958, Lucky Chemical formed a new company, Goldstar Co Ltd, to manufacture electrical appliances, and the company made the first Korean radio

Korean seafood and ginseng now reach a ready and wide international audience

Increased automation has helped service sustained growth in world-wide demand for Korean automobiles

soon after this. The chemical and electrical/electronic businesses were developed in the 1960s, and in 1967, the group built the Honam Oil refinery. In 1983, Lucky Ltd became the first Korean enterprise to enter into a joint venture, forming the National Petrochemical Corp (NPC), a 500,000 tonnes/year capacity petrochemical plant, with Saudi Arabia's SABIC.

The Lucky Goldstar group subsidiaries include: Lucky Ltd, Honam Oil Refinery Co Ltd, Lucky Petrochemical Co Ltd, Hoyu Energy Co Ltd (chemicals and energy); Goldstar Co Ltd, Goldstar Information & Communication Ltd, Goldstar Telecommunications Co Ltd, Goldstar Software Ltd, Goldstar-Alps Electronics Co Ltd, Goldstar Precision Co Ltd, Goldstar Electronic Devices Co Ltd, Goldstar Industrial Systems Co Ltd, Goldstar Electron Co Ltd, Goldstar Electric Machinery Co Ltd, Goldstar Honeywell Co Ltd (electric goods and electronics); Goldstar Cable Co Ltd, Kukje Electric Wire Co Ltd, Lucky Metals Corp (machinery and metals); Lucky Goldstar International Corp, Lucky Securities Co Ltd, Lucky Insurance Co Ltd, Pusan Investment & Finance Corp, LG Credit Card Ltd, Pusan Investment & Finance Corp (trade and finance); Lucky Development Co Ltd, Lucky Engineering Co Ltd, LG Mart Co Ltd, Hee Sung Tourism development Co Ltd, LG Ad Inc, Systems Technology Management Corp (construction and services); Lucky Goldstar Economic Research Institute.

New trade relationships

Korea's overdependence in the 1980s on western markets, notably the United States, and its reliance on imports from Japan, have led to the republic increasingly focusing on intra-Asian trade when looking for new markets. The maturity of the western markets and political sensitivity over trade imbalances, have forced Korea to raise its profile in the Asian sphere, and new alliances have been formed to take advantage of the rapidly-expanding markets in this region.

The major growth areas for Korea are likely to be the highly populated nations of China, Vietnam, Thailand and Indonesia; and, as the Indian subcontinent emerges from poverty, India and Pakistan are likely to become gradually more significant importers of Korean goods. The development of non-exclusive regional trade blocs such as the APEC will intensify this trend.

China

China has emerged as an important trading partner for Korea since Seoul resumed ties with the communist nation in August 1992, shifting its allegiance from its long-time ally, Taiwan. The potential for friction began to emerge in 1993, however, as volumes of trade between the two countries spiralled: China has urged Seoul to remove trade barriers, particularly on rice and meat, and to buy more of its traditional export commodities, machinery, electronic products and finished industrial goods.

As a result, China has emerged as one of Korea's biggest trading partners in Asia. Total exports to China in 1991 totalled just over US$1 billion, but the figure rose rapidly to more than US$2.65 billion in 1992, and in the first eight months of 1993, exports totalled US$2.81 billion, suggesting that the end-of-year figure will be close to US$4 billion. Meanwhile, imports from China, which totalled US$3.44 billion in 1991, had risen to US$3.72 billion in 1992. Actual volumes of trade between the two countries

Exhibit 4.6

Korea's worldwide export and import totals, 1982-1993 (US$ millions)

	Total trade		*Exports*		*Imports*		*Exports-Imports*
Year		*% growth*	*FOB*	*% growth*	*CIF*	*% growth*	
1982	46104.23	-2.70	21853.39	2.82	24250.84	-7.20	-2397.450
1983	50637.28	9.83	24445.05	11.86	26192.22	8.01	-1747.170
1984	59876.30	18.25	29244.86	19.64	30631.44	16.95	-1386.580
1985	61418.78	2.58	30283.12	3.55	31135.66	1.65	-852.533
1986	66298.37	7.94	34714.47	14.63	31583.90	1.44	3130.570
1987	88300.74	33.19	47280.93	36.20	41019.81	29.88	6261.115
1988	112507.00	27.41	60696.39	28.37	51810.63	26.31	8885.756
1989	123841.90	10.07	62377.17	2.77	61464.77	18.63	912.402
1990	134859.40	8.90	65015.73	4.23	69843.68	13.63	-4827.950
1991	153395.00	13.74	71870.12	10.54	81524.86	16.72	-9654.740
1992	158406.80	3.27	76631.52	6.62	81775.26	0.31	-5143.740
1993	78262.50	-50.59	78262.50	2.13	82593.00	-100.00	78262.500

may exceed these figures, however, as smuggling along China's eastern coast has become common.

Total two-way trade in 1993 was expected to reach around US$7.5 billion, a rise of 20 per cent over the previous year. With the heavy Korean direct investment seen so far in China, this would make Beijing one of Korea's three most important strategic allies in terms of trade and investment. China's huge population, its shift in the early 1990s to a market economy, and growing consumer demand are likely to continue the trend. The shift from being a net importer from China to being a net exporter is likely to lead to increasing pressure for Korea to redress the balance. The surge in trade between the two countries does not just reflect the resumption of diplomatic ties, however, as trade had been increasing even before 1992. China is also a formidable rival to Korea for a share in the large western consumer markets, and it has made advances in the fields of textiles, simple electronic devices and toys, with sales increasing to the United States, Japan and the European Community. These trends are likely to continue for some years, because of China's big cost advantage over Korea in manufacturing low-priced consumer commodities. The presence of a growing number of low-cost competitors is likely to push Korea increasingly towards the development of high-tech industries, to service the growing middle-classes in the NIEs.

Eastern Europe

The resumption of ties with Russia and other eastern bloc nations has so far failed to generate the expected trade bonanza for Korea, largely as a result of the political turmoil that has followed the break-up of the former Soviet Union. Korean exports to eastern Europe (Yugoslavia, Poland, Czechoslovakia, Hungary, Romania and Bulgaria) dropped 34.5 per cent between 1991 and 1992, and exports to the former Soviet Union fell even more; a steep 41.6 per cent drop in the same period. Moreover, after running a small trade surplus with the former Soviet Union in 1990 and 1991, trade in 1992 went into the red, and that trend looks set to continue as Russia and its former partners remain in desperate need of foreign exchange.

Korea had been eager to develop ties with the eastern bloc as a springboard for developing business in central Europe and the former Soviet republics. Hungary and Korea, for instance, re-established diplomatic relations in 1989, but trade volumes have so far failed to live up to expectations, with exports and imports with Hungary dropping in 1992 after successive gains since 1986. Korean companies' expectations that they would be able to use Hungary as a base for trade and investment throughout the former eastern bloc have been hampered by political uncertainty, and by the fact that the economies of eastern Europe are competing intensely for capital and markets.

Because of its geographical proximity, Korea is emerging as a supplier of technology and expertise to underdeveloped areas in the Russian far east, and the huge oil and gas resources in this area, far from utilised as yet, could be an attractive spur to a nation like Korea that lacks significant natural resources. However, the huge infrastructure and human resource relocation that would be needed to develop the fields mean that significant trade between the two areas is not likely to be seen within this decade.

Other markets

Korea is aiming to develop more sophisticated three-way trade and investment strategies with existing business partners. In this context, France looks set to make significant gains over other European nations as a result of the selection of GEC Alsthom for the massive Seoul-Pusan high-speed rail project. France is keen to penetrate the Chinese market, notably in the railways sector where Beijing is likely to make huge investments in the coming years, and Korea is eager to expand its participation in European trade, and could benefit from stronger ties with France in terms of access to the single European market. These triangular relationships will be pursued through the private-sector, but such alliances have strong support from the Korean government. Meanwhile, although the high-speed train project is unlikely to be reflected in trade flows until 1995-1996 when the project is fully underway, President Mitterrand's visit to Seoul in autumn 1993 has provided a strong foundation for developing business and trade ties further. *Business Korea*, a weekly Korean magazine, commented that the visit had "provided a huge boost to the image of France" within Korea. The article mentioned the fact that Mitterrand had presented President Kim with a rare Korean manuscript that had been kept in the French National Library since the nineteenth century and concluded that: "In Korea and some other Asian countries, such actions are often as significant as more substantive matters". Mitterrand's warning to North Korea to comply with international nuclear inspections was also warmly received in the South.

Communist countries such as Vietnam have also seen trade ties develop with Korea. Korea registered a healthy US$378 million trade surplus with Vietnam in 1992, as exports more than doubled to US$436 million in that year from a little under US$200 million in 1991. This trend is likely to continue growing as the heavily-populated nation of 70 million develops.

Meanwhile, India made a significant shift in its foreign policy in 1993, with an official visit by Prime Minister P.V. Narashima Rao in September leading to calls for expanding investment and bilateral trade between the two countries. Rao was the first Indian prime minister to visit Korea since the two nations established diplomatic ties in 1973 (at the same time as India also established relations with North Korea). Trade is presently at a low-ebb between Seoul and New Delhi, amounting to little more than US$915 million in 1992, with Korea running a small (US$39 million) deficit. However, the diplomatic view is that the Rao visit marked a break in the Indian policy of even-handed diplomacy between South and North Korea, and there appears to be scope for expansion. Rao's free market reforms have led to higher economic growth in India in the 1990s, and trade between India and Korea grew rapidly in 1993, with a 36 per cent increase expected for end-of-year figures.

Two further areas have emerged as important new partners for Seoul during the last few years. One is a maverick: exports to Panama increased dramatically in 1992 to top US$1.84 billion, in comparison to just US$624 million in 1991. However, this looks set to return to more normal levels in 1993 at just over US$1 billion. However, Latin America as a whole is becoming increasingly important as an export market for Korea. Exports to the area rose by 72 per cent between 1991 and 1992 to US$4.96 billion from US$2.8 billion, and exports to Mexico, Argentina, Chile, Uruguay, Paraguay, Peru, Brazil, Ecuador, Colombia, Venezuela and Bolivia now account for 3.35 per cent of total Korean exports. Overall exports to the region stood at more than US$2.5 billion in 1992, nearly 10 times the level in 1980 when exports made up only 1.57 per cent of total exports.

Korean investment abroad

Korean companies have expanded their foreign direct investment (FDI) rapidly since the nation experienced its first sustained trade surpluses in 1986, and the push overseas has been actively supported by the government. Korean FDI growth was spurred mainly by mounting costs in the domestic market, and an urge to deflect criticism of the country's trade surpluses, particularly with the key American market.

Korean companies display a strong preference for 100 per cent ownership or majority control of investments, rather than joint ventures. At the end of 1992, Korean companies had equity shares of more than 50 per cent in more than 80 per cent of their total overseas investments.[14]

The twin factors of lower wage and production costs and averting trade sanctions have attracted Korean companies to two main areas: the Americas and South East Asia, which account for 79.2 per cent of total FDI funds. The average size of investment project is small (71.8 per cent of the projects involve less than US$1 million of Korean money), and the biggest projects tend to be in North America, with a total US$1,985 million invested in 524 projects, representing an average size of investment of US$3.788 million.

In North America and Europe, the trend for FDI has been sparked mainly by the urge to avoid import restrictions, and to develop or gain access to high technology. In South and Central America, obtaining preferential treatment for exports to the United States has also been a driving force. Trade friction and the spectre of a rise in protectionist sentiment that could block Korea's exports, have accelerated this movement.

In South East Asia, cost has been the key factor. Low labour costs and the region's abundant natural resources have pushed Korean companies overseas, as higher domestic wages increasingly strain the country's ability to compete with other NIEs in Asia. At the end of April 1993, Korea's cumulative direct investment amounted to US$4,720 million in 2,258 projects. Over 90 per cent of that investment has been made since 1986. During the 1987-1992 period, the number of projects increased by 49.4 per cent, while the amount of investment surged by 56.1 per cent.[15]

In its earlier phases, Korea's FDI was directed largely towards plugging the natural resources gap, particularly in the wake of the two oil shocks of 1973 and 1980. However, it is now manufacturing, mining and trade that make up the lion's share of foreign investment abroad. At the end of April 1993, slightly over half of the total value of Korea's FDI was in the manufacturing sector, representing 1,212 projects out of the total of 2,258. Most of these manufacturing projects are in labour-intensive areas such as textiles and footwear, with the average value of Korean investment reaching just US$2 million.

Trade projects came second in the FDI stakes, both in number of projects and in value. A total of 636 projects worth US$993 million had been set up by end-April 1993, representing 21.1 per cent of the total by value of investment.

The third biggest sector by value was mining, representing 13.2 per cent of Korea's FDI, with a total of US$622 million invested in 34 projects, as of end-April 1993. The average size of the investment in this area is much larger than those in the manufacturing sector, running at US$18.29 million.

Future growth areas

China has taken the limelight in Korea's FDI strategy since 1992, following the establishment of diplomatic relations between the two countries. As is the case with South East Asia, Korean companies are attracted by China's low labour costs, huge natural resources, and a large ethnic Korean population in some areas: "China is very close geographically, and we have about two million ethnic Koreans in China. They can speak Korean, they know much about China and they can communicate for our companies. Another factor is the low labour cost and abundant manpower. That's the reason investment has been soaring in 1992 and 1993."[16]

By the end of 1992, US$178.9 million had been invested in a total of 252 projects in China. The biggest investments were in textiles and clothing, and in fabricated metal projects. The former saw 61 projects initiated by the end of 1992, to a value of US$33.2 million, while investment in fabricated metals amounted to 34 projects with a total value of US$34.6 million.

These investments made China the second biggest recipient of Korean FDI in the region after Indonesia, but continued high levels of investment from Korea are dependent on wage levels remaining low within China. Wages are crucial in the Asian arena. Investment in Indonesia and Thailand has already slowed as a result of wage increases in recent years, and poorly-developed infrastructure is also a problem for many Korean firms in these countries.

Indonesia remains the biggest recipient of Korean FDI in Asia with US$398.9 million invested by the end of 1992 in 189 projects. Food and raw materials were the major targets of Korean companies: 20 petroleum projects were underway by the end of 1992, representing a total investment of just over US$100 million, while US$87.2 million had been directed towards six major food projects.[17]

The make-up of investment permits issued recently suggest that China will soon overtake Indonesia as chief beneficiary of Korean FDI. In Indonesia, investment permission had been received for a total of 214 projects worth US$442.8 million by the end of 1992. Thus, 25 new projects had been approved worth US$43.95 million, averaging US$1.75 million per project. This suggests that total new investment will expand by just 11 per cent. However, in China the speed of new investment is much faster. Total approved investment was worth US$332 million, to be divided between 401 projects. This is an 85 per cent increase in the value of investment.

Malaysia, Thailand and the Philippines are the other main Asian targets of Korean FDI, but these are mature relationships and the spectacular growth seen in China in recent years is not to be expected in these markets.

Korea's FDI in Malaysia totalled US$138.842 million at the end of 1992, with approval being granted to a further 18 projects worth about US$50 million. The Philippines received US$102.483 in 1992 which was invested in 76 projects. A further 39 projects were approved, but these were relatively small-scale, worth a total of only US$26.78 million. Investment in Thailand at the end of 1992 totalled US$80 million, with approval for a further 11 projects bringing the total up to US$118.4 million. Due to its active infrastructure development programme, several Korean construction firms are looking at Thailand as a possible growth market.[18]

Despite its investment potential, the Russian Far East has not greatly benefited from Korean FDI, reflecting the value attached by Korean firms to political stability and strong legal frameworks to protect their investments. The status of the so-called "Free Economic Zones" (FEZs) in this area, which have a large ethnic Korean population, has become a particularly vexed issue. So far only Sakhalin and Kalanigrad have been designated as FEZs, with the status of other areas being reduced to "bonded zones". Meanwhile, poor transport facilities, technological difficulties due to the region's extreme cold and the emergence of nationalist sentiment in the region have all aggravated problems for Korean companies.[19]

Korean sources say it will be many years before the area is equipped with reasonable infrastructure and the power supply, transportation and telecommunication resources that are needed. However, as political developments in Moscow unravel, the Russian Far East remains a wildcard which could become a winner for Korean companies.

[1] Sakong Il, *Korea and the World Economy*, pp.56-57, Institute for International Economics.
[2] Bello and Rosenfeld, *Dragons in Distress: Asia's Miracle Economies in Crisis*, Penguin, 1990.
[3] *Industry in Korea*, Korea Development Bank.
[4] Sakong Il, *Korea and the World Economy*.
[5] Sakong Il, interview with author.
[6] Agence Française Presse.
[7] Wakabayashi and Sumita, "South Korea's Semiconductor Industry", *NRI Quarterly*; Nomura Research Institute.
[8] *The Petroleum Industry in Korea*; Korea Petroleum Association, 1992.
[9] Datapro, a subsidiary of McGraw-Hill.
[10] Sakong Il, interview with author, November 1993.
[11] Steers, Shin and Ungson, *The Chaebol: Korea's New Industrial Might*.
[12] *Business Korea*.
[13] *Business Korea*.
[14] *Business Korea Yearbook 1993/94*.
[15] *Korean Direct Investment Abroad*, Bank of Korea, July 1993.
[16] Bank of Korea official, interview with author.
[17] *Overseas Direct Investment Statistics Yearbook 1993*, Bank of Korea.
[18] *Business Korea Yearbook 1993/94*.
[19] Ed. Jehoon Park, *Russia's Reform and Economic Cooperation between Korea and Russia*, Korea Institute for International Economic Policy.

Additional sources: Korea Company Handbook (Autumn 1993); "The World of Samsung" Annual Report; Daewoo Annual Report.

현대해상
한진택배
한일은행

Chapter Five

The banking system

Banking institutions

The commercial banks in Korea are classified by the Bank of Korea into four broad categories whose functions overlap considerably. These are:

- nation-wide commercial banks;
- regional banks;
- foreign bank branches; and
- specialised banks.

There are currently 14 nation-wide commercial banks, 10 regional banks, 74 foreign bank branches, and six specialised banks. All these institutions must comply with the provisions of the General Banking Act and regulations issued by the Monetary Board of the central bank under the Bank of Korea Act.

The nation-wide commercial banks run a branch banking system, with branches throughout the country totalling 2,194 at the end of 1992. The 14 nation-wide commercial banks include: Cho Hung Bank; Commercial Bank of Korea; Korea First Bank; Hanil Bank; Bank of Seoul; Korea Exchange Bank; Shinhan Bank; KorAm Bank; Donghwa Bank; Dongnam Bank; and Boram Bank.

The nation-wide commercial banks occupy a commanding position, with total assets of about won107 trillion, representing a 75 per cent share of total commercial bank assets (including regional and foreign banks) at the end of 1992. Most of their money comes from deposits in domestic currency, although they also borrow from the central bank to cover persistent shortfalls in their loanable funds. At the end of 1992, 11 per cent of total funds were borrowed from the Bank of Korea, with 45 per cent coming from won deposits. About 44 per cent of bank funds are used for loans and discounts.

The 10 regional banks also have a branch banking system but this is focused within a particular province, and each bank also has three branches in Seoul. The main clients of these banks tend to be small- and medium-sized companies in their province. The regional banks are: Taegu Bank; Pusan Bank; Chungchong Bank; Kwangju Bank; Cheju Bank; Kyonggi Bank; Chonbuk Bank; Kangwon Bank; Kyungnam Bank and Chungbuk Bank. Foreign exchange business plays a smaller part in the activities of regional banks than it does for commercial banks, and securities investment a rather larger share, but otherwise both types of banks operate in a similar fashion.

The foreign banks largely specialise in wholesale banking. The major source of funds for these banks is the interoffice account which, at the end of 1992, represented 46 per

Opposite:
Seoul: Korea's financial heart

cent of their total sources of funds, with deposits in domestic currency making up only 5 per cent. Loans in domestic currency accounted for 35 per cent of total use of funds, foreign currency loans made up about 20 per cent and foreign assets about 10 per cent.

Six specialised banks in Korea aim to provide funds allocated to sectors specifically targeted by relevant legislation. These banks were created to fill the gap for sectors whose funding from the commercial banks was insufficient, either due to limited availability or low profitability. The six specialised banks are: the Industrial Bank of Korea, Citizens National Bank, Korea Housing Bank, the National Agricultural Cooperative Federation (NACF), the National Federation of Fisheries Cooperatives (NFFC) and the National Livestock Cooperatives Federation (NLCF).

These banks have diversified and expanded their business into commercial banking since they were established in the 1960s. They rely heavily on deposits from the public for their sources of funds, in addition to the issuing of debentures and borrowing from the government, and compete directly with the commercial banks in acquiring deposits. The banks are directed and supervised by the government, but certain areas of their business are governed by the Monetary Board of the Bank of Korea.[1] The specialised banks play a major role in the economy: in June 1993 they held 33 per cent of all banking assets in the country and 42 per cent of deposits and were responsible for 41 per cent of outstanding loans and discounts.

The Industrial Bank of Korea was set up in 1961 under the Industrial Bank of Korea Act to provide financing for small- and medium-sized industries. This sector has had little access to funds from commercial banks, and the Industrial Bank aims to bridge this gap.

The Citizens National Bank, was established in 1963 with more than half of its paid-up capital subscribed by the government. It was set up to make small loans to households and small-scale businesses. Prior to this, households had little access to banking services and used the *Kye* cooperatives as private mutual savings and lending organisations. These, however, suffered from a lack of creditworthiness and were consolidated into a forerunner of the Citizens National Bank in 1962.

The Korea Housing Bank was founded in 1967 to offer housing loans to low-income families. Such loans had previously been handled by the Korea Development Bank on a long-term, low-interest basis, but growing demand for government housing funds led to the establishment of a specialised institution with half its paid-up capital subscribed by the government. The bank lends money for the construction and purchase of houses and housing sites, and lends to local governments and small- and medium-sized companies producing housing materials.

The credit and banking departments of the three federations were set up to make loans in the agricultural, fisheries and livestock sectors, and are bound by the General Banking Act and the Bank of Korea Act. The NACF was formed in 1961 under the Agricultural Cooperatives Act, by the merger of the cooperatives with the Agriculture Bank; the NFFC was formed in 1962 under the Fisheries Cooperatives Act; and the NLCF was established in 1981 under the Livestock Cooperative Act through the merger of cooperatives in the National Agricultural Cooperative Federation and the former Livestock Industry Development Corporation, and was authorised to engage in banking business in 1983.

Non-bank financial intermediaries

Non-bank financial intermediaries (NBFIs) in Korea can be broken down into four main categories according to their business activities: development institutions, savings institutions, investment companies and life insurance companies. Many NBFIs were established in the 1970s and there have been significant gains in both the number of institutions and the volume of funds handled since this date.

The development institutions consist of the Korea Development Bank (KDB), the Export-Import Bank of Korea (Eximbank) and the Korea Long-Term Credit Bank. These provide medium- or long-term credit or loans for the development of key sectors which are considered to be of benefit to the national economy including exports and the development of heavy and chemical industries. Government funds, foreign capital and money raised by issuing special bonds are widely used by these institutions.

The KDB was founded in 1954 under the Korea Development Bank Act to promote industrial development and to stabilise the economy by providing long-term credit to the major industries. The KDB helped fund the early development of Korean industry in the period immediately after the Korean War, took an active role in industrial development after the launching of the first five-year plan in 1962, and channelled funds for the development of the machinery, electronics, shipbuilding, petrochemicals and steel industries during the HCI promotion of the 1970s. In 1980s and 1990s, it has increasingly focused on the development of Korean research and development; the fostering of high-technology industries, notably factory automation; infrastructure projects such as gas and electricity; and supporting anti-pollution facilities investment by domestic industries.

The KDB has 29 domestic branches and 17 sub-branches, one overseas branch office in Tokyo and representative offices in New York, London, Frankfurt, Hong Kong, Toronto, Budapest, Jakarta, Sydney, Bangkok and Beijing. Domestic subsidiaries include: Korea Development Securities Company Ltd, Korea Technology Finance Corporation, Korea Management and Credit Rating Corporation, Saehan Merchant Banking Corporation and Korea Industrial Leasing Corporation.

The KDB has recently taken a more active role in fund-raising for major projects and corporate customers, and has strengthened its presence in the international markets ahead of the government's financial liberalisation. It raised a total of US$1.9 billion in 1992 which included fees for arranging syndicated loans to countries in Eastern Europe and South East Asia, and the issuance of a US$500 million Euro Medium Term Note (EMTN) which the bank says set the stage for other financial institutions to enter the EMTN market. The KDB is also financial advisor to some major infrastructure projects, including the Seoul-Pusan High Speed Rail Project and the Yongjong airport project.

Eximbank was established in 1969 to provide medium- and long-term credit to facilitate trade and external cooperation. Its business was handled by the Korea Exchange Bank until July 1976 when it was established as a separate entity with capital of won50 billion.

Eximbanks's core activities include medium- and long-term financing of capital goods exports, including industrial plant and ships, and providing support for overseas investment and major natural resource development projects. The underwriting of export insurance for domestic companies and financial institutions had originally been part of the organisation's mandate, but this was transferred to Korea Export Insurance Corporation in July 1992. Eximbank has also been entrusted by the government to administer the Economic Development Cooperation Fund (EDCF) and the South and North Korea Cooperation Fund (SNKCF). Cooperation with the international financing agencies, including the World Bank and the Asian Development Bank, in co-financing large-scale projects is seen as a target for the 1990s, and the bank expects to play a bigger role in providing export and import credit support for small- and medium-sized firms.

The Korea Development Finance Corporation was established in 1967, but in 1980 its name was changed to the Korea Long Term Credit Bank (KLCB), when its paid-in capital was increased to won50 billion from won10 billion. The KLCB is allowed to engage in fully-fledged development banking services and extends medium- and long-term credit to businesses, in the form of loans, discounts, equity investments and guarantees, for equipment purchases and long-term working capital.

In addition to these development institutions, NBFIs in Korea include savings, investment and insurance companies. In mid-1993 there were about 7,400 savings institutions in Korea, consisting of mutual savings and finance companies, mutual credit facilities, *Saemaul* (new community) finance associations and post offices. These companies grant small loans which are financed by their deposits. There are 39 investment institutions: 24 investment and finance companies; six merchant banking corporations; eight investment trust companies; and the Securities Finance Corporation. These companies act as financial intermediaries in the money and capital markets. There are 33 insurance companies in Korea, including 20 domestic life insurance companies, seven joint-venture life insurance companies, two foreign companies' branches, three foreign subsidiary companies and post office life insurance outlets.

Other institutions that do not function as financial intermediaries, but perform supplementary financial functions include securities companies, credit guarantee funds, credit management funds, non-life insurance companies, leasing companies and venture capital companies.

The central bank

The central bank, the Bank of Korea, was established in June 1950. Its headquarters are in the heart of Seoul, a short distance from the Namdaemun (South Gate). The head office is organised internally into 31 departments, of which 19, including a research institute, are in the headquarters; and 11 in the Office of Bank Supervision; with the Auditing department housed on its own. The Bank has 16 domestic branches in the major cities within Korea, and nine representative offices in major financial centres around the world.

The Bank's capital was originally won1.5 billion, but under an amendment to the Bank of Korea Act in 1962, it was reconstituted as a special juridical entity with no capital. The profits of the Bank are paid into the government's general revenue account after allowances for asset depreciation and the crediting of the authorised reserve funds.

Structure

The Bank of Korea's supreme policy-making body is the Monetary Board. The Monetary Board has responsibility for the execution of monetary policies and supervision of the activities of the Bank of Korea and all other banking institutions. The Monetary Board consists of nine members appointed by the president, and the board is chaired by the minister of finance or the governor of the Bank of Korea in his absence. The finance minister and the governor are appointed for four-year terms, with the seven other members being appointed for three-year terms. These are recommended by banking institutions, the Economic Planning Board, the Minister of Trade, Industry and Energy and the Minister of Agriculture, Forestry and Fisheries.

The governor administers the operations of the Bank of Korea and executes policy formulated by the Monetary Board. He is supported by a deputy and five assistant governors. The post of Superintendent of Banks is also decided by the president, on the recommendation of the Monetary Board. The Superintendent of Banks is in charge of supervising and examining banking institutions under the direction of the Monetary Board. The Auditor, appointed by the Ministry of Finance, inspects the business of the bank and reports to the Monetary Board.

Monetary policy

The Bank's main function is to control the nation's money supply and it is legally obliged to fight inflation and preserve the value of the currency. The Bank has a duty to ensure the efficient use of national resources and maintain the sound operation of the banking and credit system. The Bank is the issuer of bank notes and coins in Korea, and acts as banker to the banking sector and the government. Korea has a managed currency system in which note and coin issues are decided by the Bank of Korea in line with its monetary policy, and no minimum ratio based on gold or foreign currency holdings is required.

Monetary policy is implemented indirectly by influencing monetary and credit conditions through changes in the availability and cost of the reserves for banking institutions. However, the Bank of Korea has also had at its disposal a wide range of direct policy measures, such as putting caps on interest rates on deposits and loans at banking institutions, and direct credit control by imposing ceilings on bank credits, the latter particularly during periods of excessive monetary expansion. These powers have been reduced since 1988 under the government's deregulation plan.

In the 1960s and 1970s the Bank primarily used direct policy measures to control the money supply and domestic credit. After the Korean War, credit ceilings were set for individual banks and approval was required for extending credit. This system continued even after 1965, when indirect controls were introduced, notably in the 1977 to 1981 period. Since 1982, formal caps on bank credit have been abandoned, although even in 1990, the Bank of Korea commented that "this instrument has evolved into a form of moral suasion". Informal controls on credit through the system of "guidance" rather than explicit regulation remains a potent tool in the hands of the authorities.

The Bank of Korea set up a new system of monetary control in 1967, in the form of the Monetary Stabilisation Account, in which banking institutions were required to deposit certain amounts. This had the same function as varying the reserve requirement, but interest was paid on the funds, which were not considered to be reserves. This instrument was widely used in the early 1980s, but the government allowed banks to withdraw their deposits in May 1989.

Since the late 1980s the central bank has moved increasingly towards indirect control systems, with open market operations becoming the principal instrument of control since 1986. This was the main tool used by the Bank to absorb the large volume of money entering the country from abroad during the 1986-1989 period of balance of payments surplus.

In recent years, the Bank has exercised its monetary policy through: changes in the terms of loans and rediscount, open market operations, and changes in reserve requirement ratios. Because of chronic excess demand for bank credit, the Bank of Korea's rediscount policy has focused on determining rediscount ratios and changing eligibility requirements on bills presented to the central bank for rediscount. This has placed greater emphasis on open market operations in determining credit costs and, thus, demand. The wide gap between market and issue rates on government securities had in the past discouraged the issuance of government debt, with fiscal deficits being funded by direct borrowings from the Bank of Korea. Provisions for the issuing of Monetary Stabilisation Bonds (MSBs) were made in the Bank of Korea Act, and these were introduced in 1961, although they were never really sold on the open market.

In the 1990s, the Bank of Korea has attempted to expand its open-market operations in the conventional sense, with MSBs being sold direct to the public and also to the non-bank financial intermediaries, and the government increasingly relies on bond issuance rather than direct borrowing from the central bank.

The central bank can also exercise control of the money supply by altering the banks' reserve requirements, and during periods of pronounced inflation, banks can be required to hold up to 100 per cent of any increase in deposits in the form of reserves. In the 1960s and 1970s, reserve requirements were actively used as a way to control the money supply and credit volumes, but their high levels affected bank profitability, and were therefore reduced in the 1980s.

The Bank of Korea is responsible for some aspects of foreign exchange control under powers entrusted to it by the Ministry of Finance under the Foreign Exchange Control Act of 1962, including intervention in the foreign exchange market and approval of foreign exchange transactions. Until the early 1980s, foreign exchange dealings had largely been the prerogative of the Ministry of Finance, with the Korea Exchange Bank handling the foreign exchange transactions of businesses. The central bank's role in foreign exchange management is likely to diminish further with the deregulation of the foreign exchange sector planned for the 1993-1997 period.

Supervisory functions

The supervisory functions of the Bank of Korea are executed through the Office of Bank Supervision, subject to instructions from the Monetary Board. The Office of Bank Supervision is responsible for supervising and examining the activities of the commercial banks in Korea, and, under powers delegated by the Ministry of Finance, it also examines the specialised banks and non-bank financial institutions. The Superintendent of Banks examines each year, and without prior notice, the operations of all banks and non-bank financial institutions, and may take disciplinary action based on these findings.

The Office of Bank Supervision is also involved in authorising the opening or closing of banks and their branches, as well as changes in the bank's domicile, capital requirements or articles of association, and the expansion of banks into non-banking areas, under powers entrusted to it by the Monetary Board.

The responsibilities of the Office of Bank Supervision and the Monetary Board are detailed in the Bank of Korea Act and the General Banking Act, the two key regulatory blueprints for the banking sector in Korea. Banks must maintain minimum levels of paid-in capital and reserves as a percentage of their liabilities, and are restricted from making loans or payment guarantees above a specified percentage of their assets; the banks' compliance with these requirements is monitored by the Office of Bank Supervision. Maximum limits on credit extended to both individuals and individual conglomerates can also be imposed, and the Superintendent of Banks can require banks to adjust book values of their assets, as well as set up reserves or write off assets that are deemed to have no effective value.

The deregulation of banking

The impetus for reforms in the banking system has intensified in the 1990s as the size and complexity of the Korean economy have grown. Korea's financial sector still lags behind its corporate sector in terms of efficiency[2] and bank lending tends to reflect government policy rather than commercial decision making.

The roots of the need for deregulation date back to the early growth years of the Korean economy, notably during the HCI promotion drive between 1973 and 1979. The system of government-controlled credit allocation characteristic of this period has been variously cited as being the secret of Korea's economic success, and as the key structural deficiency now afflicting the country. There is an element of truth in both versions of the story: Korea's financial industry has contributed heavily to the high economic growth rates seen over the last 30 years, but it has acted mainly as a conduit for funding, rather than as an independent and autonomous sector determining the allocation of funds.

The government began to reform the banking system in 1980, when it presented the Programme for Deregulation of Commercial Banks' Management, under which government stakes in commercial banks were sold off. Hanil Bank was privatised in June 1981, Seoul Bank and First Bank in September 1982, and Chohung Bank in March 1983. Two new banks were licensed to encourage competition in the bank sector, with Shinhan Bank opening its doors in July 1992 and KorAm Bank in March 1983.

The Temporary Act on Bank Administration, enacted by the military government in 1961, under which the banking system had been effectively nationalised to prevent oligopolistic controls in the financial sphere, was abolished in December 1982, and this was accompanied by substantive amendments to the General Banking Act under which the powers of the banking authorities were curbed and those of shareholders enhanced. Under these reforms, the Office of Bank Supervision's power to appoint and dismiss senior bank officials was removed, and a threshold of 8 per cent of total shares and voting rights for any one private shareholder was introduced, to make sure that large stockholders could not interfere unduly in a bank's management after privatisation. A limit was also placed on the level of credit permitted to individual creditors to stop loans being unevenly allocated.

Towards the end of the 1980s, licences were granted for the establishment of three new nation-wide commercial banks; Donghwa Bank, Dongnam Bank and Daedong Bank, and the status of the Korea Exchange Bank was changed from that of a specialised bank to that of a national commercial bank. The scope of banking activities was gradually increased: the commercial banks were allowed to expand their business fields, with dealing in credit cards allowed in 1981, public sale of commercial bills in 1982, certificates of deposit in 1984 and trust business in 1984.[3] Finance and investment companies were also allowed to do business in a wide range of new areas, and had greater freedom than banks in deciding interest rates, allowing the rapid growth of these institutions at the expense of the banks.

The success of this denationalisation and deregulation programme was extremely mixed, however, and it proved difficult to shake off the country's long history of government control and ministerial guidance, particularly in credit allocation. Key bank executives were still nominated by the government, and the distinction between regulation and interference was not always evident: "In addition to official rules, there are many unofficial procedures or irrational conventions. In many cases, financial regulations were executed arbitrarily or rigidly without consistency."[4]

Foreign bankers even now target the system of "administrative guidance" as the biggest threat to full-scale deregulation of the banking sector. They argue that the Ministry of Finance cannot have its cake and eat it: liberalising the banking system piece-meal, while still keeping *de facto*, if indirect, administrative controls in place will simply not work. The government's phased approach to deregulation, however, is due to its concern that loosening the reins too rapidly could risk the destabilisation of the banking sector.

The Bank of Korea's attempts to move from a direct to an indirect system for controlling the money supply have not been entirely successful. In December 1988 the government announced that direct control over the granting of loans would be abolished, and that interest rates on loans and some long-term deposits would be partially freed, in a bid to spur competition but: "Implicit intervention in loan-granting continued even after the announcement."[5]

In 1993, Korea introduced a three-stage deregulation plan for the banking sector, due to be completed in 1997. The aim of the Three-Phased Financial Liberalisation Plan is little different from those of the previous reforms, and its main intention is to respond to structural changes in the international economic environment by boosting the competitiveness of the banking sector and reducing government control.

The government's wider aim is to shift the onus for economic development away from the technocrats in the ministries into the hands of the private sector; reforming the banking sector is seen as an essential element of this. The three distinct phases of the plan set out the targets to be met in 1993, 1994-1995 and 1996-1997 for the deregulation of foreign exchange and interest rates. The plan was designed to allow Korean entry to the OECD by 1996.

The foreign exchange market

In December 1992 the government passed the revised Foreign Exchange Management Act, which changed the basis for regulation from a positive system to a negative system, allowing many regulations to be abolished. This establishes the principle that all transactions are permitted by law except those explicitly prohibited, rather than *vice-versa*, which was previously the case.

The government has now adopted a strategy of gradually expanding the fluctuation limits of the Korean won and the size of positions banks can take on the foreign exchange market, at the same time as easing the rules on documentation requirements for foreign exchange dealings.[6]

In March 1990, the government introduced the market average exchange rate system (MAR) to eliminate government influence on foreign exchange rates. By 1993, the daily interbank foreign exchange rate fluctuation limit had been raised to 1 per cent. The fluctuation limits are to be expanded gradually in 1994-1995 with a view to setting up a free-floating exchange rate system by 1996-1997.

The ceiling on banks' overall foreign exchange oversold positions was raised from won10 million to won20 million in 1993. The government aims to adjust the oversold position limits on spot transactions during 1994-1995. In the early stages of liberalisation, a substantial improvement in foreign exchange position management systems was necessary, and this has been achieved by setting up systems that simultaneously consider bills bought and net worth.

The streamlining of documentation has been swiftly implemented. Under the plan, the ceiling on foreign currency deposits without the need to present underlying documentation was raised from won200 million to won300 million, and the time limit for submitting the documents was also extended from 30 to 45 days. In 1994, the government plans to exempt forward transactions in foreign currencies from the need to present underlying documents, and to abolish the ceiling on foreign currency deposits exempted from underlying documentation. Ceilings on forward transactions between foreign currencies and the won are to be raised in the period 1994-1995. The Bank of Korea says that its aim is, by 1996-1997, to exempt normal foreign exchange transactions from underlying documentation requirements, while maintaining the principle of "real" demand ie transactions in foreign exchange should be determined by economic activity such as foreign trade, rather than speculation on the currency markets.

By 1993 visible export or import settlements in Korean won were permitted up to a value of US$100,000, and non-residents were allowed to open accounts in won without restriction. The ceiling on the settlement in won for visible transactions is to be raised gradually between 1994 and 1995, and by 1996 or 1997 the aim is to allow full settlement in domestic currency for both visible and invisible transactions.

The private sector banks

The private Korean banks have been characterised by low profitability and a relatively high incidence of non-performing assets (largely due to government-led credit allocation policies in the 1970s). The banks have also suffered from competition from non-bank financial institutions, which have been given greater freedom to set lending rates and to provide fee-based financial services. As a result, banks have lost market share relative to the non-bank sector, while at the same time profits have been squeezed by bad loans and low average earning rates on loans.

Korea has 24 Korean private banks: 14 are nation-wide commercial banks and 10 are regional banks. Total assets held by the national commercial banks at the end of 1992 amounted to won106,975 billion or 75 per cent of total commercial bank assets, while the regional banks held won23,459 billion in assets, equivalent to 17 per cent of the total.

The market share of the commercial banks has shrunk considerably while that of the non-bank financial institutions has grown rapidly: in 1975 banking institutions held 79 per cent of all won deposits, but by 1992 63.8 per cent of the total were with the non-banking institutions. Investment trust companies have been among the main beneficiaries of this trend. In terms of loans and discounts, the market share of the banking institutions reflected a similar pattern, dropping from just under 75 per cent in 1975 to about 45 per cent in 1992, while the share of the NBFIs picked up from around 25 per cent to 55 per cent during the same period.

These variations were caused by changes in regulatory treatment: NBFIs were afforded more control over their management of assets and liabilities, and were allowed to apply higher interest rates on their deposits and loans than the banking institutions.

The growth of the commercial banks has been hampered by strong government control at almost every level, and this has generated the need, not only for financial deregulation, but also for fundamental structural changes within the banks themselves.

As Professor Chung Un-Chan from Seoul National University noted:

"The opening of the financial market is inevitable, and the gains that will follow are not negligible. But the opening also represents a potential threat to Korean financial

BYC

institutions, which have never been efficiently managed as private firms in the true sense of the word".

The banks are still suffering the burden of non-performing assets (NPAs) and low net interest earnings which were a result of the government's HCI initiative. To make matters worse, "domestic banks still remain passive in writing off bad loans and have made little efforts to strengthen their credit assessments in order to prevent new loans going sour".[7]

Seoul-based banks had won2,772 billion in problem loans at the end of June 1993, up 22.2 per cent from the end of 1992. Problem or non-performing loans are defined as those on which the principal and interest have been overdue for six months. Heading the list was the Commercial Bank of Korea, which registered a rise of 91.7 per cent in bad loans over six months: from won4.5 billion in December 1992 to won8.746 billion at the end of June 1993. A large proportion of this rise is accounted for by loans to Hanyang Corporation, which has filed for court protection.

Seven other commercial banks saw their problem loans rise in this period, with Korea Exchange Bank, Korea First Bank, Shinhan Bank, Daedong Bank, KorAm Bank, Dongnam and Hana bank all registering increases.

Regional banks also saw their problem loans rise, to won175.5 billion at the end of June 1993, up won6.4 billion from the end of 1992, bringing the total for all Korean banks to just under won2,950 billion. Domestic commercial banks suffered from the same problem at their foreign branches, with problem loans reaching US$160.2 million in August 1993 compared to US$77.1 million at the end of 1992.

Although the overall value of bad debts has risen, the bad debt ratios for all banks have fallen substantially in the last five years, dropping from around 5.5 per cent of all loans in 1987 to around 1.8 per cent at the end of 1992. However, it is unclear whether this drop is due to writing off loans or merely caused by an increase in the total volume of loans. It is also possible that the real level of bad loans is considerably higher than the 1.8 per cent disclosed: some sources suggest that non-performing loans could account for up to 10 per cent of all loans.

In the past the top managers of banks were often appointed by the government, which has led to structural problems, particularly within the larger banks. As a result of this, and the bad debt problem, it is often the smaller and newer banks which are among Korea's most profitable.

The larger banks have recently been making efforts to improve their efficiency: notably, the number of staff per branch in the five major city banks has declined consistently since 1980, at the same time as deposits increased.[8] This trend towards greater productivity is likely to continue under the government's plan for regulating and internationalising the financial sector.

In common with many other Asian banks, Korean banks tend to post high spreads between loans and deposits, and it has been estimated that 80-90 per cent of banks' income comes from loan interest. However, given the growing tendency of corporations to go direct to the capital markets to raise funding, there is the prospect that this source of income could be seriously eroded. The foreign banks pose a significant threat to the Korean banks in this context and it is likely that the domestic institutions will need to diversify their activities and develop a bigger and broader base of fee-based income in the future.

Opposite:
More sophisticated clients need more sophisticated banking

Foreign banks

In 1993, a total of more than 70 foreign banks were represented in Korea. Korea had initially allowed the banks in to encourage foreign capital investment through the foreign institutions' network of contacts in the international financial markets, but as worries about the fitness of the domestic banking sector emerged in the 1980s, the aim has been to encourage competition, to force the domestic banks to improve their banking practices and to develop managerial skills.

Chase Manhattan was the first into the Korean market, setting up a branch in Seoul in 1967. Since July 1977, foreign banks have been allowed to open additional branches in Korea, but so far only Citibank has made efforts to form a branch network.

Approval for the setting up of a foreign bank branch must be granted by the Monetary Board of the Bank of Korea, under the recommendation of the Superintendent of Banks. Foreign banks have been placed on an equal footing with the domestic banks since 1984, and like domestic banks they are regulated under the provisions of the General Banking Act.

Foreign banks have gradually been accorded the same rights as domestic banks. In 1984, foreign banks were allowed to join the Korean Federation of Banks, and in March 1985 they were allowed to make use of the Bank of Korea's rediscount facilities for export financing – the scope of rediscounts was expanded to include general commercial bills in July 1986. From September 1985, foreign banks were allowed to handle the business of money in trust, and in September of the next year, negotiable certificates of deposit. Since August 1988, foreign bank branches have been able to borrow funds form the central bank to finance possible shortages of reserve requirement or settlement funds.

These banks have not been exposed to the problem of non-performing assets, largely because they are not subject to government-induced "policy" loans, and also because they apply more strict criteria in the loan-granting process.

[1] *Financial System in Korea*, May 1993, Research Department, The Bank of Korea.
[2] "Banking in Asia Survey", *Far East Economic Review*, September 1993.
[3] Chung Un-Chan, *Is Financial Deregulation a Panacea?* Lecture Paper, September 1992.
[4] *Ibid.*
[5] *Ibid.*
[6] Bank of Korea officials, interview with author.
[7] Cho Jae-Hyon writing in *The Korea Times*, 5 October 1993.
[8] Schroders.

Additional sources:
"How To Trade With Korea" 1993/1994, Korea Trade Promotion Corp (KOTRA).
"Korea Annual", Yonhap News Agency.
Kim Jin-Chun, "Korea's Recent Foreign Exchange Rate Systems: MCBP vs MAR System", Korea Institute for International Economic Policy.

Chapter Six

The equity and capital markets

The stock exchange

The Korea Stock Exchange (KSE), the only stock exchange in Korea, opened for business on 3 March 1956, and moved to its present site in Youido on 2 July 1979. In 1988, the Exchange was restructured into the present non-profit organisation. The Exchange is a full member of the International Federation of Stock Exchanges (FIBV) and the East Asian and Oceanian Stock Exchanges Federation (EAOSEF) and in 1992, it joined the International Organisation of Securities Commissions (IOSCO) as an affiliate member.

The country's stock market has grown with the economy, and in 1992 there were 688 companies listed on the Exchange. Market capitalisation has lagged behind the growth in GNP of recent years, however, dropping from its peak of 67.3 per cent in 1989 to 36.6 per cent in 1992.

The Exchange has two subsidiary companies: the Korea Securities Depository Corporation, which acts as a central settlement and custody organisation; and the Korea Securities Computer Corporation, which serves as the computer centre for securities-related activities. In addition to the Exchange and its two affiliates, the Korea Securities Finance Corporation provides funding for stock purchases, and there are two securities-related associations: the Korea Listed Companies Association, and the Korea Securities Dealers Association.

Under the government's deregulation and internationalisation policies, the KSE has opened its doors to foreign investors since January 1992; extended international cooperation to other stock markets worldwide; and has plans to diversify its business to incorporate derivatives trading, and to develop the under-utilised bond market. To meet the expected expansion of business, construction of a new building began in 1993, and is expected to be completed by mid-1996.

As part of its efforts to internationalise, the KSE is developing its links with other stock exchanges. In May 1993, the KSE hosted EAOSEF's 12th General Assembly and in 1994, it will play host to the General Assembly of the FIBV. Together with the Securities and Exchange Commission (SEC), the Exchange has provided consultancy services to other emerging stock markets, notably Dhaka and Teheran.

The KSE is an order-driven market, with the Exchange acting as an intermediary to execute orders under the auction system. The fluctuations that marked the early development of the stock market have now largely disappeared, and the government's long-term plans for liberalising the stock and bond markets are having a positive effect on the trading system. However, the Exchange has no market makers, which often function as a stabilising force during times of volatility.

In 1992, the United Kingdom's Securities and Investments Board (SIB) designated the KSE an Approved Securities Market (ASM) and a Designated Investment Exchange (DIE), both of which confirm the KSE's status as a reputable stock market.

Daily stock price movements in won are limited by a sliding scale which is proportional to the share price. Thus, higher priced stocks have higher daily fluctuation limits, ranging from won100 to won12,000 depending on the previous day's closing price; the number of categories of fluctuation limits depending on the previous day's closing price has been extended from 13 to 17, and stocks are now categorised in 17 levels ranging from won3,000 to won500,000.

Several regulatory bodies are involved in the administration of the Korean securities industry, but ultimate control is vested in the Ministry of Finance (MOF). The SEC acts under the broad guidance of the MOF as a central regulatory body. It supervises the other security institutions and companies, as well as being responsible for issuing securities and establishing fair trading practices. The Securities Supervisory Board (SSB) is the executive organ of the SEC, and is involved in inspecting securities firms under the direction of the SEC. The SSB has nine commissioners, six of whom, including the chairman, are appointed by the president on the recommendation of the finance ministry. The other three commissioners are regarded as *ex officio* and include the governor of the Bank of Korea, the chairman and chief executive of the KSE, and the vice minister of Finance.

The Korean stock market appears to be gradually emerging from a protracted bear trend since the turn of the decade, largely as a result of an inflow of foreign funds since 1992. The key Korea Composite Stock Price Index (KOSPI) slumped from its all-time high of 1,007.77 on 1 April 1989 to a low of 459.07 on 21 August 1992. However, the KOSPI now appears to have shaken off its three-year slump, closing at 678.44 at the end of 1992, and rising above 800 in 1993.

This more positive scenario should lead to an increase in new listings on the Exchange. In 1992 only four new companies were listed, but by mid-1993 another five had already registered for listing. These low levels are partly the result of the strict policy on listing requirements introduced in July 1992, under which approval for listing is granted on a very selective basis, mainly to rising stars in the manufacturing sector.

The development of the equity market contrasts with a relatively under-developed and under-utilised bond market. This is a reversal of the earlier pattern of securities business

Exhibit 6.1

Listed stocks, 1982-1992 year-end (millions of shares/won)

Year	*No of companies*	*No of issues*	*No of shares*	*Capital stock*
1982	334	416	4705	2811317
1983	328	422	5444	3238872
1984	336	455	7047	4336163
1985	342	414	7955	4665388
1986	355	485	9410	5649718
1987	389	603	1519	7594879
1988	502	970	2511	12560366
1989	626	1284	4242	21211524
1990	669	1115	4796	23981636
1991	686	1013	5102	25509634
1992	688	1014	5412	27064657

in Korea, which saw a much greater focus on bonds than on stocks. Despite the slow progress so far, several securities firms expect that the bond market will be a key growth area in Korea as companies and the government issue debt to fund future development. The bond market trading system could be a major beneficiary of this trend, with derivatives accounting for much of the expected growth.

The KSE plans to restructure its bond market facilities following the movement of funds out of the exchange-traded market into the over-the-counter (OTC) market. Its plans include establishing a new trading floor, restructuring the trading system, extending trading hours, revising the information disclosure process, and reducing trading costs.[1] A task force was created in 1991 and upgraded in 1992 to form the Bond Market Department, which handles all business related to this market in the KSE.

Historical data and the availability of research

The KSE's information dissemination system has improved considerably since it moved to Youido in 1979, and since 1977 the Korea Securities Computer Corp (KOSCOM) has provided brokers and investors with rapid feedback on trading results, and market and corporate information. The Exchange aims to continue to expand the scope of its provision of information in line with its effort to increase market transparency.

The Exchange quotes two stock price averages, the KOSPI and, since May 1992, the revised stock price average. The KOSPI in its present form has been used since the beginning of 1983, when the calculation was changed to reflect aggregate market value, rather than the price-weighted method that had been used previously. The index currently covers 100 common stocks traded on the KSE and has a base date of 4 January 1980. The KOSPI is calculated as the ratio of the current aggregate market value to the base year value, multiplied by 100. The base index is adjusted when capitalisation changes, or new listings and delistings are introduced. This narrows KOSPI fluctuations to those created by genuine market activity, rather than incidental variations as a result of corporate activity. The KOSPI is published every minute during trading sessions.

The KOSPI remains the best known and most often quoted index of the stock market, but it has been criticised in some quarters for reflecting too limited a range of companies. As a result, the revised stock price average (also known as the adjusted stock price average) was introduced. This index is calculated by taking the sum of prices of all shares listed on the Exchange, after making technical adjustments for rights issues, stock split and other distorting factors, and dividing by the number of listed companies. No weighting is given to the capitalisation of each issue. Sub-indicators of the revised index based on industry, capital stock and first and second section stocks are also published daily. Newly listed stocks are assigned to the second section for at least one year. Qualification for the first section depends on a number of factors including net profits, the company's debt ratio, dividend payments and trading volume of the shares concerned.

Further indices are also provided. There are two section indices composed of first and second section stocks; sector indices comprise 34 industrial sub-group indices, and a daily manufacturing industry index published since 1988; and there are three indices based on capital size, for small, medium and large companies. Small companies are defined as companies with less than won5 billion capital stock, medium-size as those with capital between won5 and won15 billion and the large companies include those with over won15 billion capital.

The Exchange also publishes information on the dividend yield and the price earnings ratio of stocks. The latter has been published monthly since April 1969, and since 1974 the Exchange has provided the price earnings ratio for all listed stocks, for the individual issues and as an average for the whole market, in the Daily Official List. The Exchange also publishes daily and monthly averages of dividend yields for all dividend-paying companies.

Brokers have had access to the Exchange's manual order books since 1990, and in July 1992, the Exchange expanded the scope of information from its Electronic Order Book available to brokers to include the volume of best bid/asked prices, and the aggregate volume of bids and offers, rather than just the bid/asked prices themselves. These are communicated to the floor representatives of member brokers through information terminals on the trading floor, and the information can then be passed on to clients. The hub of this electronic flow of information is the KOSCOM computer centre located within the Exchange. This is being upgraded under a plan called "System 2000" due to be completed in 1995, which will allow the processing of up to one million orders per day.

Corporate disclosure requirements were revised by the KSE in April 1992 to reflect changes in the Securities and Exchange Law. Under the revised regulations, the Exchange has the authority to request listed companies to disclose the occurrence of any significant event when conspicuous change takes place in the price or trading volume of stocks issued by the company. The listed companies must also submit reports about their merger activities with other companies.

The Exchange has also introduced a more flexible surveillance system to spot issues that show unusual price movements. When an unusual price movement is spotted, the issue is designated first as a surveillance issue, and later as an administrative issue, to warn investors of the risk. The Exchange has revised the criteria under which such designations are made: for example, the issue can now be designated a surveillance issue if the gain exceeds eight times the daily price change limit for three consecutive days in a 10-day period and if the closing price on the third day is higher than that of the previous 30 days. This course of action can be waived if the gain is less than four times the growth rate of the KOSPI or the sector index for the stock.

The Exchange has completed a study aimed at enhancing its systems to detect abnormal or unfair transactions, and an automated system, the Integrated Surveillance System, is to be installed in due course. Two new advisory committees aimed at enhancing the fairness and efficiency of the market have also been set up: the Disciplinary Committee and the Committee on Market Operations.

Since the opening of the Korean stock market to foreigners, the intrinsic value of companies has become a much more important criterion for buying or selling shares. This has boosted the demand for corporate information, which has been sketchy in the past, particularly for the medium-sized listed companies. The KSE opened an additional Corporate Disclosure Room in July 1992, providing annual and semi-annual reports by the listed companies, as well as Articles of Incorporation and a range of magazines. The Exchange estimated that about 4,500 investors and employees in the securities field had visited the information centre in the first six months after it opened. Information on shareholders, directors, and changes in shareholdings exceeding 5 per cent of total shares issued, is available through the centre. Information about small- and medium-sized companies is still sketchy, however, and this is one of the main reasons why foreign investors tend to concentrate on the large companies.

Exhibit 6.2

Korea composite stock price index, 1979-1992 (4 January 1980=100)

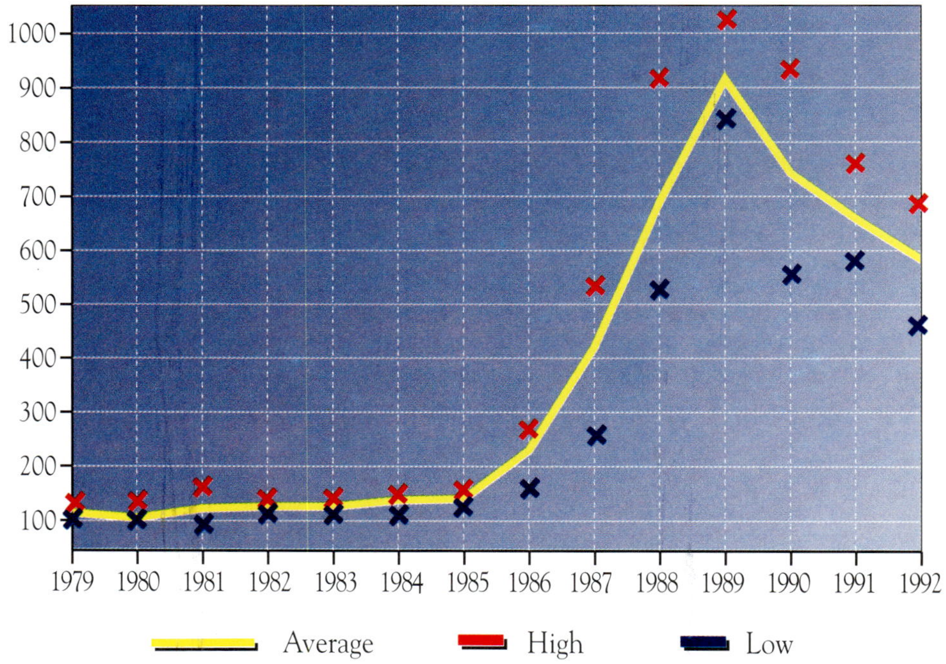

Exhibit 6.3

Stock trading value, 1982-1992 (won millions)

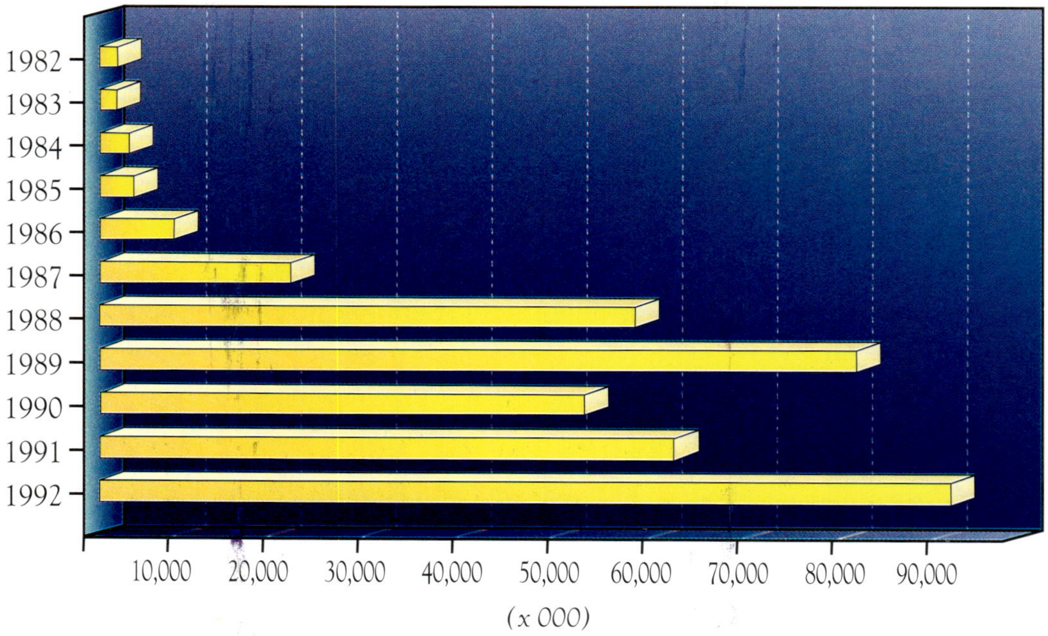

Exhibit 6.4

Stock trading volume, 1982-1992 ('000s of shares)

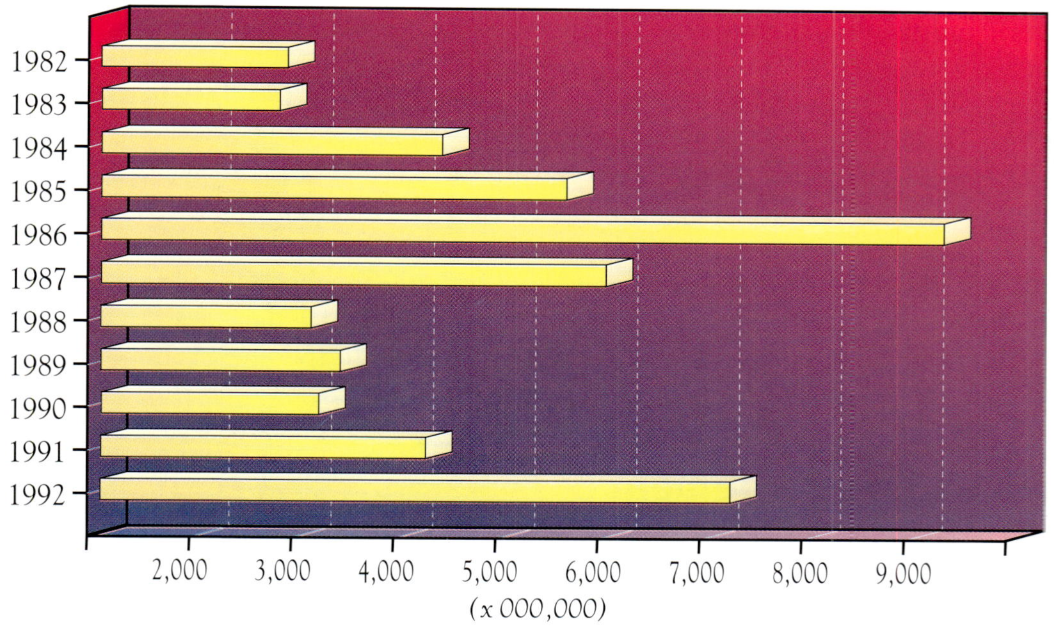

Exhibit 6.5

Market value of listed stocks, 1982-1992 (won millions)

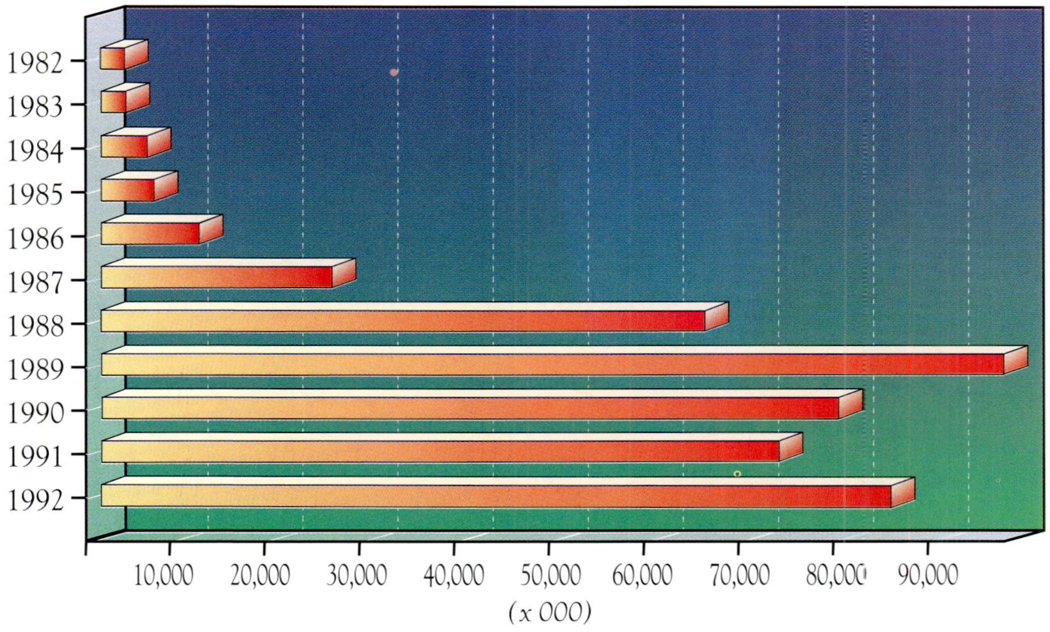

Information on the bond market, and particularly the procedures for establishing bond yields, have been singled out for further refinement. The Exchange publishes the average yield of each bond on a daily basis by subgroup, based on the issuer, terms for payment of interest and principal, and the period to maturity of the bond. The classifications divide bonds into four maturity periods (less than six months, 6-12 months, 1-3 years and 3-5 years); and two broad categories based on the type of issuer, public or corporate. The latter two categories are sub-divided further into discount, compound and coupon bonds for the public bonds, and guaranteed bonds, mortgage bonds and debentures for the corporate bonds.

The individual yields are published daily in the Official List, and a variety of averages are also published including a weighted average on a monthly basis, and arithmetic averages based on the latest yields of average issues traded on the day. Several bond indices have also been published since 1986: one on a daily and monthly basis based on the aggregate prices of selected issues compared to their prices on the base date, 30 December 1990; and a similar index published monthly with a base date of the end of the previous year.

Custody and settlement

The KSE uses the book-entry clearing system and the continuous deposit system for settlement purposes, with all transactions settled on the basis of net balance through the Korea Securities Depository Corporation, a wholly-owned subsidiary of the Exchange. The depository corporation was set up in 1974, and the book-entry system was put into operation soon after, covering all listed equity issues in 1975 and all listed bonds in 1983.

Originally called the Korea Securities Settlement Corporation, the new name was adopted on 1 August 1992. The depository acts as the clearing and settlement agent of the Exchange and for registered companies in the OTC market and stands proxy for foreign investors. It also acts as the central depository for the Exchange, receiving and making payments of dividends on stocks and interest on bonds on behalf of securities institutions with securities deposited with the corporation.

Currently the depository's custody facilities are underutilised by the securities firms, and the custody of shares is still widely entrusted to banks. Hong In-Kie, chairman of the KSE, points out that only about 56 per cent of listed stocks and 31 per cent of listed bonds are deposited with the corporation, levels which he does not consider satisfactory. Most individual investors use the depository but some institutional and foreign investors are still reluctant to use it. As a result, the Exchange is making efforts to strengthen the role of the Korea Securities Depository Corporation as a central depository. In 1992, its custody services were extended to include a depository for securities certificates on the OTC market and for some unlisted bonds. Its status will be changed in 1994 from that of a commercial entity to a public entity under the Securities and Exchange Law, in the hope of increasing public confidence. The government also plans to revise relevant laws to encourage institutional investors to deposit their securities holdings with the central depository. The depository, meanwhile, will lower the deposit fee and computerise deposit-related operations. Hong hopes that these measures will increase immobilisation and reduce the social cost resulting from the physical movement of securities.

The central depository has upgraded its technology by installing a Tandem Cyclone 902-E computer system with greater capacity and a vault with a sophisticated computerised security system. Its new building is due for completion by mid-1994.

Trade comparison and confirmation for settlements are completed on the day following the transaction. The Exchange provides clearing data to its members and the Korea Securities Depository Corporation on the second business day following the day of transaction. The delivery and receipt of securities between member firms are also effected on the second business day after the transaction, by book-entry through accounts opened by members at the depository company. Member firms are not allowed to entrust the settlement of securities transactions to institutions not designated by the Exchange.

The settlement deadlines for cash transactions are 13:00 local time on the day of contract for the morning session and 16:00 on the day of contract for the afternoon session; for what the Exchange calls regular-way transactions, under which stocks and equity-related debt securities (such as convertible bonds and bonds with warrants) are traded, settlement must be by 16:00 on the second business day following the day of contract, or 13:00 if the deadline falls on a Saturday. However, these times can be changed by the Exchange if deemed necessary in order to preserve a fair and orderly market.

Having effected their transactions, members must deliver securities or cash to the KSE's clearing agent for the difference between their sales and purchases by type of transaction before the deadline for settlement, and the clearing agent then pays the sales value or makes delivery of the securities to the appropriate member. When the deadline for both regular-way and cash transactions is the same, however, Exchange members can net the total value of transactions and pay the balance in full.

The system allows a simple book-entry transfer of securities without any physical delivery from the seller to the buyer. Under the system, the securities firms must deposit at least 90 per cent of the shares held in their own, and their customers, accounts with the central depository. Other institutional investors are also encouraged to open accounts with the depository corporation.

The Korea Securities Depository Corporation operates a continuous deposit system, allowing it to register deposited shares in its own name. This was introduced in June 1985 under a special contract between the corporation and its members. The system enables the depository corporation to ensure the proper and timely distribution of dividends, subscription and voting rights to participants and their customers. It also eliminates troublesome registration procedures and the risk involved in physically moving certificates. Similarly, bonds on the books of the Korea Securities Depository Corporation are allowed to be registered in the nominee name of the corporation, allowing delivery to be made by book-entry transfer and payment of principal and interest to be made without presentation of the securities.

The KSE employs rigorous measures, including the maintenance of a compensation fund and a strict disciplinary code, to ensure the settlement of all transactions. The Exchange is responsible for the settlement of all securities transactions on the exchange-traded market, and stands liable for damages incurred as a result of any breach of trading contracts by a member.

Stock Exchange members deposit guarantee money in the Joint Compensation Fund administered by the Exchange, and are jointly and severally liable for damages. The Joint Compensation Fund is used to make payments for damages resulting from any unsettled transactions. The deposit paid into the fund by each member is 1/100,000th of its trading value. The fund is limited to a maximum reserve of the larger of 2/300ths of the trading value per member in the last calendar year, or the amount in the fund divided by the number of members at the end of the previous business year. When that limit is reached, the payment of guarantee money is discontinued, but this is resumed when the fund is depleted below the maximum level as a result of paying compensation. In the settlement of a damages claim, funds deposited by the member who caused the damage are paid out first, and the remainder is paid from funds deposited by the other members. The Exchange retains the right, however, to recover the full amount of a compensation payment plus related costs, from the member concerned.

Funds held by the Joint Compensation Fund are deposited with banks or investment trust companies, or can be leased to the Korea Securities Financing Corp (KSFC) or used to buy bonds issued by the KSFC. Proceeds from the operation of the fund are included in the principal. At the end of each fiscal year, the proceeds are divided on a *pro rata* basis between the members, and added to the Joint Compensation Fund account of each member. If the amounts held in the compensation fund are inadequate to cover a payment, the Exchange must make up the difference from its own funds.

Stock Exchange members are required to deposit guarantee money, which the Exchange can use if members fail to meet their obligations arising from dealings on the securities market, with the amount determined by the KSE's board of directors up to a maximum of won50,000,000.

According to the strict disciplinary code, if a member fails to clear its transactions, the Exchange has the right to suspend its dealings, and if the failure results in serious disruption to the market, the Exchange can cancel the registration of the member concerned. In serious cases, the Ministry of Finance will revoke the member's licence for conducting securities business. If a securities firm is suspended, the member must complete the clearing of outstanding transactions, and the Exchange can request that a claim be filed against members who fail to clear their transactions. The Exchange takes priority over any other creditor with respect to the member's guarantee money in the case of such claims.

The derivatives market

Derivatives trading remains relatively underdeveloped in Korea, with an inadequate regulatory framework for OTC business, and no facility for futures or options trading on the official market. The government's aim is to introduce a stock index futures contract on the KSE as part of its 1993-1997 financial reform plan, with the futures market being established at the beginning of 1996. The KSE established the Stock Index Futures Market Organising Committee in October 1992 to study how this should be introduced. The committee comprises 16 members representing the Ministry of Finance, the Securities and Exchange Commission, academia and industry.

However, the KSE is taking a measured approach to this important step. It plans to publish a new index for the index futures beginning in 1994, to be based on aggregate market capitalisation of liquid blue chip stocks. Between 100 and 200 of the total of nearly 700 traded issues are likely to be represented in the index. The Exchange is also planning to set up market facilities and develop its computer system to support futures trading and clearing by the first quarter of 1995 and a simulation test will be conducted during the last half of that year. If the stock index futures prove successful, the Exchange will then consider the introduction of additional derivative products such as index options and futures.

Opposite: The Korea Stock Exchange

The trading of stock index futures will require further steps towards the internationalisation of the Korean equity market. Key questions remain as to the extent

to which foreign investors will be able to participate in the futures market: if foreign investors are allowed to trade the index, but still have limits imposed on them in terms of the ownership of individual stocks, for example, disjunctions between foreign and domestic fund flows may affect the value of the index futures as a hedging mechanism. It is likely that foreign participation will be needed to give a kick-start to trading activity, as many Korean companies and financial institutions still regard derivatives as rather risky. The value of a futures market as a hedging tool depends on a relationship existing between the futures and the underlying market. In the past, however, foreign funds have often entered the stock market at times when Korean investors were sidelined, and *vice versa*. The existing stock limits on foreign investment could result in disjunction between the futures and equities markets, exacerbating the problem. As a result, regulation of the two markets will need to be integrated, if the hedging value of the futures market is to be maintained.

The Korean government has been extremely cautious in its programme of financial liberalisation so far and has tried to avoid excessive speculation. The essence of a futures market, however, is that the hedging and speculative flows should balance: market makers take on risk and investors receive "insurance" in return. A healthy flow of speculative funds is essential, therefore, for liquidity in any derivatives market.

Where will this speculative funding come from? The Korean banks have been used to the "Korea Inc Guarantee" under which the state directed the banks' lending activities in return for an implicit guarantee that they would not allow the failure of the companies to which funds had been lent. Although the government renounced this policy in the 1990s the financial institutions still tend to be risk averse and, moreover, there is a lack of skilled traders in this field. The large Korean corporates have the clout to take on large speculative positions and they have recently shown a remarkable capacity for speculative investment, notably in land and property development, but this has been the focus of recent public criticism and may dissuade them from participating actively in the derivatives market. The *Chaebol*'s investment in the financial sector has also been a controversial issue, and their shareholdings in banks have been limited to just 8 per cent of total equity.

The absence of candidates to play a market-making function, by being able to quote buy and sell prices simultaneously, is a key problem that will be faced by the nascent futures market. The absence of the necessary expertise or the inclination to play this role is demonstrated by the largely underdeveloped state of derivatives in the OTC market, although this is also affected by the regulatory system. At present, financial institutions and larger corporations use OTC derivatives mainly to hedge their exchange risk, because the current foreign exchange controls allow firms to use the foreign exchange market only for capital flows from their ordinary business activities.[2] It appears to be the larger conglomerates rather than the banking institutions which are pioneering the use of derivatives, although accurate statistics on this kind of trading are not available.

The trading of derivatives is currently limited to forward deals and interest-rate caps and floors, and these are arranged mainly by a few Korean banks and merchant banks, although some of the more sophisticated corporate treasurers also participate. These markets are still in their infancy in Korea and by Western standards the Korean banks and corporates would seem to leave large foreign exchange exposures unhedged.

The trading of commodity swaps is of great potential value to a resource-poor nation like Korea, particularly for the Korean oil companies, which are heavily dependent on imported oil, and could use the futures or swaps markets to lock in costs and guarantee earnings. However, the continued regulation of the domestic oil market, where the "guidance" system still sets the price of domestic products, obviates the need for these hedging mechanisms, as margins on sales are effectively guaranteed by the government. As a result, the development of this market – as is also the case for the stock index futures – depends on further financial deregulation.

The way in which the derivatives market complements the swaps and over-the-counter options markets, which are basically unregulated, will determine its success. The KSE is aware of the risk that off-market derivatives trading may undermine confidence in the organised exchange market, and the issue is currently being studied by the FIBV and IOSCO.

The debt markets

The first and second stages of the market liberalisation plan, which were completed in 1993, have led to the freeing of lending rates on all bank and NBFI loans except for those provided by Bank of Korea rediscounts; rates have been liberalised on long-term time deposits and money-in-trust with a maturity of two years or longer; and short-term, large denomination deposit instruments such as CDs, trade bills, commercial paper and repurchase agreements (REPOs) have also been deregulated.

In the third and fourth stages, due for completion in 1997, lending rates on loans financed by Bank of Korea rediscounts, such as discount bills, are also scheduled to be freed, as are those applying to bank loans on special terms under which the government compensates the borrower for the interest rate gap. Interest rates on all deposits excluding demand deposits, will also be liberalised.

By November 1991, rates on corporate bonds with a maturity of at least two years had been freed and the government aimed to liberalise rates on Monetary Stabilisation Bonds, all government and public bonds, corporate bonds with a maturity of below two years and all bank debentures in the two to three years after that.

The ongoing liberalisation of interest rates is likely to increase the volatility of bond prices, diversify bond issuance conditions and develop trading techniques. The government also needs to increase the issuance of government bonds to finance its fiscal needs. These two factors should encourage individual investors to participate in the bond market, making the need for an organised exchange market where fair pricing and continuous bond quotations are possible more pressing.

The freeing of interest rates has been a necessary precursor to a wider deregulation of the capital markets, but the government is extremely cautious about loosening its grip on the reins of credit, largely because Korean corporations are already heavily indebted and the banks are suffering from the weight of non-performing assets. It is ironic that the aftermath of the system which has led to the current need for deregulation, should be the factor that prevents the government from making a clean break with it. However, the successful freeing of interest rates so far, without any significant rises in market rates (which could prove ruinous to heavily indebted companies), will hopefully encourage a faster pace of change.

In 1994, the government will allow foreigners to invest directly in equity-linked bonds issued by small- and medium-sized companies and underwrite the issuance of low-interest public bonds. In 1995, it will authorise international organisations, like the World Bank and the Asian Development Bank, to issue won-denominated bonds in Korea and allow local investment trust companies to establish and sell bond funds for foreigners. In 1997, the government will allow foreigners to invest in non-guaranteed long-term bonds issued by small- and medium-sized companies.

The potential of the domestic capital markets

Korea's gross domestic savings as a percentage of GDP is high relative to many of its Asian neighbours, with only Singapore, China and Indonesia surpassing it in 1992, when the savings ratio stood at 34.9 per cent of GDP.[3] The rapid growth of the economy in the earlier stages of development led to large foreign debts, amounting to 38 per cent of total funds raised in the latter half of the 1960s; but foreign debt has declined steadily as economic prosperity has increased, and accounted for only 2 per cent of total funds raised in the late 1980s.[4]

The prospects for domestic savings are mixed. Savings as a percentage of GDP have decreased in the last few years, having peaked at 38.3 per cent in 1988. The 1993 total is projected to be just a shade over 30 per cent and this is expected to reach 35.6 per cent in 1994: these figures may be affected by the rapid growth of the middle classes in the country, which will tend to encourage higher spending despite the government's campaign against conspicuous consumption.

Corporate profits have been slim recently, due to intense competition for market share, making it difficult to reinvest profits; and the tendency for large conglomerates to invest in land and property during the late 1980s appears to be changing now as slumping property prices have led to a channelling of funds into more productive areas.

In the 1980s the funding requirements of the business sector were increasingly met by internal rather than external sources: the share of external funding decreased from 77 per cent of the total in the latter half of the 1970s, to about 60 per cent in the late 1980s. This was a result of the business sector's growing ability to accumulate capital and savings in the form of reserves. At the same time, companies have moved from indirect to direct financing, by issuing shares, bonds and commercial paper.

Between 1970 and 1974, indirect financing provided 56.3 per cent of external funds raised by the business sector, while direct financing accounted for just 23.9 per cent, with the balance of 19.8 per cent made up by foreign borrowings. By the late 1980s, these figures had virtually reversed: in 1985-1989, indirect financing accounted for 44 per cent of external funds raised, and direct financing for 53.7 per cent of the total.[5]

As a result, the securities markets' share of total funds rose sharply from 11.1 per cent in 1970-1974, to 27.1 per cent in 1985-1989, with stocks accounting for 16.4 per cent and bonds 10.7 per cent respectively. The share of the banks has declined commensurately, dropping to just 20.3 per cent in the 1985-1989 period compared to 29.2 per cent in the earlier period.

These figures need to be viewed in the context of the highly developed "kerb" market that existed in Korea until the real name system introduced in 1993 effectively abolished it. The kerb market was an unofficial market, in which depositors could invest money often anonymously and which remained largely unregulated. The huge size of the kerb market means that government figures, which do not take it into account, are bound to be distorted. It would appear, however, that the equity and capital markets have reaped the greatest benefit from the ending of the kerb system, demonstrated by the sharp rise in share and bond prices at the end of 1993. Further growth in the KSE bond market is expected due to this and to the liberalisation of interest rates.

The KSE bond market was characterised in 1992 by low trading value and a decline in market yield. The value of corporate bonds issued in 1992 fell to US$14.2 billion in 1992 from US$17.3 billion in 1991, largely as the result of reduced investment in plant and equipment by leading companies. The trading value of corporate bonds also dropped

Exhibit 6.6

Public and corporate bond trading volumes, 1982-1992 (won millions)

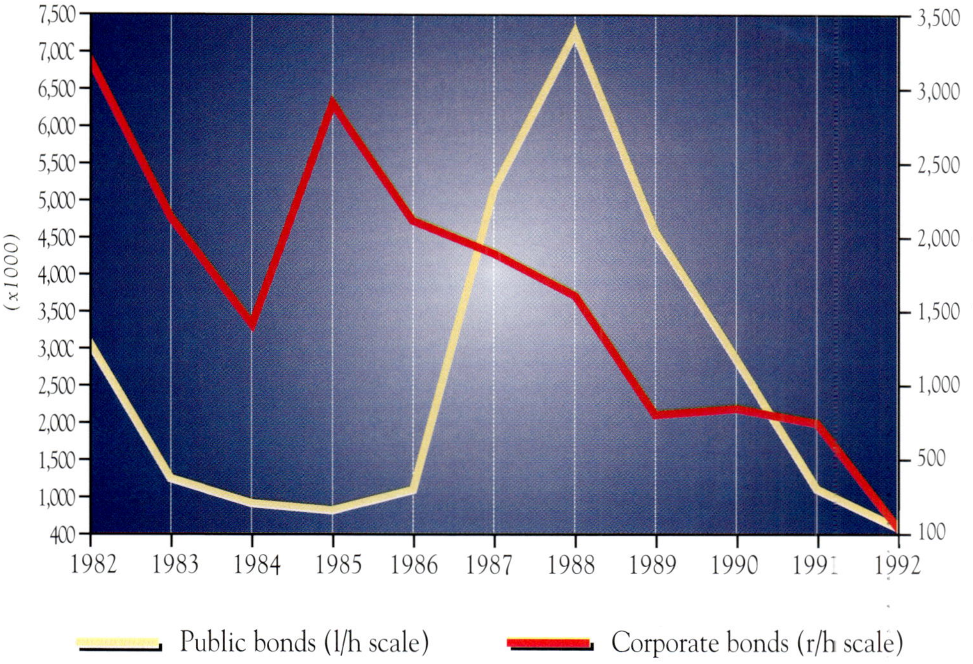

to just US$774.8 million in 1992 from US$2.9 billion in 1991, as liquidity moved out of the exchange market and into the OTC market, with the 1992 value of OTC bond trading surging 35.7 per cent between 1992 and 1991.

The drop-off in trading on the KSE bond market has been blamed mainly on the prevalence of institutional investors in this field. Bond trading in Korea is generally conducted between institutional investors on a negotiation basis with little participation from individual investors, resulting in a preference for OTC dealing and a neglect of the KSE bond market. However, the liberalisation of interest rates and bond rates should stimulate greater volatility in this area, and savings from domestic investors should increasingly find a home in the sofar under-utilised official bond market, rather than the exclusive channelling of funds into bank deposits and the kerb market which was so prevalent in the past.

This could become an important funding source for the many small- and medium-sized enterprises and the KSE chairman agrees that all firms, regardless of size, should have an equal opportunity to take advantage of the securities markets. The KSE is now looking into the possibility of opening a parallel market with more liberal listing requirements to open up funding for the small- and medium-sized companies, as a possible alternative to easing requirements for listing on the existing market. If they are unable to issue equity, however, the ability to raise funds through bonds may provide an attractive opening for both the companies and individual investors, although this would require more detailed credit rating information than is currently available.

The government needs to find new and better ways to absorb the high domestic savings level of Koreans, as well as to encourage more savings. The stock market is one vehicle

Exhibit 6.7
Public bond statistics, 1982-1992

Year	*No of issuers*	*No of issues*	*Amount listed (won millions)*
1982	12	401	2496546
1983	14	627	3026337
1984	14	916	4193550
1985	12	979	4737782
1986	17	1305	8638218
1987	21	1856	15093840
1988	19	1717	22159016
1989	25	2072	28094655
1990	24	2648	29049113
1991	24	2831	32248691
1992	46	2943	32446520

Exhibit 6.8
Corporate bond statistics, 1982-1992

Year	*No of issuers*	*No of issues*	*Amount listed (won millions)*
1982	519	1244	3303830
1983	734	1680	4371130
1984	1065	2168	5286620
1985	1213	2749	7263250
1986	1354	3103	8474349
1987	1457	3311	9972864
1988	1467	3372	11521035
1989	1504	3622	15395469
1990	1603	4243	22068214
1991	1862	5527	29241009
1992	2070	6496	32696632

for investment, but a higher degree of individual participation in bonds of all kinds will also be needed to diversify the spread of capital, and to allow the diffusion of risk between different instruments.

The prospects for raising capital internationally

Fixed-rate bonds remain the most important method of raising funds for Korean companies, with floating rate notes another popular method of taking on debt.

The convertibles market took off slowly in Korea with the issue in 1985 of one US$20 million issue, followed by two US$30 million issues in 1986 and a yearly US$30 million issue in 1987, 1988 and 1989. In 1990 and 1991 volumes increased substantially, with four issues totalling US$150 million in 1990 and 15 issues worth US$596.43 million in

1991. Towards the end of 1993 the total had climbed to US$510.98 million, bringing total yields from 1983 up to almost US$1.7 billion. Most of the convertibles issued since 1988 are long-term (that is, about 15 years) debt with the maturity in 22 out of 37 issues being beyond the year 2005.

Between 1988 and 1992 Korean companies issued a total of US$4.401 billion in fixed-rate debt and in 1993 alone the figure leapt to US$4.404 billion, reflecting lower worldwide interest rates. 1993 was a heavy year for borrowing all round: a total of US$5.693 billion Korean bonds were issued, with the balance made up of convertibles (US$510.98 million), and floating rate notes (US$728 million). Equity warrants made up a further US$50 million.

The US dollar is by far the most popular currency for bond issues, accounting for US$4.271 billion of the total in 1993, compared to US$1.182 billion in yen and US$240 million in Swiss francs. This reflects both the close trade and investment links with the United States and the negative trade balance with Japan.

The late 1990s saw a dalliance with the Deutschmark and the European Currency Unit (Ecu), but these were short-lived. Deutschmark issues totalled the equivalent of US$352.5 million between 1990 and 1992, and Ecu issues reached US$126.7 million in the same period, but there have been no further issues since the end of that year.

[1] KSE Chairman, Hong In-Kie, interview with the author.
[2] *Ibid.*
[3] Asian Development Bank data.
[4] *Financial System in Korea*, The Bank of Korea, December 1990.
[5] *Ibid.*

Chapter Seven

Foreign investment

History of foreign investment

Foreign investment in Korea before 1980 was largely in the form of loans, but after this date the rules on the formation of joint ventures were eased and the negative-list system for approving foreign investment in projects was adopted. Investment in the stock market has increased substantially since 1992, when the stock exchange opened its doors to foreign investors.

In the thirty years to 1992, 68.2 per cent of all foreign investment was directed towards the manufacturing sector, US$5.35 billion in total. Just over 20 per cent of this went to the electric/electronic and chemical industries, which received between US$1.1 and US$1.2 billion each.[1]

The service sector absorbed US$2.44 billion in foreign investment in the same period, of which almost half was invested in hotels, and the rest in banking. Foreign investment in mining, agriculture, forestry and fisheries has been extremely limited, mainly because of domestic barriers, and accounted for only 0.5 per cent of total foreign investment.

The value of foreign investment has been rising since 1983, when it totalled just US$122 million; it peaked at US$1.177 billion in 1991, but dipped sharply to below its 1988 level in 1992, when it reached only US$803 million.

The government passed the Foreign Capital Inducement Promotion Law in 1960 to encourage foreign direct investment in Korea through a series of incentives, largely focused on giving tax breaks and allowing profits to be remitted. These were extended in 1966 and a new round of investment promotion efforts began in 1969. The government established the Office of Investment Promotion at the Economic Planning Board in a bid to reduce the red tape involved in securing approval for investment projects. Despite this gradual easing of the rules, the bulk of foreign financing continued to take the form of loans throughout this period. The low level of direct foreign investment was a result of the government's strict regulatory procedure, which prevented foreign companies exercising autonomy over the joint ventures in which they were investing and "the general fear of foreign domination of Korean industries was too widespread for the government to be accommodating on this matter".[2] Majority control of joint ventures was allowed only in specific high-technology projects or projects which were wholly export-oriented.

The Confucian legacy of a paternalistic government with strong bureaucratic checks allowed the Korean market to remain heavily protected in almost all areas. One recent study suggests that state controls on foreign investment have been much tighter than the regulations in the foreign investment code would indicate: "not only were foreign investors banned from many sectors of the economy, but the screening process weeded out

Opposite: Catch the equity market right and the returns are high

applications from many sectors that were supposed to be open. Applications were viewed not only from the vantage point of the letter of the law but were judged according to unpublished guidelines."[3]

Foreign direct investment remained at a low ebb until the revision of the Foreign Capital Inducement Act which went into effect in July 1984. This set up a negative list system for approval of investment projects, under which all sectors were in theory open to investment except those named as restricted sectors. This was accompanied by a relaxation of the rules on ownership, with foreign companies allowed to invest up to 100 per cent of the equity in specified sectors. Bureaucratic red tape was reduced, and the rules on dividend remittance eased.

The negative list system resulted in a gradual increase in the number of sectors in which foreign companies could invest. The liberalisation ratio, which reflects the percentage of sectors in which foreign companies can invest relative to the total number of sectors available for investment, for the manufacturing sector has risen from less than 80 per cent in 1980 to 97.8 per cent in 1992, and the overall liberalisation ratio from below 50 per cent to a little over 80 per cent in the same period. The negative list will be further reduced by 1997.

Of the total foreign investment in Korea between 1962 and 1993, more than 60 per cent of this was invested between 1987 and 1993. Despite the attempts at liberalisation, however, foreign investment as a percentage of GNP remains low. It has been estimated that the share of foreign direct investment in foreign capital inflow has averaged just 5 per cent, and its share in gross capital formation has averaged just 1 per cent.[4] The average size of investments in individual projects has grown considerably since the 1960s, when typical inputs averaged less than US$1 million; in the late 1980s and early 1990s, investments tended to be to the order of US$3 million or US$4 million.

Sources of foreign investment

Historically, Japan has been the most important investor in Korea, with a cumulative total of US$2.256 billion invested since 1962.[5] Japan's population of 700,000 ethnic Koreans has contributed a significant part of this sum. Sakong Il cites one Korean study claiming that more than a third of Japanese direct investment in the 1962-1991 period came from this source. The rate of Japanese investment accelerated in the early 1980s as the appreciation of the yen forced Japanese companies to look elsewhere for lower cost production bases; higher domestic wages and Japan's large trade surplus encouraged the trend. Japan's share of investment has, however, been declining since 1988, partly due to rises in Korean wages.

In 1991 the United States and Europe were the major foreign investors, with Europe recording a massive rise from just US$200 million in 1991 to US$678 million in 1992. The United States total has fluctuated between US$234 and US$269 million since 1988.

Foreign equity investment

The final guidelines allowing direct investment in the Korean stock market were announced on 3 September 1991. Under these guidelines, foreigners were allowed in principle to invest in all listed stocks up to a general limit of 10 per cent of the total outstanding shares, with the limit on individual shareholdings being set at 3 per cent. Exceptions were made for public utilities which the government felt needed to be protected for an unspecified period of time. Two companies currently fall under this category: Korea Electric Power Corporation, the state utility firm, and Pohang Iron and Steel Company, the main steel company in Korea. These companies are subject to a maximum total foreign shareholding of 8 per cent, with a maximum of 1 per cent allowed to be held by any one individual.

In 1991 the Securities Supervisory Board announced guidelines allowing foreign investors to buy up to 25 per cent of shares in Korean companies registered abroad which have floated bonds (such as convertibles) overseas.[6]

The equities market opened to foreigners on 3 January 1992, when it met with a warm response. Total inflows of funds in the first year totalled US$2.73 billion, and the pace of foreign investment quickened in 1993, reaching US$5.65 billion by the end of October. Net inflows by the end of October 1993 were US$6.21 billion. The British were initially the most enthusiastic investors, closely followed by the United States. Total investment from the United Kingdom in 1992 was US$784 million, compared to US$581.7 million from the United States. By the end of October 1993, however, the level of US investment (US$1.41 billion) in that year had surpassed that originating from the United Kingdom (US$1.24 billion).

The share of total trading accounted for by foreigners is rising: in 1992 it was 1.8 per cent, with foreigners making a net purchase of 150,830 million shares, by October 1993 the figure was 470,380 million, or 2.3 per cent of total trades. The shares held by foreigners at the end of October 1993 amounted to 6.2 per cent of total market capitalisation. This has been achieved without the disruption to the market the authorities had feared.

The key growth area has been portfolio investment while direct investment has increased much less rapidly. In 1992, portfolio investment by foreigners totalled about won230,000 million, representing 2.71 per cent of the total market value, while direct investment was close behind at 2.19 per cent of the total market value: in 1993 increased buying by the funds led to a sharp rise in portfolio investment, which accounted for 6.16 per cent of the total market value, while direct investment remained little changed at just 2.16 per cent.

New orders dropped sharply in 1993, as foreign investors had reached the permissible limits for investment in the top 200 companies, and the government has come under increasing pressure to raise the ceilings on foreign stock buying. The surge in the KOSPI towards the end of 1993 seems to have been sparked by speculative buying ahead of the expected increase, along with an inflow of funds from the unofficial market following the implementation of the real name financial system earlier in the year.

By November 1993, perhaps 170 issues had hit their ceilings on foreign stock holding. As a result, the issuing of warrants having KOSPI as the underlying index, became a popular way of satisfying the foreign companies' demand for Korean equities in late 1993, and this trend looks set to continue.

Hong notes that the investment strategy of foreigners has brought about desirable changes in the attitude of domestic investors: "among others, the intrinsic value of individual stocks has become an important consideration in selecting stocks for investment. This move resulted in a keen interest in the blue-chip stocks undervalued until then".

The opening of the stock market has seen a steady increase in the number of registered foreign investors, from 565 at the end of 1991 to 2,049 at the end of June 1993. The rise in the number of investors has been largely the result of registration by institutions (1,285 out of 2,049).

Since the market has been open to foreign investors, they have spent US$6.35 billion investing in Korean stocks, buying 327 million shares worth a cumulative total of won4,425 billion; they remitted just US$1.582 billion, resulting in a net inflow of US$4.57 billion. Net buying accounted for 2.95 per cent of the total market value at the end of June 1993. This has been absorbed by the market without causing inflationary pressure.

Portfolio investment and listed funds

As discussed previously, portfolio investment by foreigners accounts for 6.16 per cent of the KSE's total market value. A number of funds were established in the early 1980s to allow foreigners to invest indirectly in the Korean capital market, and the investment trust companies offer similar funds for domestic investors.

The Korean investment trust companies were formed in the mid-1970s, following the 1969 enactment of the Securities Investment Trust Business Law, which created the legal framework for the type of investment trust now in operation. Korea Investment Trust Company Ltd (KITC), founded in August 1974, was the first, and there are currently eight such management companies. The big three are the KITC, Daehan Investment Trust Company and Citizens Investment Trust Company. Six merchant banks are also allowed to carry out investment trust business, but this is limited to the management of bond funds.

Exhibit 7.1
Foreign investment by industry, 1962-1992

	Value		*Capital sources (US$ millions)*			*Capital sources (%)*		
	US$ millions	*% total*	*Cash*	*Capital goods*	*Technology*	*Cash*	*Capital goods*	*Technology*
Agriculture, forestry & fisheries	35	0.45	29	6	0	82.86	17.14	0.00
Mining	11	0.14	7	4	0	63.64	36.36	0.00
Other	1	0.01	1	0	0	100.00	0.00	0.00
Manufacturing	**5354**	**68.25**	**3845**	**1506**	**2**	**71.82**	**28.13**	**0.04**
Chemical	1181	15.05	923	261	0	78.15	22.10	0.00
Machinery	518	6.60	368	150	0	71.04	28.96	0.00
Electrical & electronics	1130	14.40	687	442	1	60.80	39.12	0.09
Transportation equipment	678	8.64	398	279	0	58.70	41.15	0.00
Other	1847	23.54	1469	374	1	79.53	20.25	0.05
Services	**2444**	**31.15**	**2126**	**318**	**0**	**86.99**	**13.01**	**0.00**
Hotels	1208	15.40	943	265	0	78.06	21.94	0.00
Banking	613	7.81	612	1	0	99.84	0.16	0.00
Other	623	7.94	571	52	0	91.65	8.35	0.00
Total	**7845**		**6008**	**1834**	**2**	**76.58**	**23.38**	**0.03**

Regulation of the investment trust market is tight, and management companies are not allowed to instruct trustees to invest more than 10 per cent of their total assets in one company, or to buy more than 20 per cent of a company's total shares. Investments must be in listed securities which have been traded on the KSE on at least five out of the last 30 days; and in companies which have either paid or are expected to pay a dividend.

The Korean funds can broadly be divided into domestic and international funds. The former marketed within Korea and the latter abroad.

Within the domestic sector, approval was granted in November 1981 for the issuing of beneficiary certificates to foreigners, initially up to a limit of US$30 million. The Korea International Trust was established by KITC with a total value of US$15 million and Daehan set up the US$15 million Korean Trust. Since then, the market has expanded rapidly, and beneficiary certificates to a value of US$1,288 million have been issued to foreigners. A US$500 million fund was later created by KITC and Daehan through which it is possible to invest in unlisted companies.

Beneficiary certificates allow foreigners to invest in the Korean market, with the local investment companies issuing and managing the fund, while investors bear the exchange risk of won-denominated certificates. The investment principal and proceeds are unredeemable.

Since 1984 the government has launched three international funds. These are closed-end joint venture fund management companies, allowing investors in the United States, Europe and the Asia Pacific region to invest in the Korean market.

The first of these, the Korea Fund Inc, was established in the United States and is subject to US law. The fund was publicly offered on 22 August 1984 and simultaneously

Exhibit 7.2

Foreign direct investment by South Korean companies abroad (total and permitted), 1982-1993 (US$ millions)

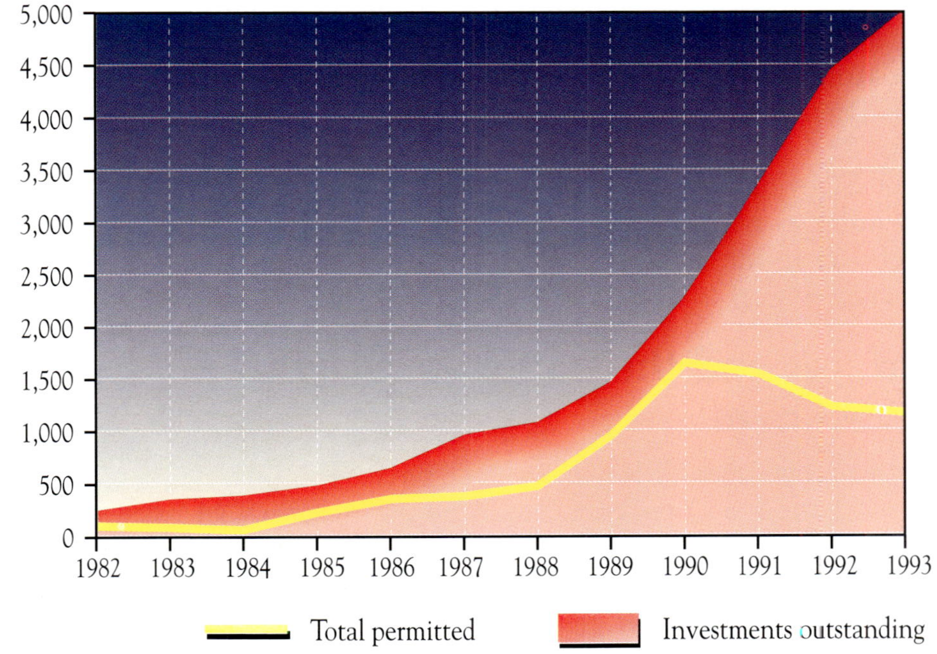

listed on the New York Stock Exchange. The Korea Fund is a foreign corporation, and trades in domestic securities as a large foreign investor.

The fund is capitalised at US$150 million. The initial offering of five million shares at US$12 each generated capital of US$60 million; a second tranche in May 1986 offered 1.24 million shares at US$32.25 each, boosting capital to US$100 million; and a third tranche of 1.42 million shares at US$35.25 was issued in 1989, increasing capital by a further US$50 million.

The Korea Europe Fund was launched in London on 24 March 1987. The fund is currently capitalised at US$110 million, made up of a first tranche of three million shares worth US$30 million, a second tranche of 1.13 million shares worth US$30 million and a third tranche of 8.02 million shares issued in 1989 and worth US$50 million.

The Korea Europe Fund is managed by Korea Schroder Fund Management Ltd. The launch of the fund allowed Korean securities houses their first taste of lead-managing, with the 44-member underwriting group led by Britain's Baring Brothers and the Korean firm, Ssangyong Investment and Securities. The launch of this fund attracted widespread interest, as the Korean stock market had been booming and the economic outlook was bright. As a result, the premium on the US$10 shares in the initial tranche had more than doubled by the signing date.

The third international fund was the Korea Asia Fund, aimed at investors in the Asia Pacific region. The US$100 million offering was concluded on 10 April 1991 and the fund was listed on the London and Hong Kong stock exchanges the next day.

Matching funds were issued from 1990, which allowed portfolio investment by investors residing outside Korea in the Korean securities market and by Korean residents in overseas securities markets. The government authorised three local investment trust companies to issue US$100 million each in matching funds, as part of a bid to stabilise the then rapidly-declining stock market. Daehan Investment Trust led the way with the first local matching fund, Daehan Asia Trust, on 28 June; Korea Investment Trust set up the Korea Pacific Trust on 6 July; and Citizens Investment Trust issued the Seoul Asia Index Trust on 20 July. Each of the trusts have a 60:40 split between investors residing outside Korea, and Korean residents and nationals living abroad. A variety of Korean offshore mutual funds are quoted in the financial press.

There are a total of 33 Korean foreigner funds run by the big domestic fund management houses such as Daehan, Citizens and Korea Investment Trust. Initial investment in the 33 trusts was US$1.47 billion; as of mid-September 1993, the net asset value of the funds had reached US$1.74 billion. These have tended to underperform the market in recent years, but the influx of new foreign portfolio funds looks set to change this situation by adding competition to the market.

Joint ventures and the opportunities for direct investment

Total foreign direct investment in Korea stood at US$10.847 billion at the end of September 1993. Of this total, about 31.3 per cent came from the Americas, 44.1 per cent from Asia and 22.9 per cent from Europe. The base of foreign investment in Korea is relatively narrow: over 90 per cent of investment funds originating in Asia are accounted for by Japan and the United States provides 94 per cent of all funds from the Americas. Total foreign investment in 1993 has improved slightly on the previous year's figure, but remains well below its peak level of 1988 (US$1.283 billion). In the year to the end of September 1993, foreigners had invested US$683.75 million in Korea in 192 projects, compared to US$655.9 million in 174 projects during the same period of 1992, according to figures from the Bank of Korea.

Rising labour and rent costs mean that new investment appears likely to continue to be geared mainly towards the service industries, in line with the government's plan to liberalise the financial sector and to expose domestic financial firms to stiffer foreign competition.

The government has adopted the so-called negative list system to encourage greater investment; in principle, all projects are open to foreign investment, unless they are specifically investors listed as restricted. Under this system, almost all manufacturing is open to foreign investment, with just 14 out of 585 sectors in this area still restricted. In the mining sector, 22 out of a total 27 business areas are open to foreign investment, and in the key services sector, 320 projects out of a total of 495 have been liberalised.

However, a total 224 sectors remain restricted, mainly in the fields of agriculture, education and culture. Particularly in the politically sensitive field of agriculture, the Korean market remains highly protected.

The government plans to reduce the number of restricted projects gradually under the Five-Year Foreign Investment Liberalisation Plan, issued on 1 July 1993, until 93.4 per cent of all projects are open to foreign investment.

Under the schedule, 113 sectors will be fully opened to foreign investment, with a further 19 sectors, including trust and a number of other financial services, partially opened to foreign investment. The remaining 92 sectors excluded from the liberalisation plan will be considered after 1997.

The government's drive to encourage foreign investment reflects the need to develop its technological resource base. FDI is seen as a significant source of technology transfer, badly needed by Korea because of its companies' heavy dependence on licensed foreign technologies and the high percentage of foreign components in some high-technology products.

Further restrictions due to be lifted include:

- Limits on the size of retail outlets will be eliminated on 1 January 1996. The limit of 10 shops occupying a maximum 1,000 metres has already been expanded to 20 shops with a maximum 3,000 metres floorspace.
- Retail sales, currently liberalised but still subject to approval, will be subject only to notification from the beginning of 1994.
- Kyongbuk joins Pusan and Kyongnam to become one of the areas in which general local freight transport services can be operated. The limits are set to be scrapped from April 1994.

Restrictions on foreigners' equity stakes in joint ventures with Korean companies are also to be eased. The limits are currently determined by the type of industry involved, with mining projects, for instance, being subject to a maximum of 50 per cent equity share. A certain amount has already been achieved in this respect. The 50 per cent maximum share of capital funds for investment trust companies has been scrapped. The 50 per cent limit on foreign ownership in the area of freight forwarding by sea and shipping brokerage/agency services has also been removed.

There are currently still 50 areas in which foreign companies' shares are limited. The government plans to reduce this number to seven by 1997.

Watch your step

The role of foreign intermediaries

Foreign securities institutions can establish joint ventures, branch or representative offices.

A joint venture allows a company to conduct a wide range of activities such as dealing, brokerage and underwriting, and other related business. However, this method can prove somewhat costly, and so far only one company has elected to enter the Korean market under a joint venture arrangement.

Foreign securities trading or financial institutions with capital of over won300 billion (the average equity capital of domestic securities firms), are allowed to set up joint ventures with Korean companies, provided these are not affiliated with any of the top 30 conglomerates. Two or more foreign companies may form a joint venture with a Korean securities firm provided that at least one of the companies has won300 billion capital. The joint venture must have capital stock of at least won50 billion, and the contribution of the foreign partner must be between 40 and 50 per cent of the total joint venture, or in the case of two or more partners entering into a joint venture, the major partner must contribute a minimum of 20 per cent.

Exhibit 7.3

South Korean direct investment by industry and region, end September 1993 (US$ millions)

	Asia		*Middle East*		*North America*		*Latin America*	
	Cases	*Amount*	*Cases*	*Amount*	*Cases*	*Amount*	*Cases*	*Amount*
Mining	9	317.241	1	48.746	9	114.792	2	9.861
Forestry	8	32.496	0	0	2	1.250	1	3.60
Fisheries	29	11.706	0	0	13	29.618	53	78.538
Manufacturing	1087	1310.571	9	17.703	139	916.174	103	96.934
Construction	30	12.864	14	14.294	18	36.169	1	1.530
Transport	23	8.019	2	0.435	15	11.156	4	6.420
Trade	247	146.804	1	0.098	276	711.371	8	8.375
Others	44	73.308	5	1.151	68	231.640	9	6.486
Total	**1477**	**1913.009**	**32**	**82.427**	**540**	**2052.17**	**181**	**211.744**

	Europe		*Africa*		*Oceania*		*Total*	
	Cases	*Amount*	*Cases*	*Amount*	*Cases*	*Amount*	*Cases*	*Amount*
Mining	3	45.454	3	24.124	9	85.083	36	645.301
Forestry	0	0	0	0	5	44.149	16	81.495
Fisheries	3	1.525	3	0.187	5	3.417	106	124.991
Manufacturing	51	223.758	16	15.618	25	17.816	1430	2598.574
Construction	1	0.045	3	1.463	3	1.688	70	68.053
Transport	2	0.932	0	0	0	0	46	26.962
Trade	104	175.769	6	2.240	17	4.416	659	1049.073
Others	11	7.331	5	57.124	21	42.141	163	419.181
Total	**175**	**454.814**	**36**	**100.756**	**85**	**198.710**	**2526**	**5013.630**

Exhibit 7.4
Foreign investment by country, 1981-1992

		US$ millions				*% total*			
Year	***Total***	*Japan*	*USA*	*Europe*	*Others*	*Japan*	*USA*	*Europe*	*Others*
1981	**150**	31	62	9	48	21	41	6	32
1982	**129**	21	60	14	34	16	47	11	26
1983	**122**	39	36	11	36	32	30	9	30
1984	**193**	79	57	17	40	41	30	9	21
1985	**236**	78	120	36	2	33	51	15	0
1986	**477**	267	161	32	17	56	34	7	4
1987	**626**	373	101	80	72	60	15	13	12
1988	**895**	443	234	156	62	50	25	17	7
1989	**812**	399	244	130	39	49	30	16	5
1990	**895**	362	269	200	64	40	30	22	7
1991	**1177**	204	262	678	33	17	22	58	3
1992	**803**	174	268	291	70	22	33	36	9
Total	**6515**	**2470**	**1874**	**1654**	**517**	**38**	**29**	**25**	**8**

To set up a joint-venture, the foreign partner must have been engaged in the securities business for the last 10 years and have no disciplinary record for the last three. Foreign companies operating branch offices in Korea are not allowed to take part in joint ventures.

The Ministry of Finance issued a business licence to the Dongbang-Peregrine Securities Company in 1992, making it Korea's first joint venture securities company. The Ministry of Finance set out the guidelines under which foreign securities firms are allowed to set up joint ventures and branch offices in November 1990; however, the establishment of local subsidiaries by foreign firms has not yet been allowed.

The branch office has so far proved a more popular option than setting up a full joint venture. The branch's required minimum capitalisation depends on the area of business in which it is engaged. To participate in dealing, brokerage and underwriting, a branch must have a minimum capital of won20 billion; for two out of three of these activities, the requirement is lowered to won15 billion; and for just one activity, the minimum is won10 billion.

To achieve branch status, the foreign firm must have maintained representative offices in Korea for a minimum of two years, have conducted securities business in their own country for at least 10 years, and must have no record of being disciplined in the last three years.

The first branch offices were opened in Seoul by two British securities firms, Baring Securities and Jardine Fleming. Since then, the number of branch offices has expanded to eight. In May 1991, the Ministry of Finance issued guidelines for the establishment of representative offices in Korea by the foreign securities companies. The guidelines require these companies to have paid-in capital of at least won50 billion or shareholders equity of won100 billion. As is the case for both joint ventures and branch offices, foreign securities firms need to have conducted business for the past 10 years or more, and have no record of being disciplined in the past three years. Under a principle of reciprocity, the country in which the company is established must also allow Korean securities firms access to the local market. The securities subsidiaries of financial institutions are allowed to set up a domestic office in Korea, although institutions engaged in banking and securities are not allowed to set up additional offices.

Nomura Securities of Japan became the first foreign securities institution to set up a representative office in Seoul in March 1981. Since then, 27 representative offices have been established.

The foreign brokers have contributed to the rapid development of the Korean securities market, adding both trading volume and value to the market following its three-year bear trend, but it is in the area of research skills and expertise that the foreign securities firms are likely to have their biggest impact on the Korean exchange.

Korean securities firms have also launched a drive to boost their own overseas networks by setting up overseas offices. Daewoo Securities set up the first overseas office in Tokyo in 1984 and 18 other securities companies have since opened a total of 54 overseas bases.

The future for international investment in Korea

The two principal patterns of foreign investment in Korea have been through foreign direct investment, and more recently through the securities market. The latter has attracted the greatest inflows of foreign money in the 1990s, while foreign direct investment in Korea has lagged behind, largely as a result of bureaucratic problems.

The opening of the stock market has been met by a heavy flow of foreign funds, to the extent that many companies have reached their equity investment limit. The government has been slow to raise the ceiling, despite repeated requests from foreign investors, but there are signs that the limit will be raised by 3-5 per cent between 1994 and 1995[7] as proposed in the new five-year plan. The timing will be decided by the government after considering conditions in the stock market and the national economy.

Despite these problems Korea is being widely touted as Asia's next major bull market.[8] A strong rebound in the economy, surging exports and rising capital expenditure are all cited as reasons for expanded corporate earnings, which have been at a low ebb since 1991, to show handsome gains in 1994. Global investment flows are focusing on the emerging markets in Asia and Latin America, and US investors increasingly turn to Asia as the preferred place to lodge their funds.

Future foreign investment in Korea is likely to be concentrated on stock buying, with only about a third of the US$12 billion expected to be invested in Korea in 1994 set to find a home in direct investment; foreign institutional flows into the stock exchange are projected at US$5 billion, with the remainder to be raised by international equity offerings by Korean companies.

[1] *How to Trade with Korea*; Korea Trade Promotion Corp (KOTRA).
[2] Sakong Il, *Korea in the World Economy*; Institute for International Economics, 1993.
[3] Bello, W. and Rosenfeld, S., *Dragons in Distress: Asia's Miracle Economies in Crisis;* Penguin, 1992.
[4] Lee Chon-Pyo and Kim Kwang-Doo, *Economic Changes in Korea and its Relation with the Asia-Pacific Region*, in *Evolution of the Asia-Pacific Economies*; Asian and Pacific Development Centre.
[5] *How to Trade with Korea*; Korea Trade Promotion Corp (KOTRA).
[6] *Securities Market in Korea 1993*, p. 97, Korea Securities Dealers Association.
[7] Hong In-Kie, KSE chairman, interview with author.
[8] For instance, in the *Straits Times*, December 1993.

Chapter Eight

The legal environment

Shin & Kim, Attorneys at law

Introduction

This chapter presents an overview of Korean law which, although by no means comprehensive, discusses areas of law which have been selected as being of potential interest to non-Korean readers.

Sources of law

The constitution and the set of five legal codes (the Civil, Criminal and Commercial Codes and the Codes of Civil and Criminal Procedure) constitute the core laws of Korea. They are supplemented by statutes passed by the legislature, decrees issued by the president and the various ministries, regulations of the ministries, their subordinate agencies, other state authorities and local governments, and international agreements. The Korean legal system, which has absorbed many of the concepts and traditions of European civil law, emphasises codified statutes as a source of law, and unlike in common law countries such as the United Kingdom or the United States, court precedents are not formally recognised as binding law. The decisions of the Supreme Court are, however, customarily followed by lower courts.

The constitution

In 1948 Korea adopted its first Western style constitution. It created a presidential system of government with a unicameral legislature and provided for civil and personal liberties, universal suffrage and economic rights. However, a democratic constitutional tradition found in Western nations, characterised by popular participation, the separation and balance of powers between branches of government and the primacy of strict adherence to constitutional law, has taken some decades to fully take root in Korea. Prior to the presidential elections of 1987, the presidency was the centre of political power. During that period, the constitution was amended several times for the purpose of consolidating the powers or extending the rule of an authoritarian president.

In 1987, the constitution was amended for the ninth time in response to popular protests for greater democracy. In a departure from the previous revisions, the new constitution strengthened the power of the National Assembly, bolstered individual rights and provided for the popular election of the president who was limited to a single five-year term. With the peaceful transfer of power to a civilian president in 1992, Korea's future as a stable constitutional democracy seems assured.

The branches of government

The constitution grants to the National Assembly the power to enact laws, pass the national budget, approve treaties, declarations of war and the dispatch of armed forces abroad, inspect affairs of state and impeach public officials, including the president. The National Assembly passes bills by the affirmative vote of a majority of members voting. The president has the power to veto a bill passed by the National Assembly, which in turn can override a veto by a two-thirds vote with at least half of its members in attendance.

The president, as the head of state, conducts foreign policy, commands the armed forces, enters into treaties and can declare martial law in times of crisis subject to *ex post* approval by the National Assembly. The president also exercises significant control over national policy by initiating legislation, issuing presidential decrees for the enforcement of laws and appointing and removing heads of ministries and other public officials.

The constitution vests judicial power in the Supreme Court and any inferior courts. Justices of the Supreme Court, including the chief justice, are appointed by the president and approved by the National Assembly. All other judges are appointed by the chief justice. As the court of last resort, the Supreme Court has power of ultimate review over all court-adjudicated controversies. The constitution, however, grants the Supreme Court only partial power of judicial review. It can declare administrative decrees and other executive actions unconstitutional, but only the Constitutional Court, composed of nine judges serving for six-year renewable terms, can declare laws passed by the National Assembly unconstitutional.

The bureaucracy

Legislation passed by the National Assembly sometimes tends to be broadly worded, stating general policy goals and leaving many substantive issues to be determined by presidential decrees and administrative discretion. Exercise of discretion by a regulatory authority must conform to the law, but in some cases, unbounded by specific legislative mandates, government officials make decisions based on loose guidelines or broad policy or practical considerations. Overturning such use of discretion by judicial review requires a finding that a decision cannot reasonably be supported by the relevant statute or that it constitutes clear abuse or misuse of discretion. A significant proportion of governmental power is thus wielded by the Korean bureaucracy, that is, by the various ministries. Listed below are the major ministries and the areas under their control:

- The Economic Planning Board manages the preparation and implementation of the nation's plans for economic development, the national budget and the nation's resources. It coordinates the actions of ministries dealing with economics and finance.
- The Ministry of Foreign Affairs is responsible for matters related to diplomacy, relations with foreign countries, treaties and other international agreements. It supervises the dispatch of diplomats and consuls and maintains relations with diplomatic and consular representatives from foreign countries.
- The Ministry of Home Affairs is responsible for a wide range of domestic matters including the protection of the lives and property of citizens, naturalisation and the administration of local affairs.
- The Ministry of Finance (MOF) is responsible for the government's financial affairs, a variety of issues related to the nation's financial system, the foreign exchange laws, government bonds, taxation and customs.

- The Ministry of Justice conducts civil and criminal prosecutions, and administers the prison system and immigration.
- The Ministry of Commerce, Industry and Resources is responsible for foreign trade, export and import regulations, patents, trademarks and the administration of unfair competition laws.
- The Ministry of Health and Social Affairs is responsible for public health, sanitation, regulation of pharmaceuticals, family planning and various social welfare programmes.
- The Ministry of Labour issues labour standards, reconciles labour disputes and overseas programmes for employee welfare.
- The Ministry of Environment administers and enforces environmental protection laws.
- The Ministry of National Defence deals with the nation's military affairs.

Other ministries include the Ministry of Education, the Ministry of Transportation, the Ministry of Agriculture and Fisheries, the Ministry of Science and Technology, the National Unification Board, the Ministry of Culture and Sports, the Ministry of Communications and the Ministry of Construction.

The Foreign Capital Inducement Act

Direct investment in Korea by a foreigner intending to participate in the management of a Korean enterprise is regulated primarily by the Foreign Capital Inducement Act (FCIA). Korea enacted its first foreign investment law in 1960 to encourage and regulate the inflow of foreign capital. Efforts by the government to boost foreign investments, which have faltered in recent years, have resulted in many revisions to laws and regulations governing foreign investment. Major amendments to the FCIA which took effect in March, 1994 have significantly simplified the process of obtaining government approvals and expanded the permitted scope of foreign investors' activities. The current FCIA has, however, retained the abiding principle of Korean foreign investment law which is that all foreign investments must obtain prior authorisation. Receiving such authorisation guarantees the remittance abroad of dividend profits within the parameters of the approval, makes the remittance of principal possible and guarantees the property rights of the foreign investor.

Government approvals

A foreign investor must invest a minimum of won50 million (about US$62,000) in a single project, or if a joint investment, at least won25 million per investor. For all foreign investments, the FCIA requires an application for approval to be filed with the MOF or a notification of investment to be submitted to one of the banks in Korea authorised to receive such notifications (the Korea Development Bank, the Industrial Bank of Korea or, effective 1 July 1994, other selected foreign exchange banks). A notification is processed more quickly and will generally receive less scrutiny than an application for approval. An acceptance of a notification or an approval of an application does not relieve the foreign investor from having to obtain authorisations required under other laws.

From among the 1,196 businesses classified under the Korean Standard Industrial Classification system, a negative list promulgated under the FCIA categorises projects as ineligible, prohibited or restricted with respect to foreign investments. A foreigner can

Deregulation and liberalisation: to let private enterprise flourish

invest in a restricted project only if criteria for government approval exists and the MOF approves the investment. The MOF is also charged with approving, after consulting with the Ministry of Labour, investment of a foreigner who has previously violated labour laws. All projects not appearing on the negative list are open for investment, and for such projects a notification must be submitted. Unless the foreign investor applies for a tax exemption or reduction simultaneously with the notification (the only case in which notification must be made to the MOF) the foreign investor must notify an authorised bank. The Korean government has announced the Five-Year Foreign Investment Liberalisation Plan which will by 1997 remove 113 of 224 restricted businesses from the negative list and partially liberalise 19 others.

The application for approval or notification must be accompanied by the business plan of the company receiving foreign investment, a certificate of nationality of the foreign investor and a power or attorney authorising a proxy to file the relevant documents in Korea. In addition, the foreign investor must submit the joint venture agreement, if a joint venture project, or either the corporate resolution authorising the investment or a letter of intent, if a non-joint venture project. Any documents not in Korean must be translated.

A notification of foreign investment is immediately accepted upon submission unless the authorised bank which has received the notification determines that it requires more time to review the proposed investment. In that case, the notification must be rejected within five days, otherwise it is deemed accepted.

For application for approval of an investment of less than won1 billion in a manufacturing industry or won300 million in a non-manufacturing industry or an investment in which the foreign investment ratio is less than 10 per cent, the period of review is five days which can be extended to 10 days if necessary. Otherwise, the application will require consultation with another ministry in which case the review process takes up to 15 days or up to 25 days if extended.

Recent amendments to the FCIA have harmonised Korea's criteria for rejecting a foreign investment with the Code of Liberalisation of Capital Movements of the OECD. Specifically, the government will reject a proposed foreign investment, which is not otherwise restricted under the negative list, only if such investment would undermine national security, public order, public morals, fulfilment of obligations relating to international peace and security or the protection of health and environment.

Any reinvestment by a foreign investor in a previously approved foreign investment project, including reinvestment of dividends, requires the authorisation of the MOF or an authorised bank. Procedures for obtaining authorisation for reinvestment are essentially the same as those for the original investment. The foreign investor must also report certain significant changes in the particulars of an approved project, such as a change in the investor's nationality, in the amount, method or ratio of foreign investment or in the business of the company.

Introduction of capital

Once an investment is authorised, the foreign investor must make the investment within one year if the investment amount is less than US$1 million and in a service business, within three years if the investment amount is over US$10 million, or otherwise within two years. Investment may take the form of cash or capital goods. If the capital goods are used goods or are given a tax exemption or reduction, the ministry which oversees the type of business the project will engage in must review and approve the goods. Cash investments must be placed in foreign exchange banks and withdrawn in won and can only be used for approved purposes.

Tax exemption or reduction

The FCIA provides tax incentives for foreign investments accompanied by certain advanced technologies which are deemed to be beneficial to the economy or to enhance Korea's industrial competitiveness. The FCIA lists 83 businesses which may be eligible for these tax incentives. If technology to manufacture the same or similar products has already been introduced more than four years previously, such technology cannot qualify for tax incentives unless the foreign investor can show improvements over existing technology.

Application for tax exemption or reduction must be made within the tax year in which the business receiving foreign investment commences. In the application for such tax benefits, MOF regulations require the submission of a number of documents containing details of the technology and its economic impact. It is through these documents that the investor must convince the authorities of the technology's value to Korea.

Upon receipt of an application, the MOF will decide within 30 days whether or not to grant tax benefits. The MOF may extend this review period for a further 30 days. The MOF will generally refer the application to the Ministry of Science and Technology for comment before making a decision.

Once approved, the FCIA confers a number of tax benefits. The FCIA exempts the income from the business approved for the tax benefits from corporate income tax in proportion to the foreign investment ratio. For the first three years following the tax year in which the business commenced, 100 per cent exemption applies, then a 50 per cent reduction for two years thereafter. During this period, the foreign investor also benefits from a reduction in taxes on dividends, on land acquired to run the approved business, on royalties and on the salaries of expatriate staff and defence taxes. In certain cases, capital goods used in the approved business are eligible for a reduction in tariffs, value-added and consumption taxes.

Company law

While such issues as government authorisations and tax incentives relating to foreign investments are governed by the FCIA, laws with regard to corporate governance and structure are contained in the Korean Commercial Code (KCC). The KCC provides for four types of companies:

- *Chusik Hoesa*, a stock corporation;
- *Yuhan Hoesa*, a limited liability company;
- *Hapmyung Hoesa*, a general partnership company; and
- *Hapja Hoesa*, a limited partnership company.

The key feature distinguishing the classes of companies from each other is the nature of the liability of the members or stockholders. The liability of a stockholder of a *Chusik Hoesa* is limited to the amount of his stock subscription. Likewise, the liability of a member of a *Yuhan Hoesa*, which is similar to a closely-held corporation, is limited to the amount

Seoul is still one of the most populous cities in the world

of his contribution to the company. All members of the *Hapmyung Hoesa* have unlimited liability, while members of the *Hapja Hoesa* can have either limited or unlimited liability.

Incorporation

A company can be incorporated by preparing and notarising the articles of incorporation and registering the company with the court. The KCC requires that directors of the *Chusik Hoesa* and the *Yuhan Hoesa* be elected prior to registration with the court. In order to protect creditors of the company, the promoters or initial members of these limited liability companies must pay, or cause to be paid, the full amount of the initial capital (at least won50 million for the *Chusik Hoesa* and won10 million for the *Yuhan Hoesa*) before registration with the court. The *Hapmyung Hoesa* and the *Hapja Hoesa*, however, have members with unlimited liability (at least one for the *Hapja Hoesa* and at least two for the *Hapmyung Hoesa*), affording creditors greater protection. Accordingly, the KCC does not require that initial capital be paid into these companies. Moreover, as members with unlimited liability have direct responsibility for the management of these companies, directors need not be elected prior to registration with the court. Upon registration with the court, the company comes into existence.

Transfer of membership interest

Given that all members of a *Hapmyung Hoesa* have unlimited personal liability, the identity and character of the members are important business considerations. Consequently, the KCC limits the transfer of membership to exceptional cases. A member who withdraws from the company remains personally liable for the company's debts and obligations for two years after the withdrawal. If a member commits a dishonest act with respect to the administration of business or representation of the company, or engages in conduct giving rise to conflicts of interest, a majority of the other members can demand from the court an order of expulsion of that member. The transfer of membership rules applicable to *Hapmyung Hoesa* apply also to the unlimited liability members of a *Hapja Hoesa*. Limited liability members of a *Hapja Hoesa* may transfer their interests with the unanimous consent of the unlimited liability members.

There are no legal restrictions on the transfer of *Chusik Hoesa* shares. Any provision of the articles of incorporation restricting such transfers are void. Shares or interests in a *Yuhan Hoesa* may only be transferred with the consent of at least half of the members, who must collectively own at least 75 per cent of all outstanding voting shares or interests. With freely transferable shares, unrestricted by any ceiling on the number of shareholders and with the option of going public, the *Chusik Hoesa* is generally more suitable for large, open-ended business ventures.

Corporate control and management

All unlimited liability members of the *Hapmyung Hoesa* and *Hapja Hoesa* have one vote, without regard to the level of financial contribution to the company. The unlimited liability members also manage the company, as the nature of the liability of such members renders the delegation of managerial duties to third parties inappropriate. In the *Chusik Hoesa* and *Yuhan Hoesa*, since the stockholders and members have limited liability, the management function is delegated to directors. In the *Chusik Hoesa* and the *Yuhan Hoesa*, voting is generally on a one share, one vote basis. However, the articles of a *Yuhan Hoesa* may provide differently.

An ordinary general meeting of shareholders of the *Chusik Hoesa* must be called once per fiscal period. Extraordinary general meetings may be called whenever required. Stockholders may vote by proxy, so long as a proxy statement has been filed at the general meeting at which the proxy voting will take place. The requisite quorum for ordinary resolutions is the presence, in person or by proxy, of a majority of outstanding voting shares. Some matters, such as the amendment of the articles of incorporation, the sale of a significant part of the company's business, the acquisition of another company's business, merger with another company or removal of a director or auditor, must be passed by special resolution, requiring the affirmative vote of two-thirds of the voting shares present or represented. Amendments to the articles of incorporation adversely affecting holders of a different class of shares, and mergers and transfers of whole businesses also require the two-thirds vote of the shares of such different class at a separate meeting. Ordinary resolutions, such as appointing directors and auditors, determining their remuneration and approving financial statements require a majority vote. Voting requirements for ordinary resolutions, except for the appointment of directors, can be altered by the articles of incorporation. Some matters, such as the release of directors, auditors or promoters from various types of liability, require the unanimous consent of all stockholders, voting and non-voting.

Directors of the *Chusik Hoesa* determine corporate policies and conduct the business of the company, except with regard to those matters reserved for the resolution of shareholders by the KCC or the articles of incorporation. The directors elect from among themselves a representative director who represents the company in all business affairs and oversees the day to day business of the company. Directors act by passing resolutions at meetings of the board of directors. A majority vote of the directors present at a meeting can pass a resolution unless the articles of incorporation provide for a more stringent requirement. A lower voting requirement is not permitted. A director must physically attend a meeting in order to vote. Voting by proxy or by writing is not allowed, although meetings through conference calls are permitted. Aside from limiting their power through the articles of incorporation, shareholders exercise control over directors in a number of other ways. They can appoint a statutory auditor or an inspector to inspect the directors' activities, remove directors by special resolution, or cause the company to sue to enjoin or recover damages for a director's violation of the law, of the articles of incorporation or for neglect of duty. A 5 per cent shareholder can also bring such suits derivatively on behalf of the company.

Auditors

Every stock corporation must appoint a statutory auditor. The appointment is by majority vote of the shareholders in which a single shareholder cannot vote shares in excess of three per cent of total outstanding shares. The statutory auditor audits and monitors the company's business affairs as carried out by the directors and also audits the company's financial statements and accounting documents before they are presented to the annual general meeting of shareholders. The statutory auditor may also attend meetings of the board of directors and is authorised to bring an action on behalf of the company to enjoin or seek damages for any illegal actions by the directors.

A stock corporation with assets of won6 billion (about US$7.5 million) or more at the end of the latest fiscal year is required to have its financial statements audited by an independent accountant. Independent audit is also required for companies listed on the Korea Stock Exchange (KSE) with regard to any financial statements submitted to the Korea Securities and Exchange Commission (KSEC) or the KSE. Unlike the statutory auditor, an independent auditor verifies the company's assets and liabilities as they appear in accounting documents, but does not audit the company's conduct of business.

Dividends

A stock corporation may declare dividends once every accounting period, which cannot exceed 12 months and for most companies is the year beginning the 1 January. To prevent excessive withdrawal of company assets, the KCC requires dividends to be paid out only from what are called "distributable profits". This is the net asset value of the corporation minus stated capital, legal reserves and profit reserves of at least 10 per cent of cash dividends. Dividends in stock are permissible but only up to half of the dividend amount. Although the FCIA affirms the right of foreign investors to remit dividends overseas, a permit for such remittance must be obtained from a foreign exchange bank. A foreigner may also need government approval for receipt of dividends in stock.

Company law issues facing foreign financed ventures

The *Hapmyung Hoesa* and the *Hapja Hoesa* are generally not appropriate corporate forms for an enterprise receiving foreign investment for two reasons. First, the KCC prohibits companies from assuming the status of unlimited liability members of these companies; unlimited liability membership is only available to foreign individuals. Secondly, the restrictions on the transfer of membership severely limit the liquidity of any such investment. In most cases, the corporate forms most suited for a foreign financed enterprise are the *Chusik Hoesa* and the *Yuhan Hoesa*.

The *Chusik Hoesa* is by far the most common corporate form. The *Chusik Hoesa* strictly separates ownership and management functions, facilitates the acquisition of large amounts of capital, and is the only form suited to taking a company public. A disadvantage of this form is that partners in a project who seek to structure their relationship solely by agreement between themselves must contend with, and work around, mandatory KCC provisions regarding the structure and management of stock corporations. For most purposes, however, an agreement between partners to vote in a particular way is a legally valid and effective way of accomplishing this. Parties can even enforce agreements to restrict transfer of shares through suits for contract damages.

Due to its more private and closely-held nature and its informal decision-making process, the *Yuhan Hoesa* may in many cases prove a superior vehicle for some projects. However, the prevalent view in Korea is that the *Chusik Hoesa* is more prestigious than the *Yuhan Hoesa* which is seen as a corporate form more appropriate for small businesses.

Withdrawal by a foreign investor

If a foreign investor wishes to withdraw from a Korean enterprise, three courses of action are generally available. The foreign investor may sell its shares to a Korean partner in the enterprise, to a Korean third party or to a foreign third party; the foreign investor may cause the company to be liquidated; or the foreign investor may redeem its shares in the company through a capital reduction.

If the foreign investor enters into a contract to sell its shares to a Korean party or a foreign party, it must submit, a report of the sale to the MOF within 30 days after the execution of the share sales contract. Along with the report of a sale the foreign investor must submit the sales contract, certificate of nationality of the purchaser (if the purchaser is a foreigner) and a document from the Korean tax authorities confirming any taxes payable. With the recent repeal of provisions requiring prior approval of sales and an appraisal of the price of shares sold to Korean parties, the withdrawal of a foreign investor has become significantly easier.

Liquidating a company is a much more complicated and time consuming process. Liquidation can be initiated by a special resolution of shareholders, pursuant to a dissolution mechanism in the articles of incorporation, or by a court order. A decision to liquidate a company benefiting from foreign investment would provide grounds for the MOF to cancel the approval for foreign investment. After cancellation the foreign investor must sell its shares to a Korean purchaser within six months. If a purchaser cannot be found within that time, the MOF will force the company into liquidation.

Under the KCC, a liquidator is appointed by resolution of a meeting of shareholders or, alternatively, by the board of directors or as the articles of incorporation may otherwise provide. The liquidator must submit a list of the company's assets to the court and issue public notices of liquidation for a period of two months, inviting creditors to submit claims for payment. After the sale of assets and payment of all debts, including required payments to employees, the remaining proceeds are distributed to the shareholders.

A third option is for the foreign investor to cause the company to reduce its capital by an amount sufficient to redeem all of the foreign investor's shares. Capital reduction requires a special resolution at the meeting of shareholders. The MOF treats the reduction of capital as though it were a sale of shares and the same reporting procedures apply. As is the case with liquidation, two months notice to creditors is also required. If any creditor objects to the capital reduction, the company must satisfy the claim of such a creditor or otherwise address the creditor's objections. After the submission of the report of capital reduction and the fulfilment of the notice requirement, the company must purchase, then cancel, the foreign investor's shares.

The repatriation of proceeds from an approved sale or redemption of shares requires a permit from a foreign exchange bank, which is usually readily available. Repatriation of liquidation proceeds, however, is not specifically provided for by law and is not so assured.

Foreign exchange

The Foreign Exchange Management Act (FEMA) supplemented by presidential decrees and MOF regulations controls and regulates the foreign exchange rate system, foreign exchange transactions (including the payment and receipt of foreign exchange which take place in Korea or involve a Korean resident and the underlying transactions which call for such payments and receipts) and capital movements. In general, to remit payments in foreign currency, there must be approval at two stages: approval for the transaction in which the conversion of won into another currency for payment to a non-resident is contemplated and, at the time of exchanging currency to effect payment, a payment authorisation from the MOF, the Bank of Korea or a foreign exchange bank.

The Korean government has recently announced plans for liberalising the foreign exchange rules over five years. In the past, the government exercised tight control over the amounts of foreign currency individuals and companies could hold and used the foreign exchange laws to channel hard currency to selected sectors of the economy. The liberalisation plans are aimed at shifting control over capital flow to market forces. Under the changes proposed in the reform plan, Korean institutional investors will be free to invest in overseas securities, as will individual investors, subject to certain limitations. Overseas branches of Korean companies will be freely allowed to borrow funds outside Korea to finance their overseas businesses. The documentation required for purchasing or selling foreign currencies or obtaining authorisation to remit foreign currencies will be simplified and the limits on the amounts of foreign currency held or used by Koreans and Korean companies will be, if not eliminated, raised.

Securities law

Like the securities regimes of most modern countries, the touchstone of Korean securities regulation is the disclosure of information. The Securities and Exchange Act (SEA) and its enforcement decrees and regulations govern Korea's securities market, and the MOF is charged with administering and enforcing the securities laws. The SEA regulates, among other things, the registration of securities, public offerings, tender offers, securities brokerage and investment advisors. It is also pursuant to this law that the KSE and the KSEC were established.

Registration

As its key disclosure measure, the SEA requires issuers of securities to prepare a registration statement and prospectus before selling securities. Unless an issuer has filed a registration statement with the KSEC, and the KSEC has accepted the statement, the issuer cannot make a public offering or a secondary distribution. An issuer may file a shelf registration covering a specified period during which the issuer can issue securities from time to time by filing a supplement to the shelf registration statement with each offering. Generally, a public offering or a secondary distribution is deemed to occur if solicitations of offers to purchase newly issued securities, in the case of a public issue, or outstanding securities, in the case of a secondary distribution, are made to more than 50 persons under uniform terms and conditions.

Once filed, a registration statement becomes effective after a specified waiting period of 5 to 20 days. The KSEC may request amendments to the registration statements, or changes may have occurred since the original filing occasioning an update of the statement. In either case, the waiting period begins from the date of any additional filing.

A registration statement must contain certain information about the offering and the issuer: it must describe the offering and specify how the proceeds will be used. Unless exempted, companies not listed on the KSE must submit the report of a rating agency. With regard to the issuer, the registration statement must contain a description of the issuer's history, its paid in capital, shares, dividend history for the past five years, affiliated companies, transactions between the issuer and interested parties and a list of its officers and their remuneration. Concerning the issuer's business, the statement should generally include a description of the issuer's products, business capabilities, contractual relationships, projects and research and development. Information about the issuer's financial condition is also required, along with the opinion of an independent chartered accountant.

For any offering which requires the filing of a registration statement, an issuer must also file a prospectus with the KSEC. The prospectus generally contains the same information as the registration statement and serves as the primary source of information for potential purchasers. No statutory or regulatory guidelines exist for the performance of due diligence in the preparation of a prospectus, and lawyers are rarely involved in the process.

The prospectus must be made available to potential purchasers at the offices of the issuer, the KSEC and the KSE. A preliminary prospectus may be used by the issuer during the waiting period. An issuer may make offers to sell securities after the filing of a registration statement and before it becomes effective. An actual sale, however, cannot occur until after the registration statement has become effective.

Liabilities

The SEA imposes civil liability for false statements, misstatements or material omissions in a registration statement or prospectus. Liability can attach to a wide range of actors involved in a securities issue, including officers, directors and promoters of the issuer, underwriters, dealers and anyone who has delivered the prospectus, accountants or any other expert who has certified facts in the registration statement or prospectus. An injured purchaser is entitled to damages equal to the difference between the actual value of the shares bought and the purchase price.

The Korea Stock Exchange

Established in 1956, the KSE had 693 listed companies and listed stocks with a total value of won104,918 billion (about US$130 billion) as of 31 November 1993. The Exchange is a non-profit corporation, chartered by the SEA, owned and managed by a number of securities brokerage firms under authorisation from the MOF. The MOF must ultimately approve any resolutions or rules of the KSE, and may order the KSE to amend its articles of incorporation or its rules in order to further public interest or to protect investors. Although the SEA allows trading of securities over-the-counter, trading on the Exchange dominates the securities market. All trades on the Exchange must be made through one of the member brokerage firms which are closely regulated. For instance, the commissions they charge to clients cannot exceed 0.6 per cent for transactions in equities and 0.3 per cent for transactions in bonds and investment trust certificates.

Only the stock of companies listed with the KSE may be traded on the Exchange floor, and a company must apply to the KSE to have its stock listed. Listings in the KSE are divided into two sections. A company being listed for the first time must list in the second section. To be listed, a company must meet a number of standard requirements concerning the size and performance of the company and other factors to ensure the liquidity and marketability of the company's shares. The company must, among other things, have at least a five year operating history, a paid in capital of at least won3 billion, a minimum of 300,000 issued shares, a debt to equity ratio of less than 150 per cent and average gross sales over the previous three accounting periods of at least won20 billion.

A company must have been listed in the second section of the Exchange for at least one year in order to be eligible for listing in the first section. In addition, the company must meet numerous stringent conditions, including, among others, requirements with regard to a recent record of profits and dividend distribution, the number of shareholders, the trading volume of the company's shares on the Exchange, paid-in capital and debt to equity ratio. A listing in the first section allows margin trading in the company's shares.

A listed company is required to file annual and semiannual reports with the KSEC. The reports must include general information about the company, its financial condition and the opinion of an independent chartered accountant as to the company's financial statement. In addition, a listed company must report to the KSE the occurrence of certain material events or facts affecting the company. The KSE may request a listed company to disclose information following unusual trading activity or to confirm rumours. Under certain circumstances, a company can be moved from the first section to the second section or delisted altogether. In another important regulatory measure, exchange rules control fluctuations in stock prices by setting limits on the amount by which the price of a stock can increase or decrease from the previous day's closing price.

Market manipulation and insider trading

The SEA prohibits a wide variety of practices in the trading of securities in which deception or misrepresentation are used to obtain financial gain. A person may not buy or sell a security for the purpose of creating a misleading impression as to the trading activity in the security or for the purpose of causing the price of the security to fluctuate in order to induce another person to buy or sell the security. A person may also not make a wilful misrepresentation to induce someone to buy or sell a security.

The SEA also prohibits trading by an insider on the basis of non-public, material information about a listed or registered company. An insider is defined as a director, officer, employee, agent, principal shareholder of the company, or any other person with authority over the company pursuant to law, anyone having a contractual relationship with any of the foregoing persons, or anyone who has received the relevant information from any of the foregoing persons. A listed or registered company or the KSEC may also bring an action to recover from an employee, officer or a shareholder with more than 10 per cent of the outstanding shares, any profits made by such person in transactions in the company's shares within any six month period.

Tender offers and takeovers

To make a tender offer for a company's shares outside the KSE, the offeror must first file a tender offer disclosure statement with the KSEC and wait 10 days until the statement becomes effective. The offeror must send the tender offer statement to the issuer and must announce the tender offer in at least two daily newspapers after it has become effective. The offeror can then purchase the securities by tender offer but not by any other means during the period of effectiveness of the tender offer.

There are several safeguards against a listed company being taken over by the purchase of shares. The SEA prohibits a shareholder from beneficially owning more than 10 per cent of the outstanding voting shares of an issuer. A shareholder can maintain, but not exceed, the percentage of outstanding voting shares (in excess of 10 per cent) owned at the time of listing or at the time of a subsequent sale of shares. A shareholder can obtain shares in excess of these limitations only through a tender offer, a direct purchase from a shareholder with 10 per cent or more shares, or through purchase from the government. These limitations, however, are due to be abolished after 1 January 1997. Any person who acquires 5 per cent of the outstanding voting shares of a listed company must file a report of share ownership with the KSEC and make subsequent filings whenever ownership changes by 1 per cent.

International aspects of securities regulation

In order to raise funds in foreign financial markets, a Korean company must comply with a number of qualifications designed to ensure the soundness of the company. The proceeds raised abroad may only be used to import manufacturing equipment not available in Korea, to finance an overseas business or as oversees working capital. KSEC regulations also place strict limits on the number of shares which may be issued abroad as a percentage of all outstanding shares. Before proceeding with the issue, the company must obtain approval of the issue plan from both the MOF and the KSEC. The Securities Supervisory Board (SSB) must also approve the terms of the issue such as the issue amount, price, and interest rate and the price of exercising a conversion or warrant.

A foreign individual or organisation wishing to invest in the Korean securities market must obtain an investment registration card from the SSB. A foreign investor must designate a Korean foreign exchange bank through which the transfer of funds for share transactions will take place. A single foreigner may not hold more than 3 per cent of an issuer's outstanding shares of any class. In addition, no more than 10 per cent of the issuer's outstanding shares of any class may be held by foreigners. The MOF has announced that these ceilings on the foreign ownership of shares will be increased in 1994. With a few exceptions, foreigners may buy and sell shares only on the KSE and may not engage in margin transactions. The foreigner must entrust its share certificates to an authorised custodian in Korea.

Labour law

Wages and benefits

The Labour Standards Act sets out the rules which regulate the terms and conditions of employment and working conditions in all businesses in Korea. Coupled with the Industrial Safety and Health Act, which focuses specifically on securing a safe and healthy work environment, Korean workers are accorded safeguards and protection comparable to any industrialised country.

The hours worked by the average Korean worker have declined over the years. With its revision in 1989, the Labour Standards Act shortened the standard working week to 44 hours from 48. Apart from the 17 days of national holidays, the Labour Standards Act guarantees workers 10 to 20 days of paid annual leave per year. The actual number varies according to worker attendance and the number of years worked at the company. Management must also provide one day paid leave each month. Women are guaranteed maternity leave.

The Labour Standards Act also protects workers from unfair dismissal: employees may be discharged only with legitimate cause and with at least one month's notice. The employee is entitled to receive severance pay equal to at least the monthly salary for each year worked at the company. The Gender-Equal Employment Act prohibits discrimination based on gender. The Labour Standards Act provides for inspectors nation-wide to monitor compliance with these and other labour rules. Inspectors also investigate petitions by workers and oversee any administrative or judicial actions resulting from those investigations.

Labour organisations

The Korean constitution guarantees workers "the right to independent association, collective bargaining, and collective action to improve working conditions". The statutory provisions specifically dealing with these issues are contained in the Trade Union Act and the Labour Dispute Reconciliation Act. Various administrative bodies under the jurisdiction of the Ministry of Labour monitor businesses and enforce these laws.

The Trade Union Act guarantees the right of workers to freely establish and democratically operate trade unions. To establish a trade union, workers need simply submit a notice to the district administrative office, which issues a final decision on approval, within three days. Collective bargaining between unions and management are also governed by the act. The term of collective agreements on wages are limited to one year and agreements on other issues to two years to ensure that agreements are renegotiated frequently to conform to changing conditions.

The management's rejection of, or failure to respond in good faith to, legitimate collective bargaining demands is considered an unfair labour practice. Other forms of unfair practices include discharging or otherwise bringing disadvantage to workers based on their union activities and making employment conditional on a worker's non-participation in union activities. Management is also prohibited from controlling or otherwise influencing the operation of unions. Violations of these measures may result in imprisonment or fines.

Collective bargaining in Korea typically takes place at the company level. Agreements at the industry level have generally failed because of the reluctance of trade unions at the company level to relinquish their right to conclude bargaining and due to the differences in wage levels and working conditions between companies in the same industry. As a result, the Labour Management Council, made up of representatives of the employer and of the employees, which is established for each enterprise with over fifty workers, is accorded a large measure of responsibility for managing issues which arise in collective bargaining in order to prevent strikes and confrontations between unions and management. The Council deals with a number of other issues including worker welfare, the work environment, personnel management and worker education and training.

When disputes do arise, the Labour Dispute Reconciliation Act recognises the principle of self-regulating resolution; that is, labour and management are to resolve the dispute between themselves. This act grants immunity to unions for financial damage incurred by the company and prohibits the employment of replacement workers during strikes. To enjoy this protection, unions must follow certain guidelines, and their actions must be legally recognised as being legitimate. Unions must submit a report of the labour dispute to the relevant Labour Relations Commission at the outset, observe a cooling-off period (generally 10 days), and obtain majority approval of the union membership through secret ballot. The Labour Relations Commission, consisting of representatives from labour, management and the public interest, mediates in disputes between unions and management and provides administrative relief for unfair labour practices.

Environmental law

During the last 30 years, Korea's rapid industrialisation and economic growth have generally overshadowed efforts to create effective laws to protect the environment. The deterioration of the environment due to the expansion of heavy industries prompted the passage of Korea's first major environmental law in 1977. Since then, the continuing environmental decline, an increasingly affluent population who want a cleaner environment and the rising political effectiveness of environmental groups have encouraged the promulgation of more stringent and sophisticated environmental laws.

In 1990, the Ministry of Environment was created at the cabinet level. This consolidated responsibility for the administration of environmental laws, which had been fragmented throughout several ministries and one subcabinet level agency. In 1991, the National Assembly passed a set of laws aimed at providing a comprehensive legal regime for the protection of the environment.

Under the Basic Environmental Policy Act, environmental standards are promulgated by presidential decree, and environmental conditions are monitored. Before proceeding with a major project, a developer must prepare an environmental impact assessment and consult with the Ministry of Environment. The Ministry then monitors the project for compliance with its guidelines. This act also imposes liability on the operators of industrial facilities for any environmental damage, regardless of fault. The Environmental Damage Dispute Mediation Act provides a forum for alternative dispute resolution for claims for damages arising out of damage to the environment.

Under the Air Environment Preservation Act, the Minister of Environment issues standards for the emission of air pollutants. This act mandates the installation of emission control devices in air pollutant emitting facilities. The act provides for enforcement through criminal sanctions against violators of emission regulations and also through a system of charges levied on facility operators who release pollutants in excess of emission standards. There is also a set of regulations on automobile emissions which apply to manufacturers as well as owners of automobiles. The Water Environment Preservation Act regulates effluent pollutants in much the same way. It also contains provisions to protect inland sources of drinking water. There is also the Sea Pollution Prevention Act which protects against pollution of the seas surrounding Korea from ships and seabed development

The Toxic Chemical Substances Management Act subjects the import or manufacture of toxic substances to risk assessment by the Ministry of Environment. An importer or manufacturer must submit information and material to assist the Ministry in the assessment, and can only proceed with the importation or manufacture after assessment has been completed.

In 1991, the Waste Management Act was significantly amended with the aim of promoting the recycling of waste. Among other things, the Act provides for a system of deposit of return for a wide range of materials, such as car batteries, tyres and industrial oils. Manufacturers or importers of such materials must pay a deposit and a charge for treatment or recycling expenses. When these materials are returned to government prescribed facilities, deposits are refunded.

Placing much emphasis on economic and industrial development, Korea has not until recently given high priority to environmental protection. With the increasing awareness of the importance of effective management of the environment, the government is devoting more resources to this task. As this issue continues to gain importance, further developments in environmental policy and laws can be expected.

Intellectual property

Although Korea has had statutes protecting intellectual property rights (IPR) since the turn of the century, it is only recently that Korea has put in place a legal system for the protection of IPR comparable to that of other modern countries. Korea joined the World Intellectual Property Organisation in 1979, the Paris Convention for the Protection of Industrial Property in 1980, the Patent Cooperation Treaty in 1984 and the Universal Copyright Convention in 1987. In 1987, major revisions to all the statutory laws governing IPR were carried out, providing a solid legal foundation for the protection of IPR.

The Korean constitution provides for the protection of intellectual property. The actual laws for this purpose are encompassed in various acts, depending on the types of intellectual property: the Patent Act and the Utility Model Act for inventions, the Design Act for industrial designs, the Trademark Act for trademarks, the Copyright Act for literary, scientific or artistic works, and the Computer Programme Protection Act for computer programmes.

Patents

The protection of inventions is provided for by the Patent Act and the Utility Model Act. The two acts are similar, both granting property rights to inventions of sufficient novelty and non-obviousness, but differ in the required degree of inventiveness and term of protection. A patent requires a much higher degree of innovation and inventiveness than a utility model and lasts longer. An application for a patent can be converted to that for a utility model, and *vice versa*, while retaining the original application date for purposes of priority. As the two are similar, the discussion below will focus on patents, noting any differences between patents and utility models as necessary.

The Korean Industrial Property Office (KIPO), under direction from the Ministry of Trade, Industry and Commerce, is the agency responsible for the administration of patents, from processing patent applications and reviewing appeals against rejected applications to conducting trials involving the validity of patents. Patent rights become effective only upon approval by and registration with the KIPO.

During the application process, the first-to-file rule applies in the event that more than one application has been filed for an identical invention. That is, the first applicant to file is entitled to patent the invention, irrespective of which applicant first conceived or completed the invention. If conflicting applications are filed on the same date, the right to patent is determined by agreement among the competing applicants; the failure to do so results in no patent right being granted.

After a final rejection, the applicant has 30 days to appeal to the Appellate Board of KIPO. An amended or corrected application is first sent to the examiner who rejected the application. If the examiner does not withdraw the rejection, the Appellate Board will consider the application.

If approved, the patent application is published in the Official Gazette of Patent Publication for a period of two months for the purpose of public inspection and opposition. At this point, the applicant is granted patent rights and is entitled to claim damages from infringers. A patent utilising an invention previously granted a patent, utility model, or design right must receive a licence from the owner of such an invention or design prior to any working of the patent.

A patent lasts for a term of 15 years from the publication date of the patent application and may be extended for one additional period of up to five years. The term for utility model rights is ten years and may not be extended. As property rights, both types of rights may be assigned or pledged. However, assignments and pledges take legal effect only upon registration with the KIPO.

Foreigners residing in Korea may apply for a patent under the same conditions as Korean nationals. If the foreigner is a non-resident but a national of a member country of the Paris Convention, or of a foreign country which allows the granting of patents to Korean nationals, the foreigner may apply for a patent but must be represented by a local patent lawyer. Foreign applications may claim priority on the basis of a prior filing of a patent application in another country; that is, the date of the foreign application will be considered the date of application in Korea. For this provision to apply, the filing in Korea must be within one year of the first foreign application date and must satisfy other procedural requirements. Finally, applicants for international patents under the Patent Cooperation Treaty desiring the extension of rights to Korea should submit a translation of their application to KIPO within 30 months of the earliest application date.

Designs

The Design Act protects rights to industrial designs and is structurally similar to the Patent Act and the Utility Model Act. In deciding to grant property rights in designs, KIPO looks to the novelty and non-obviousness of the shape and form of an item, not its functional uses, as is the case with patents and utility models. However, as design and function may not be easily distinguished in practice, conversion among the three types of application is possible.

A prior licence must be obtained to use or incorporate a registered design. In the event of multiple applications for identical designs, the first-to-file rule applies. Conflicts between design applications and patent or utility model applications, however, are resolved by allowing both to be filed, as the criteria for the two types of approval are essentially different. Once granted, design rights remain in effect for a term of 10 years. Although granted specifically for use with respect to the particular article, a design right extends to any similar design used in a similar article.

Trademarks

The Trademark Act grants property rights in "signs, characters, figures or a combination thereof which are used on goods by a person who produces, manufactures, processes, certifies or sells goods in order to distinguish his goods from those of another". Whether the right is granted depends on the distinctiveness of the trademark, servicemark or business emblem under consideration.

Trademark rights are registered with KIPO. Trademark applications may be submitted irrespective of whether the trademark has actually been used; materials evidencing the use of the trademark are unnecessary for initial trademark applications. Applications must specify the class of goods or services for which the mark will be used from among the 53 classes of goods and the 12 classes of services in the Korean national classification system. The first-to-file rule applies, and a prior licence must be obtained to use items previously granted IPR protection. The term of the trademark is 10 years from the registration date and may be renewed every 10 years on the condition that the renewal application provides sufficient evidence of use.

Once a trademark is registered, the use of a mark identical or similar to the registered trademark with respect to goods identical or similar to the designated goods of the registered trademark constitutes infringement. Licences must be registered with KIPO by submitting an executed trademark licence agreement. However, in accordance with the Foreign

Exchange Management Act and Foreign Capital Inducement Act, only royalty-bearing trademark licences require approval from KIPO.

The *de facto* owner of an unregistered trademark does not have any rights under the Trademark Act against infringers. However, if the unregistered trademark is widely known, the owner may take action against infringers by alleging a violation of the Unfair Competition Prevention Act. This process involves considerable time and expense, as the owner must prove that the mark is widely known in order to recover damages.

Copyright

The Copyright Act provides for the protection of literary, scientific and artistic works. Property rights in such works arise upon creation, but are formally established and better protected by registration with the Ministry of Culture and Sports. The term of a copyright is the life of the author plus 50 years. For stage performances, phonograph records and broadcasts, the term is 20 years after release, to be extended to 50 years effective from 1 July 1994. Copyright holders may assign or pledge the right but such assignment or pledge is not effective until registered with the Ministry of Culture and Information.

A copyright holder is entitled under the Copyright Act to claim for the cessation of infringement and the destruction of the infringing articles. Copyright holders may also claim for damages and any other remedy to restore the holder's reputation against an infringer. Foreign works are entitled to copyright protection if protection is called for under a treaty which Korea has entered into; the work is authored by a Korean resident or a company which has its main office in Korea; or if the foreign work is first published in Korea or is published within 30 days after it was first published in the foreign country. Korea joined the Universal Copyright Convention in 1987 and protects foreign works pursuant to the Convention.

The Computer Programme Protection Act provides for copyright protection of computer programmes. Programme copyright applicants may register within one year after the creation of the programme with the Ministry of Science and Technology. The term of a computer programme copyright is 50 years from the date of the creation. Assignments or pledges of a programme copyright are effective only after registration with the Ministry of Science and Technology. The Semiconductor, Integrated Circuit Layout Design Act provides similar protection for computer chip designs.

Trade secrets

The Unfair Competition Prevention Act contains provisions for the protection of trade secrets. The Act prohibits the acquisition of trade secrets through larceny, coercion or other dishonest methods. It also prohibits revealing or using trade secrets in breach of contractual obligations. The owner of the trade secret can obtain injunctive relief to enjoin an infringer or a potential infringer. Seizure and destruction of goods is also available as a remedy, as well as compensation for damages. The violation of these provisions can also result in fines or imprisonment.

Conclusion

After the sea-change in Korea's political and constitutional order of recent years, Korea's legal system is again in the midst of significant transformation. The political and bureaucratic systems in Korea are being overhauled under President Kim Young Sam's campaign to eliminate corruption in government. In addition, the government has declared its intention to relinquish some of its control over the economy to the private sector. This is in part due to a recognition that Korea is nearing a stage when it can fulfil its ambition to shed the status of a developing country and take its place among the leading developed nations. Furthermore, Korea's loss of its reputation as a low wage manufacturing haven has led to a recent decline in foreign investment. Consequently, many changes in the laws have followed recent announcements by the government of its plans to liberalise and internationalise Korea's economy. If the gathering forces of reform do carry the day, many of the laws discussed in this chapter may soon become obsolete.

Chapter Nine

Tax and accounting

Mr Yong Kyun Kim[1], Samil Accounting Corporation

Introduction

There are two levels of taxation in Korea, national and local. National taxes are levied by the government and can be divided into internal taxes, customs duties and the education tax. Local taxes are levied either by the provinces or by the municipalities.

The Korean tax system may be divided into direct and indirect taxes. The value-added tax (VAT) constitutes the primary form of indirect tax, which is supplemented by direct taxes such as individual and corporate income taxes. Since Korea introduced and effectuated the VAT system in July 1977, as part of an effort to maximise the tax revenue while minimising the conflict between the tax authority and taxpayers, the Korean tax system has focused on indirect taxes.

Direct national taxes include individual income tax, corporate income tax, inheritance and gift tax, asset revaluation tax and tax on the excessively increased value of land, while indirect national taxes include VAT, special excise tax, liquor, telephone, and stamp taxes and securities transaction tax.

Corporate income tax

Taxpayers

Companies are classified for corporate income tax purposes primarily as domestic or foreign entities. A domestic corporation is one whose head or main office is located in Korea. An entity having its head or principal office in a foreign country is classified as a foreign corporation. Domestic corporations are taxed on their worldwide income, whereas foreign corporations are subject to tax only on Korean-sourced income.

A foreign corporation that has a permanent establishment (PE) in Korea is subject to tax on its Korean-sourced income attributable to the PE, applying the same tax rates and the same taxation method as a domestic corporation. On the other hand, a foreign corporation without a PE in Korea is subject only to stipulated withholding taxes on its Korean-sourced income.

A PE includes, but is not limited to, a branch, sub-branch, shop and any other fixed sales place, workshop, factory, warehouse, site of construction or installation or assembly, or place for furnishing the directions or supervision or engineering services of such works, and any mine or quarry or place for prospecting and gathering natural resources and any other resources.

Taxable income

Taxable income is gross income minus deductible expenses. Taxable income plays a basic role in determining the tax base of a corporation. Calculation of gross income and deductible expenses under the Corporate Income Tax Law (CTL) does not always have to be in accordance with the Korean Generally Accepted Accounting Principles (GAAP) for the following reasons:

- The period of time for recognising gross income and deductible expenses under the CTL may differ from that under the GAAP;
- Certain items that should be included in revenue under the GAAP may be excluded from gross income under the CTL, and *vice versa*. For example, interest received on a refund of overpaid national or local taxes is treated as an extraneous receipt under the GAAP, while such interest is excluded from gross income under the CTL. On the other hand, capital gains on donated assets are not treated as revenue under the GAAP, but are included in gross income under the CTL unless the gains are reserved to offset accumulated net operating losses; and
- Certain expenses allowed under the GAAP may be treated as non-deductible expenses under the CTL, and *vice versa*. For example, the total amount of entertainment expenses can be considered under the GAAP, whereas only a limited amount of such expenses is deductible under the CTL. On the other hand, investment reserves or overseas investment loss reserves are deductible under the CTL, while GAAP does not consider these to be deductible expenses.

Therefore, a tax reconciliation procedure is required to determine taxable income for each taxable year. This procedure should be performed in such a manner that related items are added to or deducted from the pre-tax net income calculated under the GAAP.

Tax base

The tax base for corporate income tax is the taxable income as determined by the aforementioned procedure minus the deduction items listed below. The deductions must be applied in the order listed and only up to the limit of taxable income earned during the year.

- The carry-over of net operating losses incurred in any of the five years prior to the current taxable year and not previously deducted in calculating the taxable income or tax base since the year such loss was incurred;
- Nontaxable income stipulated in the CTL or the Tax Exemption and Reduction Control Law (TERCL); and
- Income deductions under the CTL and TERCL. The term "income deduction" refers to the tax principle under which an amount of money is directly deducted from the taxable income in the calculation of the tax base to grant a tax incentive to a corporation performing a certain transaction or earning a certain item of income.

  The following are examples of the permissible income deductions under the tax laws:

- A corporation that has made a qualified capital increase is entitled to an income deduction for the capital increase; and
- A corporation earning income from the transfer of a patent right, technical services, an overseas business or livestock farming is entitled to claim an income deduction.

Gross income

Gross income refers to all revenue from corporate transactions that create an increase in the net assets of the corporation, except for any payment of capital or equity and certain items to be excluded from the gross income. The gross income items are listed in the CTL on an illustrative (not exhaustive) basis. On the other hand, certain income items are excluded from gross income of a corporation although they increase the net assets of the corporation. Among the major income items specifically excluded from gross income for certain tax policy reasons or for the improvement of a corporation's financial structure are:

- Paid-in capital in excess of par value;
- Gains from the decrease of capital stock;
- Gains from a merger or consolidation. (Except if a new or surviving corporation appreciates the net assets acquired from an extinct corporation, when the gains arising from the appreciation are included in gross income); and
- Dividends received by a financial institution from a listed company.

The CTL provides that gross income should be attributed to the taxable year in which it is settled, and contains specific provisions to determine the proper taxable year for each type of transaction. The provisions are intended to prevent a corporation from manipulating the corporate income tax burden by arbitrarily allocating gross income between taxable years.

The gross income of a corporation is generally determined on an accrual basis. However, interest, insurance premiums, instalment payments, guarantee fees or commissions received by a domestic banking institution are attributed to the taxable year in which such payments are actually received, ie on a cash basis. According to cash basis accounting, the above items received should be included in gross income in the taxable year of actual receipt. However, if the payments are received in advance, they are not included in gross income until the taxable year they were to be paid. As an exception to the cash basis accounting principle, if a banking institution recognises a receivable for these items as gross income in the taxable year in which the receivable was accrued, then such receivable should be regarded as a part of gross income for that taxable year.

Deductible expenses

Deductible expenses refer to the expenses arising from transactions that create decreases in the net assets of a corporation, except for the distribution of capital or equity, the appropriation of retained earnings or other transactions specified under the CTL.

The CTL lists the deductible expense items on an illustrative, rather than exhaustive, basis. Therefore, even if an expense item is not listed in the CTL, it shall be deductible if it creates a decrease in the net assets of a corporation. On the other hand, items excluded from deductible expenses are listed in the CTL on the enumerative or exhaustive concept. Hence, a payment that can be established as decreasing the net assets of a corporation may not be deductible if the payment is classified as an item excluded from deductible expenses. Samples of major non-deductible items enumerated in the CTL include the following:

- Criminal fines, administrative fines, interest on late tax payment and expenses incurred in settling taxes in arrears;

- Public imposts other than those specifically described under the CTL;
- Expenditures deemed not directly related to a corporation's business;
- Bonuses paid by a corporation to its officers who are shareholders; bonuses paid to employees (including officers who are minority shareholders of a listed company and officers who are not shareholders) through an appropriation of retained earnings; any portion of the severance pay exceeding the prescribed limit that is paid to officers (including those who are not shareholders and minority shareholders of a listed company);
- Any portion of reserves set aside by a corporation engaging in the life insurance business exceeding the allowable limit in order to pay dividends to policyholders; and
- Any portion of entertainment expenses in excess of the prescribed limit.

Depreciation

Optional depreciation

If a corporation has not written off its depreciable assets in its financial statements, the depreciation expenses are not deductible for the purpose of tax accounting. On the other hand, if the amount that has not been claimed in prior taxable years is recorded as a depreciation expense in the financial statements of subsequent years, such expenses may be deductible within a certain limit as prescribed by the CTL in the year concerned. In other words, a corporation is not required to complete the depreciation of fixed assets within their useful lives: if an undepreciated balance remains, the corporation is allowed to include depreciation in its deductible expenses within the said limit in calculating taxable income in respective taxable years even after the useful life of the asset concerned is over. The corporation may, thus, have an opportunity to reduce its tax burden by using this depreciation system.

However, a corporation receiving a tax exemption or reduction benefit must include depreciation expenses in its deductible expenses. Under this "deemed depreciation" system, the corporation's total allowable depreciation for the subsequent taxable years shall be limited to the acquisition value minus the amount of unrecognised depreciation which should have been recognised, even if such a corporation did not recognise depreciation expenses as deductible expense during the tax incentive period. This system is intended to prevent a corporation enjoying a tax incentive from unreasonably reducing its tax burden by deferring depreciation until the tax incentive period is over. For deferred charges, a uniform amount of depreciation expenses shall be recorded over the asset's useful life.

Scope of depreciation expenses

Depreciation expenses are deductible within limits set by the CTL. Any excess is not deductible during the current taxable year, but may be carried forward to subsequent taxable years.

Useful life and residual value

The CTL prescribes the useful life and residual value of each category of depreciable assets to avoid the inequitable tax burden that could arise if corporations were given the opportunity to determine these things by themselves.

Consistent application of depreciation methods

Once a corporation selects one of the various depreciation methods applicable to each category of assets as prescribed in the CTL, and reports this choice to the tax authorities, it shall apply that method consistently except in certain specified cases.

Special depreciation
A special depreciation benefit may be granted to fixed assets acquired by a corporation engaging in a qualified industry or performing a qualified project under the CTL and TERCL. Two types of special depreciation exist; initial depreciation and additional depreciation. Under the initial depreciation system, a certain percentage of the acquisition value of a fixed asset is deductible in the taxable year of the acquisition. Under the additional depreciation system, an amount calculated by applying a certain percentage to the ordinary depreciation expense is included in deductible expenses in addition to the ordinary amount of depreciation.

Deferred charges

Under the "deferred charges" concept, the benefit of an expense extends not only over the year of payment but also over subsequent years. The expenditure is not fully included in deductible expenses in the year of payment but is treated as if it were an asset. Items with deferred charges under the CTL include organisation costs, pre-operating costs, new stock issuing costs, R&D costs, debenture issuing costs and discounts on debentures. The amortisation of deferred charges may be classified as below.

Compulsory amortisation
The depreciation of fixed assets can be included in deductible expenses for tax purposes only where the depreciation expense is recognised in the financial statements of the company concerned. However, deferred charges must be amortised in the respective taxable year regardless of whether or not the amortised amount is recorded in the company's financial statements.

Yearly amortisation
Where a company newly acquires a depreciable fixed asset during a taxable year, the amount of depreciation to be included in deductible expenses for the year is limited to the depreciation corresponding to the number of months the asset is actually held. In other words, the deductible amount of depreciation expenses of fixed assets is calculated on a monthly basis although deferred charges may be amortised on a yearly basis. A corporation may include an amount equivalent to, or more than, the yearly average of deferred charges (except for discounts on bond issues) for a period as prescribed in the CTL in the deductible expenses for any year during the prescribed amortisation period, regardless of the month in which the payment was made.

Gains or losses on foreign exchange rates

Gains or losses on the translation of foreign currency receivables or payables should be included in, or deducted from, gross income for the respective tax year. Gains or losses on foreign exchange transactions, for example the difference between the won book value and the actual won payment of relevant receivables or payables shall be included in, or deducted from, gross income in the taxable year in which actual payment is made.

The exchange rates used in the calculation of gains or losses are T/T (telegraphic transfer) buying rate for the translation of foreign currency payables, or the valuation or collection of foreign currency receivables, and T/T selling rate for the translation of foreign currency receivables, or the valuation or redemption of foreign currency payables.

Inventory valuation

The inventory refers to assets held by enterprises for sale including goods, merchandise, semi-finished products, finished products, products in progress, or raw materials to be used for the production of goods. Real estate held by a real estate company for sale and securities held by a security company for sale are also included in inventories.

In general, the cost of sale is calculated by deducting the final inventory from the aggregate of the initial inventory and the purchases for the period. Inventory valuation means a procedure for dividing the acquisition costs of the inventories between a portion matching with revenue arising in the current taxable year and a portion to be carried over to subsequent tax years. Since the taxable income and the tax burden thereon in each taxable year may differ according to which inventory valuation method the corporation adopts, the valuation method is a very important factor for corporate income tax purpose. The CTL defines an inventory as consisting of:

- Finished goods or merchandise (including real estate held for sale by a real estate company);
- Semi-finished goods and products in progress;
- Raw materials; and
- Stored goods.

The same method of inventory valuation should be applied to the same type of inventory. Inventory valuation methods enumerated in the CTL include valuation at cost, the market price method and the cost or market method.

Allowances

Under the Korean GAAP, allowances constitute the contra account of the account to be used for recording the future (yet to be determined) expenses likely to be incurred as expenses in the current year. Since revenue and expenses should be based on the settlement of rights or obligations for corporate income tax purposes, expenses likely to be incurred in the future should not be deductible in principle. In order to achieve the purpose of the tax policy and to observe accounting practices under the GAAP, however, the CTL allows a corporation to deduct allowances for special repairs, severance pay and bad debts from its gross income in the current year.

Reserves

Reserves are the amounts retained by a corporation as deductible expenses in the current year to provide for expenditures that are likely to occur in the future. Although a corporation's taxable income decreases in the tax year if a reserve is set aside, the reserve should be included in gross income or offset against expenses actually incurred in subsequent taxable years. In this sense, a reserve may be considered an indirect tax benefit resulting from the deferred payment of taxes.

Tax rates

Normal corporate income tax rates are listed in Exhibit 9.1.

Exhibit 9.1
Corporate income rates

Tax base (won)	*Tax rate*
100,000,000 or less	18%
Above 100,000,000	won18,000,000 + 32% of the amount in excess of won100,000,000

A 7.5 per cent resident surtax is levied by local governments on the corporate income tax payable.

Special surtax on capital gains from real estate

For corporate income tax purposes, capital gains and losses are treated in the same manner as ordinary income and loss, except that capital gains arising from the transfer of real estate, including land or buildings, are subject to the special surtax at rates ranging from 25 per cent to 35 per cent of the capital gains in addition to the ordinary corporate income tax on the same capital gains. The capital gains are the net amount remaining after deducting from the sales price the original acquisition value, the incidental expenditures directly incurred in connection with the transfer and the inflation deduction amount calculated by multiplying the original acquisition value by the rate of increase in wholesale prices for the period the real estate was held.

Tax exemption or reduction

The Tax Exemption and Reduction Control Law (TERCL) and the Foreign Capital Inducement Law (FCIL) provide various corporate income tax exemptions and reductions, some of which are discussed in the section on tax benefits granted to foreign investors, below.

In exempting a corporation from corporate income tax under the TERCL and FCIL, the amount exempted is determined by multiplying the calculated corporate income tax by the ratio of tax-exempt income to the tax base for each year (which cannot exceed 100 per cent).

Tax credit

Foreign tax credit

If income from sources outside Korea is included in the tax base of a domestic corporation in a taxable year, the foreign tax paid or payable on the foreign-sourced income will be credited against the corporate income tax for the respective taxable year within the following limits:

$$\text{Limit for foreign tax credit} = \text{Calculated corporate income tax} \times \frac{\text{Foreign source income}}{\text{Tax base}}$$

Tax-sparing credit (TSC)

If a Korean corporation was exempt from taxes on its foreign source income in a foreign country with which Korea has a tax treaty, then the domestic corporation is permitted to credit the amount equivalent to the exempt foreign taxes against its Korean corporate income tax liability as if the foreign taxes were paid in accordance with the relevant provision of the tax treaty.

A domestic corporation may elect to treat foreign tax paid as deductible expenses or to credit the amount against the Korean corporate income tax. TSC is included in the amount of the foreign tax paid or to be paid for this purpose.

Tax credit for casualty loss

If it is deemed impossible for a domestic corporation to pay taxes because it has lost 30 per cent or more of the total value of its business assets due to an act of God or other disaster in a taxable year, a tax credit to make up for the casualty loss is available up to a specified ceiling.

Tax credits available under the TERCL include tax credit for the development of technology and manpower and investment tax credit for starting up a business selling new technology. These are discussed more fully later in this chapter.

Penalty tax

A penalty tax is imposed when a taxpayer fails to fulfil various obligations under the tax laws. CTL provides for various penalty taxes, extra penalty taxes and interest charges for failure to file tax returns, underreporting of the tax base, nonpayment or insufficient payment of tax, or other types of noncompliance.

Tax returns

A corporation is required to file a tax return for the respective taxable year with the government and pay the corporate income tax to the government by the due dates as prescribed by the law. A corporation's tax liability may be settled if the tax base or tax amount stated in the tax return is calculated in conformity with the tax law. The government may exercise the right to determine or adjust corporate income tax only where no tax return is filed or where the tax due stated in the tax return filed is found to be unreasonable. In cases where the government determines or adjusts the tax base and tax due of a corporation, it shall make the determination or adjustment based on the books of account or any other evidential documents (field audit method) if they are available. However, if they are false, incomplete or not available, the government may determine or adjust the corporation's tax base and tax due by estimation. The consolidation of income for tax purposes by a parent company and its subsidiaries is not permitted.

Withholding tax

A domestic corporation paying another domestic corporation income such as interest, distribution from a securities trust or other income can withhold a prescribed amount of corporate income tax and pay the tax withheld to the government. A corporation paying an individual such income as interest, dividends, salaries and other income can withhold a prescribed amount of individual income tax and pay it to the government.

A person paying Korean-sourced income, other than real estate or forestry income, to a foreign corporation without a permanent establishment (PE) in Korea shall withhold the amounts of corporate income tax indicated below, plus 7.5 per cent of the corporate income tax as a resident surtax, at the time of making the payment and pay these withheld taxes to the government by the given due date. In addition, a person paying such income not attributable to a foreign corporation's PE in Korea is also required to meet the tax withholding obligations:

- Interest, dividends, royalties or other income: 25 per cent of the amount paid.
- Rental income from ships, aircraft or registered heavy equipment, or business income: 2 per cent of the amount paid.
- Income from personal services: 20 per cent of the amount paid.
- Gains on the transfer of securities or bonds: the lesser of 10 per cent of the compensation received or 25 per cent of the gain on the transfer.

Reduced tax rate for interest, dividends and rental income under tax treaties

The withholding tax on passive income such as interest, dividends and royalties paid to a treaty country's foreign corporation not having a PE in Korea shall not exceed the amount calculated by applying the tax rates prescribed in the treaty to the gross payment of the passive income, regardless of the withholding tax as specified in the CTL. However, as the reduced tax rate for income from the rental of ships, aircraft, registered heavy equipment or automobiles is higher than the tax rate under the CTL, the tax rate under the CTL, which is 2 per cent of the amount paid, shall be applied to such income.

Individual income tax

Taxpayers and taxable income

Resident individuals are subject to Korean taxation on worldwide income, while non-resident individuals must pay tax only on domestic source income. If a foreign individual resides in Korea for one year or more, they will be classified as a resident individual under the domestic tax laws. Where a foreign individual is a resident of both Korea and a foreign country, whether or not he is a Korean resident should be determined in accordance with the provision of the tax treaty concerned. In practice, however, resident foreigners are seldom taxed on income from other than Korean sources, and thus, the taxation result is the same as that for non-residents. Non-resident individuals are taxed on domestic source dividends, interest, and royalty income etc. on a withholding basis.

The Individual Income Tax Law (ITL) specifies four categories of income. The broadest is global income, which consists (without regard for country of origin) of wages and salaries, interest, dividends, profits from real estate and business activities, and miscellaneous receipts ("occasional income"). The remaining three categories are retirement income, capital gains and profits from forestry. Where the total personal deductions for global income exceed that income, the balance may be applied to the next three categories in the above order.

Exhibit 9.2

Tax withholding rates under the tax treaties Korea has entered into with foreign countries

		Special tax rates for investment income[1]	
	Dividends (%)	*Interest (%)*	*Royalties (%)*
Australia	15	15	15
Austria	10-15	10	10
Bangladesh	10-15	10	10
Belgium	15	15	10-15
Brazil	15	10-15	15-25
Canada[2]	15	15	15
Denmark	15	15	10-15
Finland	10-15	10	10
France	10-15	15	10
Hungary	5-10	0	15
India	15-20	15	15
Ireland	10-15	–	–
Indonesia	10-15	10	15
Italy	10-15	10	10
Japan	12	12	12
Luxembourg	10-15	10	10-15
Malaysia	10-15	15	10-15
Mongolia	5	5	10
Netherlands	10-15	10-15	10-15
New Zealand	15	10	10
Norway	15	15	10-15
Pakistan	10-12.5	12.5	10
Philippines[2]	10-15	10-15	15
Poland	10-15	10	10
Singapore	10-15	10	15
Sri Lanka	10-15	10	10
Sweden	10-15	10-15	10-15
Switzerland	10-15	10	10
Thailand	10-20	10	15
Tunisia	15	12	15
Turkey	15-20	10-15	10
United Kingdom	10-15	10-15	10-15
United States[2]	10-15	12	10-15
West Germany	10-15	10-15	10-15

[1] The lower of the two rates indicated in the table applies to intercompany dividends, interest on loans for a stipulated period and income from the use of know-how, patent or confidential processing for industrial purposes except for royalties paid to United States residents.

[2] When the payee of investment income is a resident of the United States, Canada or the Philippines, 7.5% of the reduced tax rates is imposed as a resident surtax because the surtax is a state/local tax not covered by the treaties.

Capital gains on the sale of securities of listed corporations are excluded from the taxable income of a resident individual, and gains incurred on the sale of land or buildings are subject to special rates.

Individuals are entitled to tax credit for dividend income received from other than non-listed large companies. In addition, credits on all categories of income are available to Korean residents for taxes paid under the laws of foreign countries, calculated on a similar basis as for corporations. Individuals, including both resident foreigners and Koreans, who receive their salary in foreign currency from a foreign corporation (excluding a foreign corporation's PE in Korea), are entitled to a 20 per cent credit for such income voluntarily declared and subjected to monthly withholding through a Class B income taxpayers' association. The credit is given on the condition that the salary payment is not included in the deductible expenses of a PE in Korea of the foreign corporation paying the salary.

Non-taxation and tax exemption

Certain types of income that are not taxable because of their peculiar nature or government policy, are neither included on an income tax return nor subject to withholding tax. Certain qualified types of interest income, real estate income and dividend income are non-taxable. Non-taxable wage, salary and retirement income includes allowances such as the reimbursement of expenses actually incurred and wages in the nature of welfare benefits.

If the amount of global income of an individual includes tax-exempt income as prescribed by the law, the income tax amount equivalent to the amount calculated by applying the tax rate to the tax base times the ratio of the tax-exempt income against the total amount of income shall be exempt. The tax law allows tax exemptions and reductions for three types of income: employment income, business income and capital gains. In addition, wages received by qualifying expatriates are tax-exempt or non-taxable. Qualified expatriates include those as prescribed in "Incentives and grants under FCIL" (p. 17). Wages received by an expatriate who serves a foreign government agency or an international organisation as prescribed by the law are non-taxable. Also, various allowances for overseas service received by a foreigner, such as an overseas duty allowance or housing allowance, not to exceed 20 per cent of the regular monthly wage are non-taxable.

Calculation of taxable income

In calculating taxable income, the taxpayer is allowed a basic exemption equal to won720,000 per year. An additional exemption of won540,000 is allowed for a non-working spouse. An exemption equal to won480,000 per dependent is allowed for up to two qualifying dependent children who live with and are supported by the taxpayer. In the case of a non-resident expatriate, however, exemptions are not allowed for a spouse or children.

Additional deductions are allowed for qualifying insurance premiums up to won500,000; medical expenses up to won1,000,000; education expenses for the taxpayer (excluding post-graduate studies) and his dependents (excluding university and post-graduate studies); contributions to government agencies, national defence, and disaster relief funds; and certain qualifying charitable contributions of up to 5 per cent of taxable income.

A wage and salary deduction ranging from won2,700,000 to won6,200,000 per year from employment income is also available.

Tax rates

The amount of income tax on global income, retirement income or forestry income is calculated by applying the basic tax rates to the respective tax base. Capital gains are subject to special tax rates that are higher than the basic tax rates. A resident surtax is assessed at a fixed rate of 7.5 per cent of the income tax. The basic tax rates are listed in Exhibit 9.3.

Tax credits

The ITL and TERCL provide individual income tax credits for certain types of income including a foreign tax credit, credit for casualty losses, credit for dividends, credit for maintenance of books and records as required by the ITL and credit for wage and salary income. The amount of credit for dividend income, the most important type of individual income tax credit, is calculated based on the gross-up (partial imputation) system as summarised below.

If the global income of a shareholder, other than a minority shareholder of a listed corporation, or a shareholder, partner or investor of a domestic corporation, other than a listed corporation, includes dividend income received by the person from such a corporation, an amount equivalent to 9/41 of the amount of the dividend income actually received will be added to the amount of the dividend income actually received. This figure will then be used to calculate the global income tax of the person. Thereafter, the amount that was added as mentioned above will be credited against the individual income tax amount so calculated. See the formula below:

> Individual income tax to be paid = [global income other than dividend income + dividend income + (dividend income x 9/41) – various income deductions or personal exemptions x global income tax rate] – [tax credits other than dividend income tax credit + (dividend income x 9/41)].

Other significant taxes

Value-added tax

All corporations and individuals that supply goods or services, whether or not for profit, are subject to 10 per cent VAT. VAT is levied on supplies of goods and services, and on the import of goods into the country. Certain basic commodities such as farm products, health services, government transactions and other specified transactions are exempt from VAT. Exported goods are zero-rated, and no VAT is applied on the final sale. VAT is actually borne by the final consumers, because the taxpayer pays VAT on its purchases (input tax) but charges VAT only on its sales (output tax). The tax to be paid to the tax authorities is the difference between the taxpayer's output tax and input tax for a prescribed tax period.

Securities transaction tax

Instead of imposing a capital gains tax on the sale or transfer or securities, Korea currently imposes the Securities Transaction Tax (STT) at the point of sale or transfer of the stock or ownership interest.

Exhibit 9.3
Basic tax rates

Tax base (won '000s)	*Tax rate (%)*
4,000 or less	5
8,000 or less	9
16,000 or less	18
32,000 or less	27
64,000 or less	36
Above 64,000	45

The STT is imposed on the transfer of stock of a corporation established under the Commercial Code or any special Act, or the transfer of an interest in a partnership, limited partnership or limited liability company established under the Commercial Code. The transfer of deemed stocks is also subject to the STT. Deemed stocks include stocks before issuance, rights due to a subscription of stock, pre-emptive rights and a subscription certificate to a corporation established under a special law. However, the transfer of stocks listed on an overseas stock exchange and the over-the-counter transfer of stocks by and between non-residents (those holding less than 10 per cent of the total stock in the concerned corporation for the past five years) is not subject to STT.

The STT base is the total value of securities at the time of transfer. If the transfer price is unknown or lower than fair market value, the appraised value as prescribed by the Enforcement Decree will be the tax base.

In general, the tax rate imposed is 0.5 per cent of the transaction value. Where the transfer value is equal to or less than par value, the tax rate is zero. The tax rate is also zero for new or outstanding publicly offered stocks as prescribed by the law, when the transfer price is equal to or less than the publicly offered or issued price.

Education tax

Education tax is a surtax imposed on the national or local taxes as prescribed by the Education Tax Law, at rates ranging from 0.5 per cent to 30 per cent of the amount of taxes paid (or the revenue of banking and insurance businesses) depending on the category of tax subject to the surtax are shown in Exhibit 9.4.

Registration tax

A person who registers the incorporation of a company or registers ownership of real estate, vehicles, etc. will pay a registration tax. The tax rate for the registration of an incorporation is 0.5 per cent of the value of total shares, while the tax rate for the registration of ownership of an asset varies between 0.3 per cent and 5 per cent of the value of the asset. If a company is established within certain major cities, the tax rates are increased by five times the normal rate under the government's industrial decentralisation policy.

Property tax

A local property tax is assessed annually on buildings, ships, aircraft and mines, at rates between 0.3 per cent and 7 per cent. A newly built factory located in a major city is assessed

Exhibit 9.4
Education tax rates

Tax basis	*Tax rate (%)*
Liquor tax	10.0
Revenue of banks, banking corporations, and insurance companies	0.5
Special excise and automobile taxes	30.0
Property, registration, aggregate land and horse taxes	20.0

Exhibit 9.5
Commodities subject to a special consumption tax

Commodity	*Tax rate (%)*
Gasoline	100
Vehicles (by size)	10-20
Television sets, colour (by size)	15-20
Refrigerators (by size)	15-20
Other	10-100

at a rate equal to five times the normal rate for a period of five years from the date of initial payment. The tax on mines is won50 per hectare of minelot. Aggregate Land Tax (ALT), which is paid instead of property tax, is assessed annually on land registered under the Land Register Law at progressive rates ranging from 0.1 per cent to 5 per cent of the tax base depending the value of land.

Special consumption tax

Certain commodities are subject to a special consumption tax (see Exhibit 9.5).

Assets revaluation tax

Tangible fixed assets directly used for operating purposes, except for non-business assets and land (for land acquired on or before 29 December 1983, one exceptional revaluation is allowed) may be revalued. An increase of asset bases due to the revaluation is subject to a 3 per cent asset revaluation tax.

Acquisition tax

A 2 per cent acquisition tax is levied primarily on the acquisition of property such as land, buildings, motor vehicles, ships, heavy equipment, forests, and membership in a golf club or condominium. However, a 10 per cent acquisition tax is levied on the acquisition of such properties when used for the construction of plant facilities in major cities. A 15 per cent acquisition tax is levied on golf courses, residences, motor vehicles or ships of a luxury class, and on land owned by a corporation but not used for business purposes.

Tax benefits granted to foreign investors

Foreign investment in Korea is encouraged, although some degree of selectivity is exercised. Priority is given to investments that are accompanied by advanced technology, which is consistent with the country's current economic policy. Although tax incentives for foreign investment have been gradually reduced, enterprises receiving foreign investment may still enjoy privileges not extended to domestic investors. The government's current policy on foreign investment is to liberalise various restrictions on foreign investment.

The basic law governing foreign investment is the FCIL which is accompanied by the Enforcement Decrees and Working Rules specifying the matters covered by the Law and its method of enforcement. The Regulations on Foreign Investment provide the matters necessary for enforcement of the Law and Working Rules with respect to foreign investment.

Industries open to foreign investment

Under the current FCIL, foreign investment is generally permitted in any industry except for those specifically restricted or classified as sectors ineligible for foreign investment (the so-called "negative list").

Restricted industries comprise:

- Services for the public welfare normally provided by the government or public organisations, ie water supply and sewage, post, telegram and telephone services, railroad transportation, manufacturing of tobacco and red ginseng, and other industries as listed in the Regulations;
- Industries hazardous to public health and the environment, as listed in the Regulations;
- Industries hazardous to social morality, eg gambling houses;
- Industries which receive special support from the government;
- Industries which are large consumers of energy or which depend heavily on imported raw materials;
- Highly extravagant consumer-oriented industries;
- Industries related to farming or fishery business;
- Industries in the early stage of development which need protection for a period of time in conformity with national industrial policy; and
- Other industries, including newspaper publishing, radio broadcasting, grain planting and others as listed in the Regulations.

Sectors ineligible for foreign investment comprise:

- Public administration, education, religious activities, arts and other sectors as listed in the Regulations.

Foreign investment in restricted industries may be approved if the conditions for approval are met; these are specified in the Regulations.

Report or approval of foreign investment

Applications for investment under the FCIL should be reported to and accepted by the appropriate government authorities in principle. However, the applications will be subject to the approval of the Ministry of Finance (MOF) if any of the following apply:

- The project is on the restricted industry list;
- It involves reinvestment by a foreign investor who has violated Korean labour laws;
- The foreign investment project is feared to cause excessive competition or market-dominance;
- The foreign investment project may threaten the domestic industrial basis; or
- The investment is in hotels, inns, lodging, or any other form of short-stay accommodation.

If all of the following conditions are met, the foreign investment report is filed with the Bank of Korea instead of the MOF:

- The project is an industry subject to reporting;
- The company does not request a tax holiday; and
- The amount of foreign investment is less than US$1 million (US$3 million in the case of manufacturing), or the foreign ownership is less than 50 per cent.

Applications for investment must be accompanied by a description of the project, a certificate attesting to the nationality of the controlling investors and, where applicable, a joint venture agreement. Currently the application is normally acted on within 20 to 60 days, depending on the nature of the investment. From 1 March 1994, however, the approval period will not exceed 15 days.

Incentives and grants under FCIL

Corporate or individual income derived from a business eligible for tax incentives through the FCIL is 100 per cent exempt from income tax for the first tax year and the three subsequent years, and is reduced by 50 per cent for a further two years, according to the ratio of stock or shares owned by the foreign investor. In addition, acquisition tax, property tax and aggregate land tax are reduced by 50 per cent throughout the period for which the income tax is exempt or reduced and the related dividend income of the foreign investor is 50 per cent exempt from income tax for five years.

A foreign lender's interest income accruing from a public loan may be tax exempt or reduced in accordance with the provisions of the public loan agreement. Royalties paid under a technical inducement agreement accepted by the government in accordance with the FCIL, may be exempt from income taxes for five years from the date of acceptance if an application for the tax exemption is approved by the MOF and if the technology introduced under the agreement is one of the high technologies designated by the government.

Furthermore, the compensation received by a foreigner working in Korea under such a technology inducement agreement is exempt from income taxes for five years from the date of acceptance. Under the TERCL, the compensation of eligible foreign technicians employed by domestic entities in specified businesses is also exempt from income tax for five years from the date of their entry into Korea.

Incentives and grants under TERCL

A resident or a domestic corporation (including an enterprise receiving foreign investment) investing in productivity-promotion or industry rationalisation facilities, advanced technology facilities, antipollution facilities, industrial hazard prevention facilities, facilities for technology and manpower development or for the commercialisation of new technology, etc may enjoy one of the following tax incentives under the TERCL:

- Tax credit of an amount equivalent to 3-5 per cent (10-15 per cent in the case of investments using domestically produced materials) of the amount invested in the business year in which the investment is complete.
- Special depreciation of 50 per cent (or 70 per cent) of the acquisition value of the facilities.

A resident or a domestic corporation engaging in a business earning foreign currency may set aside reserves for export losses within the limit of an amount equivalent to 1 per cent of foreign currency revenue from export business for the business year concerned, or 50 per cent of the income thereof, whichever is lower. The amount so reserved shall be added back to the gains in three annual instalments beginning from the second year after the year in which the reserves were set aside to the extent that the reserves were not offset against actual export losses incurred.

If a domestic enterprise (including a foreign-invested enterprise) qualifies as a Newly Organised Small-Medium Enterprise (NOSME), then the income tax and resident surtax on its taxable income will be exempt for the first four years and will be reduced by 50 per cent for the subsequent two years. In addition to this, various reductions in local taxes such as the acquisition tax, registration tax and property tax are also granted to a NOSME. In this case, the NOSME means a newly organised enterprise whose objective is to engage in a manufacturing or mining project in an agricultural or fishery area as designated by the government or whose objective is to carry on a technology-intensive manufacturing or mining project. To qualify as a NOSME, the number of employees of the enterprise should be no more than 300 (200 for construction enterprises and 20 for wholesale and retail enterprises), and the total assets of the enterprise should not exceed a certain limit, ranging between won8 billion and won30 billion depending on the industrial sector.

A corporation operating in the agricultural and industrial areas may qualify for a tax exemption or reduction and financing support. The acquisition of land by a company with foreign investment is allowed within certain limits. Various other tax incentives are also granted to qualifying businesses under the TERCL.

Exchange controls

Virtually all transactions between residents of Korea and non-residents, and transactions by residents involving foreign currency or assets situated outside Korea, require the approval of the Bank of Korea or foreign exchange banks. Approval is based on policy guidelines laid down from time to time by the government. It is important to note that government policy in this area is constantly changing, and therefore investors should obtain detailed advice prior to entering into transactions that may involve Korea's exchange control rules.

A foreign enterprise's branch in Korea must register with the Bank of Korea and report funds received from its overseas parent to the Bank. Overseas remittance of operating income is possible without the Bank of Korea's approval if it is confirmed by the head of the designated foreign exchange bank.

Investment in securities by non-residents

The Korean stock market was opened to non-resident foreign investors on 1 January 1992. Foreign investors are allowed to invest in all listed stocks, unless restricted by other regulations. However, there are initial limitations on foreign ownership of a company: total foreign investment allowed in each listed company is 10 per cent of the total outstanding shares, with the exception that up to 20 per cent of the total outstanding shares of certain companies may be owned by foreign investors. A single foreign investor may not purchase more than 3 per cent of the total outstanding shares of each listed company.

[1] Mr Yong Kyun Kim is a tax partner with Samil Accounting Corporation which is the largest accounting firm in Korea and a member firm of Coopers & Lybrand (International). Mr Kim is a member of Coopers & Lybrand (International) Asiatax Group, responsible for tax matters affecting member offices and their clients in the region. He is a member of the Korean Institute of Certified Public Accountants (KICPA), and also a member of C&L International Tax Service Group.

Chapter Ten

Prospects

New friendships and old alliances

Korea's foreign policy has in the past focused on the unification issue, but as the country's economy develops, a more complex diplomacy is required. Along with the North Korean threat, the South is sandwiched between two much larger and potentially competing nations, China and Japan: an arms race between the two countries has been identified by Korean sources as among the biggest potential threats to national security in the Asia Pacific region.

China

The biggest shift in strategic alliances between Korea and its neighbours has been the normalisation of diplomatic ties with China in August 1992. China, a longtime ally of communist North Korea, has since been acting as a mediator between Seoul and its allies and Pyongyang in a bid to persuade the North to allow IAEA inspections of its nuclear facilities, which are suspected of being used for developing weapons.

Trade volumes have surged, and there have been discussions about cooperation in the nuclear sector; Korea has imported nuclear fuel from China on several occasions, and officials from China's State Science and Technology Commission visited Seoul in 1993 for the purpose of discussing cooperation in this area, as well as the joint manufacture of satellites. Korea is making major investments in petrochemical projects and oil and gas exploration in China.

The relationship with China created a rift between Korea and Taiwan, which the mainland still claims as its own. Korea had been Taiwan's last formal ally in Asia, enjoying a clout beyond its economic significance. Taiwan escalated trade restrictions against Korea, having previously downplayed such disputes, and prevented Korean companies from participating in Taipei's sixth five-year development programme. Unofficial ties were, however, re-established in July 1993, following secret talks between the two countries, and diplomatic missions were set up in Seoul and Taipei. Trade between the two countries was maintained at a healthy level throughout this episode and totalled more than US$3.5 billion in 1992.

Russia

Seoul and Moscow established diplomatic relations in September 1991, after decades of Cold War enmity, which date back to the Soviet Union's sponsorship of the founding of North Korea. Russian President Boris Yeltsin visited Seoul in October 1992 and promised to cooperate in bringing to light the details of the shooting down of the aircraft KAL 007, which he blamed on Moscow's former communist rulers. Seoul pledged US$3 billion in economic assistance to the cash-strapped nation, of which US$1 billion was to have been in cash and the rest in commodity loans, as part of former president Roh Tae-Woo's Northern Policy which aimed at forging ties with communist and former communist countries in a bid to isolate North Korea.

However, relations have cooled since. Russia, which took over the debt of the former Soviet Union, was unable to repay or meet interest payments on the US$1 billion cash loan, and in August 1993, Seoul cancelled almost US$1.5 billion of the promised package and rescheduled debt and interest payments on the sums already disbursed. The Russians claim that the loans from Korea have to be viewed within the context of Moscow's outstanding loans to its Paris Club creditors. The total backlog on interest payments for Korean loans and tied loans was estimated at nearly US$140 million by late 1993.[1] Russia has offered to transfer defence technology to Korea provided Seoul allows Moscow to repay the outstanding loans with military hardware, including missiles and fighter aircraft; but the offer met with a lukewarm response (even though it would have allowed the South to study at first hand the weapons used by the North), because of Korea's long-standing alliance with the United States.

In 1993 the dumping of nuclear waste in the Sea of Japan by Russia met with condemnation from both Seoul and Tokyo, although it was later alleged that Seoul had itself made such "sea burials" of nuclear waste. The unilateral suspension of Korean fishing rights in the sea of Okhotsk has exacerbated the situation and the continuing lack of a satisfactory explanation for the KAL 007 disaster in 1983, has led to a public backlash against Russia.

Against this background, and an unsettled Russian economy, the Korean business community has been reluctant to invest in the country. Only Hyundai's US$16 million logging venture has gone ahead so far, and trade dropped off to US$860 million in 1992, compared to US$1.2 billion in 1991.

What are the prospects for the future? The Russian and Korean governments have both publicly denied that relations have cooled and the two countries would appear to have great potential for trading because of the abundant oil and mineral resources of the Russian Far East. In many respects Russia is a more natural partner than China, which is a potential rival in the fields of petrochemicals, and automobiles and ship manufacture.

The United States

Korea's relationship with the United States is somewhat ambivalent: although the two countries are diplomatic allies they are also business rivals. The end of the Cold War and the break-up of the Soviet Union have undermined one of the major reasons for American strategic support for Korea, and anti-American sentiment remains a problem for Seoul. However, the presence of large numbers of ethnic Koreans in the United States, estimated at more than 1 million, and emotional ties dating back to the Korean War, ensure that the United States remains loyal to Korea.

The new administration has taken a strong stand on the North Korea issue and Bill Clinton has praised his Korean counterpart's anti-corruption and market liberalisation plans. Economic relations have also improved, and the two countries set up a new economic forum, the Dialogue for Economic Consultation, in a bid to further bilateral trade.

A 1993 visit by Clinton to the frontline between South and North Korea, in which he threatened massive retaliation if the North ever used nuclear weapons against the South, has reassured Korean diplomats, as has the fact that the United States still has 36,000 troops stationed in Korea and has cancelled all plans for withdrawal while the North Korean nuclear threat remains.

The United States urged North Korea to return to the Nuclear non-Proliferation Treaty and undergo inspections of two nuclear facilities around Yongbon suspected of developing nuclear weapons. Negotiations are still going on. The North Korean issue was also obliquely referred to in the 1993 Group of Seven economic summit, which stated that enhanced cooperation was needed to combat the spread of weapons of mass destruction, and a reference to North Korea's decision to withdraw from the NPT was made explicitly in this context.

In addition to its continued commitment to Korea, the United States has also been seeking other alliances in order to maintain security in north east Asia. China has become a strong card for Korea now that diplomatic relations have been re-established, and it was Peking rather than Washington that was credited for getting Pyongyang to postpone its decision to leave the NPT. The United States has meanwhile agreed to inform Peking of US plans related to North Korea. Pyongyang's development of the Rodong-2 missile, a version of the Scud missile with a range of almost 1,000 kilometres, also puts Japan under threat. As a result, US diplomacy over North Korea has been supplemented by Japanese and Chinese support.

Japan

Korea and Japan have strengthened their cooperation over the North Korean threat and the nuclear arms development programme, despite the fact that the Socialist Democratic Party of Japan, the largest party in the government coalition, has long refused to recognise South Korea as an independent nation. Relations with Japan have picked up despite the legacy of bitterness that remains as a result of the 1910-1945 Japanese occupation of Korea, although there are still important issues to be resolved. The Japanese elections of 1993 which saw the first non-Liberal Democratic Party government since 1955, have provided a boost to relations between the two countries. Japan's prime minister, Morihiro Hosokawa has laid emphasis on enhancing ties between the two countries, promising to do as much as he could to help promote Japanese investment in Korea. Politically, Japan's Hosokawa and Korea's Kim share the fact that they are both perceived to be leaders of political reform efforts in their respective countries, and relations in the summit between the two in 1993 were markedly warmer than in previous visits by Japanese leaders to Korea.

Hosokawa began his term in office by expressing "profound remorse and apologies" for Japan's wartime role in Asia, in remarks which were welcomed by the Seoul foreign ministry. In a July 1993 report, Japan acknowledged that its military had forced Asian woman, most of them Korean, into prostitution to serve Japanese soldiers during World War II. The report marked the reversal of a half-century of denials.

Hosokawa has ruled out any fresh compensation for war victims, claiming that Japan has fulfilled all requirements for reparations under the 1951 San Francisco Peace Treaty and bilateral agreements. Japan also settled with Korea through grants and credits when they signed a treaty in 1965 to normalise their relations. There is still pressure from former "comfort women" in Korea and their support groups to discuss further compensation, however.

In the trade sphere, as well, much remains still to be done. The Korea-Japan Parliamentarians' Union has adopted an 11-point plan to boost industrial and political cooperation between the two countries, but the issue of technology transfer remains a problem.

The Asia Pacific region

Korean trade and investment have increasingly been directed towards Asia in the 1990s, and its active participation in regional political and trade blocks is encouraging this trend. Seoul's strategy lies in developing its regional ties within the context of a continued engagement in the region by the United States to guarantee its security. As a result, Korea has acted in key worldwide multilateral organisations, participating in United Nations peacekeeping operations, and has fostered and extended its development assistance programme through a variety of bodies to third world nations. In the area of trade, Korea has taken a broadly accommodative stance on the General Agreement on Tariffs and Trade (GATT).

President Kim Young-Sam has emphasised continuity of policy with previous South Korean governments, but has moved away from the almost exclusive concern with reunification with North Korea, towards developing a wider set of bilateral and multilateral alliances with Asian neighbours. Developing a regional security system and achieving economic integration in the Asia Pacific region is one of the three key aims of Korean foreign policy, along with reuniting the peninsula through the "Northern Policy" and furthering friendly ties with the United States and Japan.

The emphasis placed on strengthening strategic ties within the Asia Pacific region comes partly from the prospect of greater regionalism in world trade, as Europe forms the Single European Market, and the United States entrenches its position within the North American Free Trade Zone. Although the GATT agreement in late 1993 laid the foundations for open trade, Korea remains very vulnerable to regionalism because of its heavy dependency on trade, which constitutes over 70 per cent of its GNP. Rapid growth within the region, which accounts for 40 per cent of the world's population, has also been a powerful incentive to develop local relationships.

Korea's private sector has been engaged in dialogue with its neighbours through the Korea-ASEAN business leaders club, set up in 1979, and the Korean chapter of the Pacific Basin Economic Council (PBEC). The Asia Pacific Economic Cooperation (APEC) forum has emerged as a key vehicle for achieving Korea's twin aims of maintaining its close relationships with Japan and the United States, and developing new links within the region.

The APEC was formed in 1989 as a loose consultative forum to promote free trade and economic cooperation among countries in the Pacific rim. Ministerial meetings have endorsed the principle of "open regionalism" making it less threatening to the United States and other industrialised countries as a potential trade bloc. The United States is the current chairman of the 15-member forum, which groups the six ASEAN countries, Brunei, Indonesia, Malaysia, the Philippines, Singapore and Thailand with the United States, Canada, Korea, Japan, China, Taiwan, Hong Kong, Australia and New Zealand.

At the APEC summit in 1993, Korea was elected to the chair of the forum's Trade and Investment Committee (to be created in 1994), which will implement a working programme for free trade and investment in the region.

Korea remains more cautious about the East Asia Economic Caucus (EAEC), a Malaysian initiative set up to give rapidly-developing East Asian nations a greater say in economic issues. The EAEC is linked to APEC, as it shares the same core members, and its status is that of a caucus within APEC.

Korea aims to use APEC as a bridge for achieving closer ties with regional economic groupings from which it is excluded, notably ASEAN. The ASEAN security summit (at which Korea is a dialogue partner) affords an opportunity to develop common policies in the political arena to supplement economic ties, as well as providing a vehicle for Seoul to develop relationships with nations diplomatically linked to North Korea.

A policy of "open regionalism" is consistent with the needs of Korea. Rapid economic growth in the region from an uneven base has led to widely differing factor endowments, and the region's overall GDP now accounts for almost 60 per cent of world production a growth of over 10 per cent since the 1970s. Furthermore, "the strong complementary relationships existing among these economies, together with an outward orientation, has led to deepening interdependencies".[2]

Korea's development in the field of high-technology goods will allow it to supply its Asian neighbours in the financial and information technology fields as the region's economies become more sophisticated. Its dominance in consumer goods, notably in the electronics sphere, will meet increasing demand from mid-tier large-population centres, such as Indonesia, China, Vietnam and Thailand. The limited infrastructure and underdeveloped natural resource sectors of Russia and China also provide a natural market for Korean heavy machinery and industrial plant exports.

On the other hand, deeper reliance on Asia is a double-edged sword: Korea is still dependent on Japan for much of its technology, and it could lose ground to the other NIEs and developing nations in the region because of relative cost structures.

The country has recently taken notice of events on the other side of the Pacific too: Korea Telecom was one of the unsuccessful bidders in February 1994 for the Peruvian telephone company.

North Korea

Kim Young-Sam announced in 1993 that he hoped the two Koreas would be able to forge a South-North confederation within his five-year term, allowing them to set up a "Peace City" in the Demilitarised Zone which still divides the two Cold War rivals. But, two years into his term, there is little sign of this happening and many Koreans remain sceptical that reunification will ever be a reality. However, the example of East Germany, and the collapse of communist regimes throughout the former Soviet Union and eastern bloc, conclude that totalitarian regimes have a limited life expectancy, and that once signs of weakness emerge, a collapse can follow much more rapidly than observers could ever have expected. The irony is that Germany's experience has given the South cold feet as regards any sudden reunification, and only a very gradual process would now be considered.

The last two years have seen a marked increase in tension between the two enemies, exacerbated by the North's threat in March 1993 to withdraw from the Nuclear non-Proliferation Treaty. The South believes that Pyongyang is planning to develop nuclear weapons at two nuclear reactor plants in Yongbon, 90 kilometres north of Pyongyang.

The abrupt shifts in diplomacy by the North have led to the development of three theories regarding its aims. These are:

- that the North, beset by food riots, and facing the prospect of political instability after leader Kim Il-Sung dies, is upping the stakes with a view to achieving concessions in the negotiation of a federalist solution to the divided Korea;

- that the North is developing a nuclear bomb in order to hold the South to ransom in the future, because it believes that the South, backed by the United States, will invade; and
- that the communist regime is seeking to extract limited concessions by forcing the United States to the negotiating table in the hope that the prospect of an eventual negotiated settlement and the threat of not negotiating with the South, will lead to a disjunction between the US and Southern foreign policies.

Which of these strategies Pyongyang is actually following is anyone's guess, however, because of the reclusive nature of the regime. The North Koreans are clearly worried by the annual military exercises held by the United States and the South, and Pyongyang made the cancellation of these events one condition of the resumption of talks in August 1993, following its boycotting of inter-Korean talks in January of that year.

The parlous state of the North Korean economy makes it likely that the stress on the military threat is largely for the benefit of the country's own population, however. Reports of food riots in the North Korean countryside, the sudden and mysterious withdrawal of some border troops from the frontline in 1993, apparently to deal with an attempted coup, and reports from defectors all paint a picture of a country that is falling apart at the seams. North Korea's recalcitrant diplomacy could be explained by the need to put the country on a war footing in order to quell internal dissent.

Exhibit 10.1

The Government's five-year plan for the new economy

	Unit	*1993*	*1994*	*1995*	*1996*	*1997*	*1998*
GNP	per cent	6	7.1	7.2	7.1	7	7
Gross consumption	per cent	6.1	6.5	6.5	6.4	6.4	6.4
Fixed investment	per cent	4.2	7	7.8	8.7	8.9	9.2
Trade balance	US$100 million	10	25	35	48	65	82
Current balance	US$100 million	-14	0	9	21	37	53
Export	per cent	9.2	8.1	8.3	8.1	8	7.8
(Commodity)	per cent	9.1	8	8.2	8	7.9	7.7
Import	per cent	5.3	6.1	7.6	8.2	8.5	8.6
(Commodity)	per cent	4.4	6	7.5	8.1	8.4	8.5
Export	US$100 million	823	901	993	1101	1226	1363
(Increase rate)	per cent	9.5	9.5	10.2	10.9	11.3	11.2
Import	US$100 million	813	876	958	1053	1161	1281
(Increase rate)	per cent	5.1	7.8	9.3	9.9	10.2	10.3
Producer prices	per cent	1.8	1.8	1.7	1.6	1.5	1.4
Consumer prices	per cent	4.9	4.3	3.7	3.6	3.2	2.9
GNP deflator	per cent	5.3	5.3	4.8	4.5	4.1	3.8
GNP	won trillion	256.7	289.5	325.3	364.3	405.8	450.5
GNP	US$100 million	3219	3643	4189	4849	5616	6480
Per capita GNP	US$	7306	8196	9339	10716	12305	14076
Savings ratio	per cent	34.7	35.4	35.6	36.2	36.8	37.5
Investment ratio	per cent	35.1	35.4	35.4	35.8	36.2	36.7

Exhibit 10.2

Current GNP based on market average exchange rates, 1992 (US$ billions)

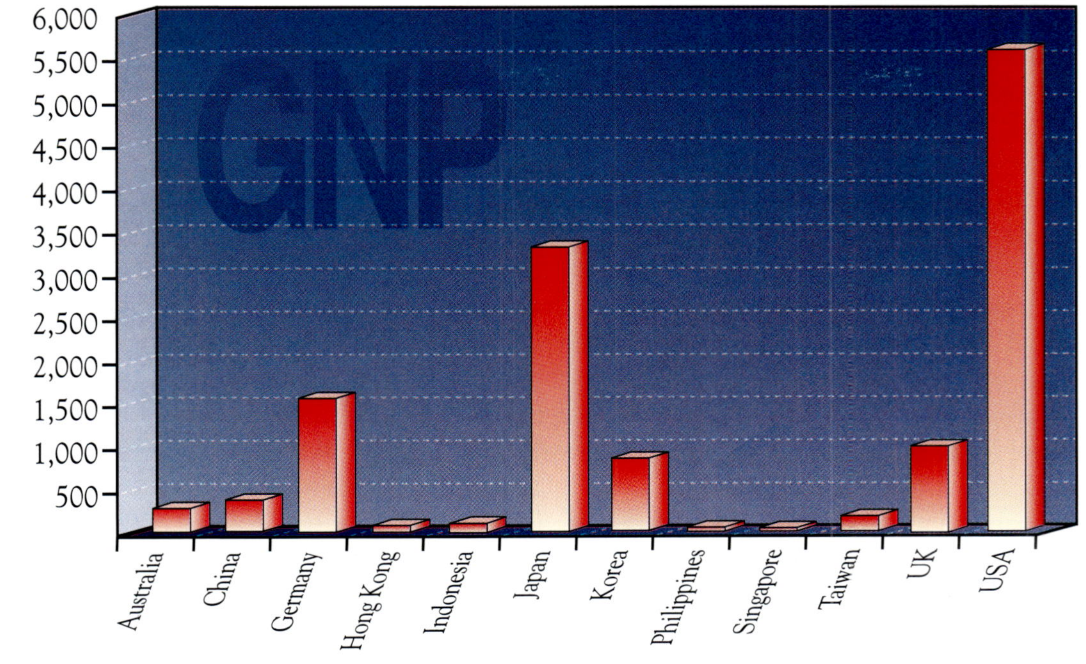

Exhibit 10.3

Per capita GNP, 1992 (US$)

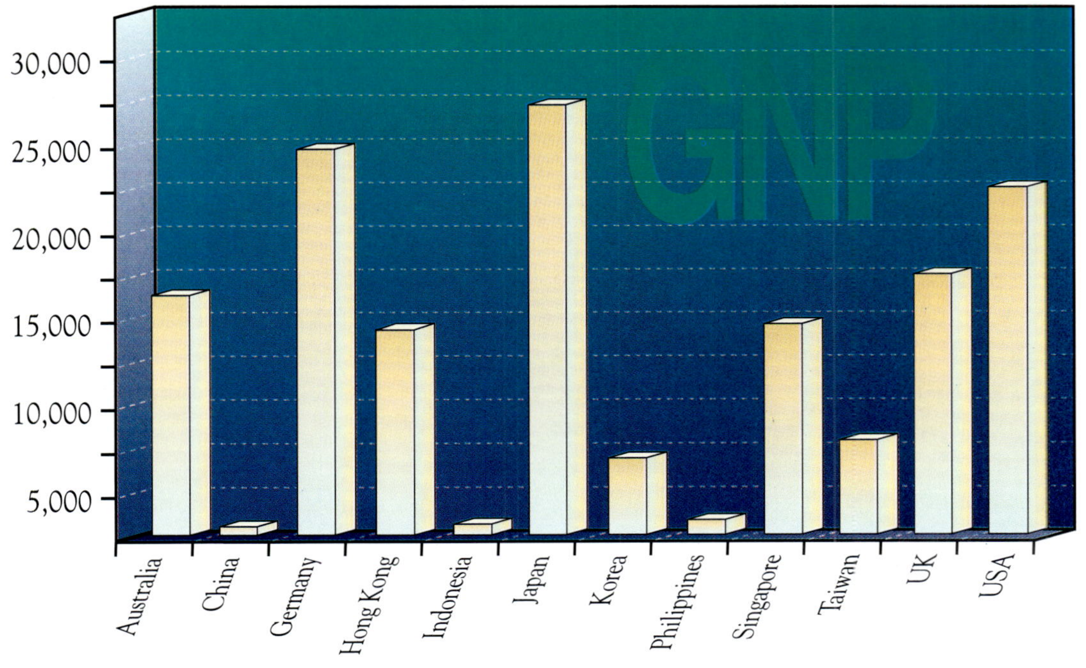

North Korea's ambition has clearly been to begin a dialogue with the United States, before resuming talks with the South; whereas the United States has equally clearly taken the firm line that the resumption of dialogue with the South must be a precondition for talks with Pyongyang, and meanwhile has threatened sanctions against the communist regime if the nuclear issue is not resolved. Implicit diplomatic recognition appears to be behind the North's strategy. The impasse on the diplomatic front remains unbridgeable, but Pyongyang has made some conciliatory gestures to the United States, by agreeing in August 1993 to set up a working-level panel to resolve the issue of servicemen missing from the Korean War.

Third parties have increasingly been involved in the diplomatic stand-off. Seoul has made a concerted effort to warm its relations with Japan: Japan's minority population of 700,000 ethnic Koreans is composed largely of former inhabitants of the North, who regularly remit money to their families in Pyongyang, and thus provide a further conduit for dialogue. The South is also seeking to strengthen diplomatic ties with its former Cold War rivals, in a bid to pressure Pyongyang and keep channels open when dialogue breaks down.

Korea has set up a number of research organisations in Seoul to prepare for unification, and now looks set to develop low-level economic contacts with Pyongyang, to avoid a scenario in which unification is achieved by the economic demise of the North. Korean technocrats say that a process of gradual federalism, in which economic links between North and South are progressively fostered, would be preferable to the North's economic collapse. Such links are being formed, albeit slowly.

Liberalisation and structured management of the economy

It is only relatively recently that Korea has emerged as a true democracy, and that the tremendous influence of the military in the corridors of power has been reduced. The government aims to give greater autonomy to the private sector, curb the monopolistic potential of the *Chaebol* and promote the small- and medium-sized firms; and yet all these aims have been on the agenda since the early 1980s. Although the government of Kim Young-Sam has acted with a speed that many political commentators found remarkable, it has nevertheless yet to show results in key areas of its election policy.

The Confucian cultural heritage, with its strong emphasis on respect for elders and a strongly patriarchal pattern of government, has often been cited as a contributory factor in Korea's rapid economic development. Ironically, it has also been cited as a factor in China's relatively low level of development since the war. Both viewpoints have some validity: Confucian beliefs can provide a tremendous vehicle for mobilising the chain of command between the government and bureaucracy, or between management and workers; but they can also stultify the decision-making process and become an excuse for the lethargic exercise of democracy.

Former finance minister Sakong Il – often identified with the pro-Confucian camp and an exponent of the benefits of having a strong leadership commitment to economic growth – is careful, however, to make a distinction between strong leadership and authoritarianism. The government commitment to economic development in the last 30 years has been both impressive and necessary; however, many argue that now is the time to loosen the reins and allow the private sector more independence and more freedom to make its own mistakes.

The government has made tremendous progress recently in liberalising the economy. However, while competition is to be welcomed, the structure of the economy remains fragile, and setting up stronger anti-trust enforcement to encourage the free-play of competitive forces will be particularly important to the success of the deregulation effort.

It is also important that the ministerial bureaucracy limits its intervention in the private sector. This is not a peculiarly Korean problem; the power of the bureaucracy has blighted liberalisation efforts in Japan, and even in Singapore – which has opened its arms to foreign investment in a way few other economies have – there is more state intervention than many care to admit.

The system of guidance, particularly in a Confucian society, is an effective way to translate policy into action; but it is also a two-edged sword. The strenuous efforts made by large Korean companies to cultivate government officials reflects both the need for government approvals for ongoing business, and the benefits of information exchange.

However, the small- and medium-size business sector has suffered from the close links between big business and the government. The liberalisation of the financial market will certainly go some way to improving funding for these enterprises, but this sector will need the continued attention of the authorities if it is to prosper. Given the huge power of the *Chaebol*, anti-trust action to allow a level playing field is critical, and in the long term will be more effective than state subsidies.

Conclusion

The Chinese character for "crisis" consists of the signs for both "danger" and "opportunity". It is in this context that the potential for crisis in Korea must be viewed. The East Asian miracle – and it is probably not too exaggerated a term for the rapid economic growth seen in the last 30 years in the "Tiger" economies of Korea, Taiwan, Hong Kong and Singapore – must be followed by structural change, if the seeds of success are to take root.

Korea came out of the 1950-1953 war virtually in ruins; since then, the country has achieved a startling growth in its exports and GNP, particularly in the 30 years following the military-led governments of the 1960s. However, the Korean "miracle" has had its costs.

The price of boosting productivity, and the relentless quest for expansion, particularly in world export markets, has been an uneven economic development, and a heavy dependence on the goodwill of international trading partners. There have also been social and political costs. In common with many other rapidly-developing Asian nations, the maintenance of domestic political stability will become a key area of concern, as concepts of authority, obedience and freedom undergo profound and irreversible changes as Korea moves towards a more pluralistic society.

Pollution remains a long-term problem, although it is one that the government has made some progress towards solving: sulphur dioxide emissions, according to statistics from the Ministry of Environment, have more than halved from 0.094 parts per million in 1980 in Seoul to 0.043 parts per million in 1991. However, much still needs to be done in this respect: sulphur dioxide pollution in other key cities such as Inch'on more than doubled in the same period, and anyone who has visited Seoul's choked streets will realise that bare statistics do not adequately reflect the whole picture.

GNP growth rates are often cited by the believers in the East Asian miracle: international investors marvel at the double-digit growth seen in the late 1980s, and even the gloomier projections of 4-6 per cent growth over the rest of this decade compare favourably with other countries. Rapid growth has, however, neglected many less quantifiable aspects of development.

Pessimists see a scenario in which Korea, squeezed because of wage-cost pressures from competing in the textile and light industrial arenas with other Asian NIEs, at the same time fails to break through into the top rank of industrialised countries because of a failure to invest in R&D. The Japanese, the argument goes, will never give up their technological edge over Korea, making available only the technologies that are near to being superseded. As a result, Korea will become an ever-higher cost assembly plant, lacking the financial clout of Hong Kong or the international and entrepôt facilities of Singapore, never quite able to catch up with Japan and the United States in terms of pioneering technology.

These negative aspects of the "miracle" should not lead one to conclude that the Korean economy is facing imminent crisis: most analysts believe growth will average 4-6 per cent in the years to 2000. The economy has also shown resilience in times of crisis, notably during the oil shocks of 1973 and 1980. The Korean economy is 99 per cent dependent on imported energy; when oil prices quadrupled after the fall of the Shah of Iran in 1980, however, the impact on economic growth, if not inflation, was modest. GNP shrunk in 1980 by about US$1 billion; but recovery was rapid, with 5.9 per cent growth registered in the subsequent year, while manufacturing growth stood at 9.9 per cent. In this context, the outward-looking development strategy can be viewed as one of the country's biggest assets, as it has led to an adaptable economic environment, in which external shocks are quickly absorbed to filter through into the structure of the economy. As Sakong Il remarks: "Some people say that because of the volatility of the external environment and the trade environment, particularly the rise and fall of protectionist trade, the outward-looking development strategy may be more vulnerable but I think it's just otherwise. And it worked out that way. We had various real tests during the oil shocks of the early and late 1970s and it turned out that economies relying on outward-looking development strategies were better [equipped] to adapt to change and the adverse environmental changes."[3]

Successive Korean governments have been characterised above all by pragmatism, rather than ideology, and this will be a crucial advantage in the years ahead. How Korea adjusts to the ongoing changes in the domestic sphere and in the world economy will be critical to its future success. The government has already made a start in the labour sphere, with the 1991 Labour Code establishing the ground for a more productive way of settling disputes between management and workers. Its programme for deregulation has also devolved the decision-making process at all levels, although the state bureaucracy remains powerful. On the international front, Korea made the supreme sacrifice in GATT negotiations of opening its rice market, despite huge internal protest which led to a wide-ranging cabinet reshuffle.

These factors encourage one to believe that Korea's economic miracle, even though it will not be repeated in the next century, will at least not prove to be an illusion.

[1] Korea Economic Report, November 1993.

[2] Sakong Il, *Korea and the World Economy*; Institute for International Economics, 1993.

[3] Sakong Il, interview with author.

Appendix

The Korea Trade Promotion Corporation (KOTRA) runs a world-wide network of offices providing Korean and foreign companies with information about trade and investment opportunities. The local KOTRA office is often a useful first-base for foreign companies to contact if they wish to do business in Korea or with Korean companies. KOTRA has 12 domestic offices within Korea, with its headquarters at the World Trade Center complex in Kangnam in southern Seoul. The following gives the addresses and contact details for KOTRA's overseas branches:

Africa

Ivory Coast
BP 3429
Abidjan 01 Plateau
Tel: +225 21 4581
Fax: +225 22 4609

Kenya
PO Box 40569
Nairobi
Tel: +254 (2) 22 0458; 22 8928
Fax: +254 (2) 33 2850

Nigeria
Plot 1388 A. Olosa Street
Victoria Island, Lagos
Tel: +234 (1) 61 4294
Fax: +234 (1) 61 1519

South Africa
PO Box 1086
Johannesburg 2000
Tel: +27 (11) 331 1076/7
Fax: +27 (11) 331 2111

Asia

Bangladesh
PMP Plaza, 2nd Floor
14 Kemal Ataturk Avenue
Banani, Dhaka 1213
Tel: +880 (2) 60 3012; 60 4866
Fax: +880 (2) 88 3086

China
Room 2317
China World Trade Centre
No. 1 Jianguo Men Wai Avenue
Beijing 100004
Tel: +86 (1) 505 2324/7
Fax: +86 (1) 505 2310

Room 1305/6
Shanghai International Trade Centre
2200 Yan an Road (W)
Shanghai
Tel: +86 (21) 219 7592/3
Fax: +86 (21) 219 6015

Hong Kong
PO Box 5573
Tel: +852 545 9500; 545 9786
Fax: +852 815 0487

India
Embassy of the Republic of Korea
703 International Trade Tower
Nehru Place, New Delhi 110119
Tel: +91 (11) 646 1312; 646 1331
Fax: +91 (11) 646 1482

Indonesia
PO Box 1362, Jakarta
Tel: +62 (21) 51 1408
Fax: +62 (21) 521 2514

Japan
7F Dai-ichi Seimei Building
4-1 1-chome Hakataekimae
Hakata-ku, Fukuoka
Tel: +81 (92) 473 2005/6
Fax: +81 (92) 473 2007

9F Nagoya International Centre Building
47-1 Nagona 1-chome
Nakamura-ku, Nagoya
Tel: +81 (52) 561 3936; 561 3946
Fax: +81 (52) 561 3945

10F Honmachi Meidai Building
5-5 2-chome Azuchimachi
Chuo-ku, Osaka
Tel: +81 (6) 262 3831
Fax: +81 (6) 262 4607

Yurakucho Building, 10-1 1-chome
Chiyoda-ku, Tokyo
Tel: +81 (3) 3214 6951/4
Fax: +81 (3) 3214 6950

Malaysia
10F, Mui Plaza Jalan P Ramlee
50250 Kuala Lumpur
Tel: +60 (3) 242 0756/9939; 248 3944
Fax: +60 (3) 242 2107

Myanmar
PO Box 445, Yangon
Tel: +95 (1) 82795
Fax: +95 (1) 86537

Pakistan
Bahria Complex, Ground Floor
24 Moulvi Tamizuddin Khan Road
Karachi 74000
Tel: +92 (21) 55 1659; 55 2219
Fax: +92 (21) 55 2190

Philippines
PO Box 1881 MCC, Makati
Metro Manila
Tel: +63 (2) 87 3244; 87 1183
Fax: +63 (2) 817 3369

Singapore
PO Box 421, Robinson Road
Singapore 9008
Tel: +65 221 3055/6
Fax: +65 223 5850

Sri Lanka
PO Box 965, Colombo
Tel: +94 (1) 57 4441/2
Fax: +94 (1) 57 5928

Taiwan
PO Box 1555, Taipei
Tel: +886 (2) 725 2324; 725 2343
Fax: +886 (2) 757 7240

Thailand
PO Box 1896, Bangkok
Tel: +66 (2) 233 1322/3
Fax: +66 (2) 237 1956

Vietnam
178 Nguyen Van Thu St, District 1
Ho Chi Minh City
Tel: +84 (8) 22 3944/3950
Fax: +84 (8) 22 3941

Europe

Austria
1/3 (Generali Centree, 3F)
Mariahilferstrasse 77-79
A-1060 Vienna
Tel: +43 (222) 586 3876/7
Fax: +43 (222) 586 3979

Belgium
World Trade Centre, 2ème étage
Boulevard Emile Joaquin 162
B-1210 Brussels
Tel: +32 (2) 218 5132; 218 5499
Fax: +32 (2) 218 7511

Bulgaria
Room 902, Interpred Building 16
Bulgaro-Sovetska Drujauba Boulevard
1057 Sofia
Tel: +359 (2) 70 3251; 70 9139
Fax: +359 (2) 70 7497; 70 8589

Czech Republic
Room 558, Koospol Building
Evropska 178, 16067 Prague 6
Tel: +42 (2) 336 2580; 336 2570
Fax: +42 (2) 336 3436

Denmark
PO Box 1520, Holbergsgade 14
DK-1020 Copenhagen K
Tel: +45 (33) 12 6658; 12 8039
Fax: +45 (33) 32 6654

Finland
Hallituskatu 15, SF-00100 Helsinki
Tel: +358 (0) 63 8122
Fax: +358 (0) 63 8611

France
25/27 Rue D'Astorg
75008 Paris
Tel: +33 (1) 4742 0017
Fax: +33 (1) 4742 0270

Germany
4th Floor, Zi-Nr. 4C5 (Box 11)
Im Internationalen Handelszentrum
Friedrichstrasse 95, D-10117 Berlin
Tel: +49 (30) 2643 2637/8
Fax: +49 (30) 305 2363

Mainzer Landstrasse 27-31
D-6000 Frankfurt-am-Main 1
Tel: +49 (69) 23 6895/7
Fax: +49 (69) 25 3589

Heidenkampsweg 66
D-20097 Hamburg
Tel: +49 (40) 23 2235; 23 2638
Fax: +49 (40) 23 3998

Greece
7th Floor, 43 Academias Street
Athens 10672
Tel: +30 (1) 362 6540; 364 4839
Fax: +30 (1) 364 1567

Hungary
PO Box 571
H-1373 Budapest
Tel: +36 (1) 117 2183; 117 2082
Fax: +36 (1) 117 2358

Italy
Via Larga 31
I-20122 Milan
Tel: +39 (2) 5830 3967; 5830 3934
Fax: +39 (2) 5830 3643

Netherlands
Strawinskylaan 767
1077 XX Amsterdam
Tel: +31 (20) 673 0555/6
Fax: +31 (20) 673 6918

Norway
PO Box 191, Okern 0510
Oslo 5
Tel: +47 (2) 272 1155/6
Fax: +47 (2) 272 1151

Poland
UL Mokotowska No 4/6
00-641 Warsaw
Tel: +48 (22) 25 3536; 25 3547
Fax: +48 (22) 252935

Portugal
Av. Eng. Duarte Pacheco, Torre 2
10° andar, Sala 2, 1000 Lisbon
Tel: +351 (1) 69 0814/6
Fax: +351 (1) 69 0814

Romania
16 Boulevard Nicolae Balcescu, Etajul 3
Sectorul 1, Bucharest
Tel: +40 (1) 614 1486; 614 0052
Fax: +40 (1) 312 0464

Russia
Hotel Mezhdunarodnaya-2, Room 747
Krasnopresnenskaya NAB.12
123610 Moscow
Tel: +7 (095) 253 1569; 253 1571/4
Fax: +7 (095) 253 1698

Room 426-428
45-A 25th of October Street
Vladivostok 690009
Tel: +7 (4232) 26 5897; 26 5019
Fax: +7 (4232) 26 4979

Slovenia
Mencingerjeva 7 61000, Ljubljana
Tel: +3 (861) 21 7600; 21 9510
Fax: +3 (861) 21 9558

Spain
Paseo de la Castellana, 140 (Edif. Lima)
6C 28046 Madrid
Tel: +34 (1) 564 6668/9; 564 7287
Fax: +34 (1) 564 7302

Sweden
4tr Box 45188, Tegnergatan 34
10430 Stockholm
Tel: +46 (8) 30 8090
Fax: +46 (8) 30 6190

Switzerland
Biberlinstrasse 6, CH-8032 Zurich
Tel: +41 (1) 422 1232; 422 1581
Fax: +41 (1) 422 4318

Turkey
Taksim, Mete Cad. Mete Apt. 25, D-7
Istanbul
Tel: +90 (1) 243 5075; 249 8223
Fax: +90 (1) 249 8571

United Kingdom
Ground Floor, Vincent House
Vincent Square, London SW1P 2NB
Tel: +44 (71) 834 5082; 828 4275
Fax: +44 (71) 630 5233

Latin America

Argentina
Av. Cordoba 456-19B
1054 Buenos Aires
Tel: +54 (1) 312 2203/6
Fax: +54 (1) 312 5218

Brazil
Av. Paulista 1439, Conj. 132 Bela Vista
Sao Paolo SP CEP 01311
Tel: +55 (11) 289 4200; 284 5984
Fax: +55 (11) 289 4684

Chile
Av. 11 de Septiembre 1901
52 Providencia, Santiago
Tel: +56 (2) 251 2236; 251 2227
Fax: +56 (2) 204 9833

Colombia
Calle 72, No 10-03, Bogota
Tel: +57 (1) 217 1393; 248 5696
Fax: +57 (1) 217 2191

Costa Rica
Apartado 929-1007, Centro Colon
San José
Tel: +506 33 4207; 33 1836
Fax: +506 55 4018

Dominican Republic
Edificio Santanita, 1 Av. San Martin
No 253, ESQ Calle 43
Local 302, Santo Domingo
Tel: +1 (809) 567 3391/2
Fax: +1 (809) 470 4493

Guatemala
Edificio Geminis 10, Torre Sur Oficina
513 12 Calle 1-25, Zona 10
Guatemala City
Tel: +502 (2) 35 3435; 35 3422
Fax: +502 (2) 35 2944

Mexico
24° piso, Paseo de la Reforma No 10
Edificio Torre Caballito, Col. Guerrero
CP 06040, Mexico City
Tel: +52 (5) 592 5071; 592 5091
Fax: +52 (5) 592 5167

Panama
Apartado Postal 87-2082
Panama 7
Tel: +507 64 8105; 64 7970
Fax: +507 64 0928

Peru
PO Box 18-0337, Lima
Tel: +51 (14) 42 2834
Fax: +51 (14) 420841

Venezuela
PO Box 5368, Carmelitas
Caracas 1010
Tel: +58 (2) 762 2130; 762 6013
Fax: +58 (2) 762 0659

Middle East

Egypt
PO Box 358, Dokkyt, Cairo
Tel: +20 (2) 302 1279; 302 1280
Fax: +20 (2) 302 1281

Iran
PO Box 11365-7877, Teheran
Tel: +98 (21) 84 2925; 85 5289
Fax: +98 (21) 85 3559

Jordan
PO Box 3471, Amman
Tel: +962 (6) 68 4253
Fax: +962 (6) 68 4254

Kuwait
PO Box 20771, Safat 13068
Tel: +965 255 4206; 257 0341-2
Fax: +965 257 0894

Libya
PO Box 91311, Tripoli
Tel: +218 (21) 34138
Fax: +218 (21) 42889

Morocco
Tour des Habous, 8ème étage
Avenue des F.A.R. Casablanca
Tel: +212 231 4280; 231 4232
Fax: +212 231 9780

Saudi Arabia
PO Box 4323, Jeddah 21491
Tel: +966 (2) 669 0031; 669 0073
Fax: +966 (2) 660 8918

United Arab Emirates
PO Box 12859, Dubai
Tel: +971 (4) 22 0643; 22 3285
Fax: +971 (4) 21 6330

North America

Canada

Suite 600, PO Box 9
The Thomson Building
65 Queen Street West
Toronto, Ontario
Tel: +1 (416) 368 3399
Fax: +1 (416) 368 2893

Suite 1710, One Bentall Center
505 Burrard Street, Vancouver BC
Canada V7X 1M6
Tel: +1 (604) 683 1820; 687 7322
Fax: +1 (604) 687 6249

United States

Suite 519, 111 East Wacker Drive
Chicago, IL 60601
Tel: +1 (312) 644 4324/4
Fax: +1 (312) 644 4879

Suite 110, 1000 Tower Lane
Bensen Ville, IL 60106
Tel: +1 (708) 350 0102
Fax: +1 (708) 350 0747

Suite 390, 12720 Hillcrest Road
Dallas TX 75230-2040
Tel: +1 (214) 934 8644
Fax: +1 (214) 934 4191

Suite 104, 4801 Wilshire Boulevard
Los Angeles, CA 90010
Tel: +1 (213) 954 9500
Fax: +1 (213) 954 1707

Suite 1620, One Biscayne Tower
Miami, FL 33131
Tel: +1 (305) 374 4648
Fax: +1 (305) 375 9332

Suite 402, 460 Park Avenue
New York, NY 10022
Tel: +1 (212) 826 0900
Fax: +1 (212) 888 4930

Suite 1905, 1 California Street
San Francisco, CA 94111
Tel: +1 (415) 434 8400; 434 8422/3
Fax: +1 (415) 434 8450

Suite 410, 1129 20th Street NW
Washington DC, 20036
Tel: +1 (202) 857 7919; 857 7921
Fax: +1 (202) 857 7923

Oceania

Australia

PO Box 275, World Trade Centre
Melbourne, Victoria 3005
Tel: +61 (3) 614 1733
Fax: +61 (3) 629 6746

Suite 1811, Tower Building
264 George Street, Sydney NSW 2000
Tel: +61 (2) 247 3369
Fax: +61 (2) 251 5826

New Zealand

PO Box 4007, Auckland
Tel: +64 (9) 373 5792/3
Fax: +64 (9) 373 2952

The co-publishers

Daewoo Securities Co., Ltd.

Daewoo Securities is proud of having the largest network in Korea, sophisticated human and capital resources, and high-quality research tailored for foreign investors

By assuming a leading role in the development of the Korean securities industry, Daewoo Securities has established itself as the premier brokerage firm in Korea. The company has been recognised for its investment expertise and quality services provided to both individual and institutional clients. It has acquired this reputation in the Korean securities industry, supported by the largest operational network, sophisticated human and capital resources, and high-quality research.

The scope of its business ranges from brokerage, underwriting and dealing, to M&A, repayment guarantees of corporate bonds and the management of financial products.

In line with the steady expansion of the Korean securities industry, Daewoo Securities has grown to dominate among local firms. Total assets have reached W1,831 billion and shareholders' equity grown substantially to W957.8 billion as of 31 March 1993. In terms of total capital, Daewoo Securities was the world's 23rd largest securities firm in 1993.

The company employs a total of 2,600 people at its headquarters, 72 local branch offices, and overseas network. The nationwide sales network continues to maintain a strong foothold thanks to the management policy that favours strong broker-client relationships and customer satisfaction.

In order to enhance its standing as an international securities house, Daewoo Securities upgraded its overseas representative offices to subsidiaries: London in September 1991 and New York in December 1992. The company has served an increasing number of corporate clients that have discovered that the domestic capital markets are too small for their financing needs. To overcome this problem, the company has stretched out its hands overseas for them through its overseas network in London, New York, Tokyo, Hong Kong, and Zurich. It also has extensive interests in Hungary, Vietnam, China and India: developing its business in emerging markets.

By the end of financial year 1993 (March), Daewoo Securities had brokered W23 trillion in stock transactions, the largest amount since the firm's inception in 1971, representing a market share of 11.58 per cent. It also underwrote 16.1 per cent of domestic bonds in the same period, unmatched by other local brokers. Moreover, Daewoo Securities had 20.1 per cent of all deposits in savings accounts opened with local securities houses.

Management strategy for financial year 1994

Daewoo Securities' management policy is designed to work in the increasingly competitive and challenging environment throughout the world. This strategy stresses innovative management internally and customer satisfaction externally. The aim of this approach is to create a unified vision for the company's employees with an emphasis on surpassing the customers' needs.

In terms of management structure, Daewoo Securities is improving its operational efficiency by allotting each division more independence and responsibility. To enhance the quality of its services, the company is developing new investment techniques, applying advanced investment models to the clients' portfolios, and actively investing in research and the training of personnel.

Daewoo Securities has established its ACE campaign: stressing the corporate aim to be the first in all business fields by providing the best services. The company's newly organised Customer Satisfaction team was designed to meet different customer demands and to develop stronger broker-customer relations via a variety of communication channels. Daewoo Securities is proud of these commitments and the acclaim it has received from its clients.

Top: Chang Hee Kim, President and Chief Executive Officer
Bottom: Daewoo Securities' corporate aim is to be the first in all business fields by providing the best services

International operation

Daewoo Securities made its practical debut in the international capital market in 1984 through co-sponsoring the launch of the Korea Fund (KF), a closed-end fund listed on the New York Stock Exchange with a current capitalisation of US$265 million. Since then, Daewoo Securities has been entrusted with a major role in the issuance of many Euro-market equity-linked securities: convertible bond issues for Daewoo Heavy Industries (US$40 million), Saehan Media (US$30 million), Jindo (Sfr25 million), Daewoo Telecom (US$50 million), Kangwon Ind. (US$40 million), and the recent Ssangyong Oil Refinery (US$150 million); bonds-with-warrants for Yukong (US$75 million) and for Daewoo Corp. (US$150 million).

The opening of the Korean securities market to foreign investors in early 1992 provided Daewoo Securities with an opportunity to leap forward in the foreign capital market and broaden its international client base. The liberalisation also brought the opportunity to compete with well-managed foreign securities firms that have had a presence in Korea for several years.

Anticipating the challenge, Daewoo Securities has sought to modernise operations and extensively train its employees. These efforts have brought excellent results in all areas in financial year 1993. Daewoo Securities' brokerage of domestic equities to foreign investors was well received, while the firm continued to expand its international underwriting activities.

Daewoo Securities has a firm commitment to brokerage of Korean equities and strives to provide high quality research, timely market information, and smooth execution of clients' orders. As a result, the firm has earned a solid reputation for its ability to execute transactions successfully: even block orders, which are very difficult to execute on the local exchange.

The firm's research on Korea's economy, industry, and individual companies has been ranked highly by many surveys of international fund managers. Daewoo Research Institute (DRI), a subsidiary of Daewoo Securities, is the source of these activities. The institute has over 100 professional analysts, studying all areas of local industry and the economy. The Daewoo Advanced Versatile International Trading System (DAVIT) was developed in-house and is already proven to be efficient and reliable in conducting settlement operations, ensuring credibility when placing orders.

Settlement and standing proxy

As the needs of foreign clients increase in line with the further opening of the Korean stock market, settlement and standing proxy service operations have become crucial to successful international brokerage. The Settlement and Standing Proxy Team offers a comprehensive range of services, including investment registration, account reporting, and notifying clients of various corporate actions. The Team also contributes papers on new developments in the Korean stock market to the bi-annual International Society of Securities Administrators.

As a leading standing agent, Daewoo Securities has registered 361 foreign investors for participation in the Korea Stock Exchange as of 31 December 1993, including various pension and mutual funds. This represented 13.1 per cent of total foreign investors registered. Moreover, Daewoo Securities had standing proxy agreements with over 283 clients.

In the settlement area, the firm is very proud of its ability to prevent default through experienced staff and the use of its automated trading system, DAVIT. As well as using international clearing houses such as Euroclear and Cedel for the settlement of international transactions, Daewoo Securities also holds accounts with most major international banks and brokerage houses worldwide.

Computerisation

Daewoo Securities' EDPS Department has developed a state-of-the-art computer system called Daewoo Advanced Reliable Worldwide Information Network (DARWIN), that provides comprehensive information services to the in-house sales staff as well as to the clients.

Among the various systems that make up DARWIN, the most important and widely-used is DIAL-VAN. DIAL-VAN collects and analyses information provided by DRI, the Investment Analysis Department, and all the company's branches. The results of this analysis are available at each broker's computer terminal. In addition, the firm's computer system gives clients quick and ready access to the latest investment information. This enables clients to place orders using home PCs and modems. Clients are able to see price quotes, corporate reports, investment analysis, economic and industrial news, and information on overseas equity markets.

Another DARWIN system, DEAL, is an operation processing tool. DEAL handles order processing, execution management, subscriptions for IPOs, and money transfers. DEAL also efficiently manages all types of client accounts, supporting operations ranging from product development to general administration.

The DAVIT system expedites settlements for the international brokerage business. Through DAVIT, brokers of Daewoo Securities' overseas network are able to place orders and to check transaction results on a real-time basis. DAVIT also ensures efficient settlement operations without default.

Lastly, Daewoo Securities is proud of having the largest database in a newly-built information and telecommunication centre housing more than 100 EDPS personnel with the most advanced equipment. This new information and telecommunication centre will further the development of computer systems to better support the needs of the company's securities activities.

We strive to maximise client' s profits

Daewoo Research Institute

Success in today's rapidly changing financial markets requires in-depth analysis of many issues. The DRI, established in 1984, is the largest private economic research institute in Korea, with capital of W3.5 billion (US$4.41 million). DRI's staff of more than 100 professionals is responsible for tracking a broad range of macroeconomic trends and forecasting the performance of domestic and overseas corporations. DRI's services also include securities analysis, economic policy research, data processing, and business consulting services for general business management, incorporation, restructuring, accounting, and taxation.

DRI works with the Investment Analysis Department of Daewoo Securities to support the company's brokerage business. Through fundamental investment research and analysis of the economy, industry, and the financial and securities markets, DRI and the Investment Analysis Department of Daewoo Securities complement each other. DRI's research is largely macroeconomic and the Investment Analysis Department's research is oriented toward providing clients with precise information on recommended stocks and practical issues.

Daewoo Capital Management Co Ltd (DCM)

DCM was established in February 1988 as a wholly-owned subsidiary of Daewoo Securities. It has a staff of 36, including 15 fund managers, and has assets under management worth W514.2 billion (US$647.6 million) as of 31 March 1993. Although DCM is a subsidiary of Daewoo Securities, it formulates policies and operates independently as an investment adviser.

DCM registered with the US Securities and Exchange Commission as an investment adviser in 1988. Since then, DCM has played a prominent role as the sole Korean adviser to the Korea Fund, and as an investment company listed on the New York Stock Exchange. With experience as investment adviser to the Korea Fund, DCM now acts as an adviser to several substantial foreign-based funds: including the Regent Korea Fund established in July 1991, an open-ended mutual fund set up in Canada, and the First Korea Smaller Companies Fund established in December 1991, and the Korea Capital Fund established in May 1993.

DCM's close relationship with the economists and securities analysts at DRI is integral to its investment decision making process. With recommendations from DRI and the in-house research staff, DCM's fund managers design portfolios to meet the particular investment objectives of each client.

Coryo Securities Corporation

Our Name Tells You We Know Korea!

Coryo Securities Corporation was established in July 1959, and has since, as an affiliate of the *Coryo Group*, grown into one of Korea's top securities houses. Coryo Securities' network consists of 32 domestic branches, subsidiaries in London and in Hong Kong, a branch in Tokyo, and representative offices in New York and Zurich. The New York office is to be incorporated as a subsidiary in 1994, making the most extensive global network of any Korean securities house.

Backed by its professional staff and strong research capabilities, Coryo Securities provides a full spectrum of services, including brokerage, dealing, underwriting, and investment banking for domestic and foreign clients.

Review of domestic operations

Brokerage

In fiscal 1993, ending 31 March, the stock market expanded greatly in volume, turnover exceeding W200 trillion for the first time in its history, up 40.7 per cent from W144.3 trillion in fiscal 1992. Coryo Securities' performance assures its status as one of Korea's blue-chip brokerage firms, and not only as a result of a bullish market climate. Coryo's brokerage performance for fiscal 1993 reached W9.9 trillion, (US$12.5 billion), up 26.4 per cent from the previous year's W7.8 trillion. Coryo benefited greatly from the large expansion of foreign investment, with its international brokerage business amounting to W250.1 billion (US$315 million).

Equity dealing

As of 31 March 1993, the equity portfolio being managed by Coryo totalled W280.2 billion (US$352.9 million). Coryo Securities also played a key role as an institutional investor for the stabilisation of the stock market. As is the case with most securities companies, Coryo's equity dealing activities act as a bridge between its brokerage and underwriting activities, facilitating client investments as well as acting as a source of profit for the company. The professionalism of Coryo's equity dealing operations has produced attractive performance in comparison with its competitors, with return on investment ranking high among the larger securities houses.

Bond trading

Since Korean bond trading volume is estimated to be only about 40 per cent of GNP – quite small compared to that of the United States or Japan – there is enormous growth potential for the Korean bond market in the near future. To make the most of this opportunity, Coryo has adopted medium- and long-term plans to cultivate professional dealers in bonds and derivatives. Coryo has put together a project team, consisting of members of the Bond Trading, Underwriting, Institutional Sales, and Treasury departments and the Coryo Research Institute, to share information and to coordinate activities for successful bond trading. In addition, Coryo is completing development of a bond trading system with a new portfolio model for forecasting the economy, interest rates, and other factors affecting the bond market.

Underwriting

Bond market

Underwriting is a particularly important area of business for the Coryo management, and as a result, the firm underwrote W1.2 trillion (US$1.5 billion) worth of bonds, giving it a market share of 6.6 per cent. Coryo was able to attract much more underwriting business in the area of government agency bonds than any other major Korean securities firm, thanks to its ability in forecasting bond yields.

In the area of corporate bonds, Coryo underwrote W658.8 billion as a lead manager, giving it a market share of 5.4 per cent and a leading position among Korean securities houses.

Stock market

As a result of the government constraints placed on new issuance to prevent over-supply, IPOs in the Korean securities market declined substantially. Given that environment, Coryo concentrated on over-the-counter (OTC) registration activities as a means of securing future IPO business. In 1993, Coryo registered eight companies in the OTC market, valued at W44.2 billion, giving it a market share of 7.6 per cent, and ranking the firm highly in terms both of number of companies registered and total value.

The Coryo Daeyungak Center – situated in the heart of downtown Seoul, and home to the Coryo Group, one of the few conglomerates in Korea devoted primarily to financial services

Technology

Coryo has proven its strength in computer technology by developing innovative systems for managing products and providing convenient services for customers. Coryo is particularly proud of its data distributor processing (DDP) system that enables front line offices to process their own data, thus streamlining the whole procedure. The DDP system makes it unnecessary for branches to send all of their data to the host computer at the head office, rendering information handling more prompt and efficient.

Coryo has already invested well in excess of some W10 billion in its technology systems, and plans to continue to upgrade its information network and to increase the responsibility and importance of the MIS Department.

Review of international operations

Brokerage

Over the past year, Coryo Securities has been enhancing the two factors important to its success in the international brokerage business handled by its International Business Department. First, Coryo has been improving the quality of its research services to meet the sophisticated needs of international clients. Through the work of the Coryo Research Institute (CRI), investment climate is systematically analyzed, while investment strategy is drawn up in meetings of the heads of CRI and key departments, and quickly distributed to clients worldwide through Coryo's well organized overseas network.

Second, Coryo has been strengthening the capability of its order execution and confirmation system. Backed by its automated computer system, the experienced staff of the settlement team is especially proud of its record of perfect settlement. Coryo's proxy team supports international brokerage activities and is responsible for a varied range of services, including investor registration, buy/sell confirmations, and buy/sell recommendations. For fiscal 1993, Coryo's international brokerage totalled W250.1 billion, a market share of 5.6 per cent.

As the Korean capital market opens wider, foreign investors naturally will increase their participation in it, and Coryo Securities is providing up-to-the-minute information and in-depth research materials for them throughout the world, while expanding its own global network.

Coryo expects to reap a bountiful harvest in fiscal 1994, thanks to a burgeoning stock market and a broad client base

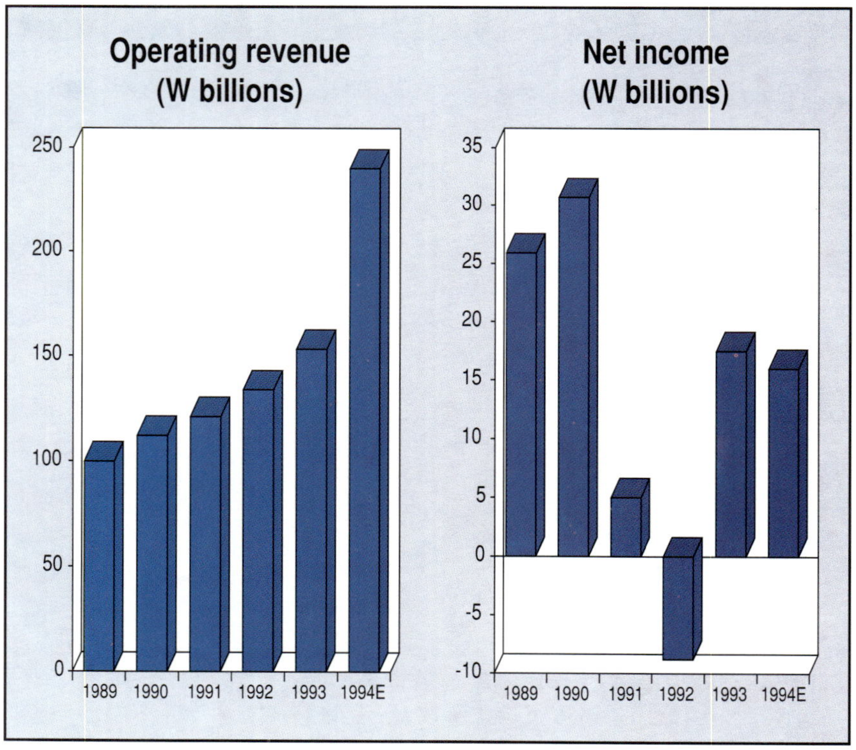

Investment banking

The International Finance Department conducts global investment and underwriting activities for Coryo. The Company's well-trained, highly-qualified corporate finance and portfolio managers have been performing excellently in international capital markets.

Between September and November 1993, Coryo Securities was actively participating as underwriter, co-lead manager or co-manager in over half a dozen issuances in overseas markets. Coryo's Tokyo branch was the underwriter for a ¥20 billion Samurai Bond issued by The Korea Development Bank in September and the co-manager of the ¥26.5 billion Samurai Bond issued by Pohang Iron & Steel Co in October – no other securities house outside the OECD has ever underwritten a Japanese issue. Its London subsidiary was co-lead manager of a US$100 million FRN Euro issue in September for Hyundai Engineering & Construction Co and co-managed Kolon International's US$20 million CB issue in November. In 1991, Coryo was lead manager for one of Korea's three country funds, the Korea Asia Fund, which is listed on the London and Hong Kong exchanges.

Coryo has actively engaged in overseas investment in Japan, the United States and Europe, while expanding its portfolio of overseas assets to diversify into other

April 1991

Placing of

10,000,000 Shares

The Korea Asia Fund Limited

Offer Price per Share: US$10.50

June 1990

Korea Pacific Trust

a securities investment trust established under the laws of the Republic of Korea

Offering of 6,000,000 International Units out of a total of 10,000,000 Units
Aggregate fund size US$100,000,000
Offer Price: US$10.50

December 1989

STC CORPORATION

(Incorporated in the Republic of Korea with limited liability)

US$30,000,000
1¼% Convertible Bonds Due 2004

October 1992

SAMSUNG

SAMSUNG ELECTRO-MECHANICS CO., LTD.
(Incorporated in the Republic of Korea with limited liability)

US$40,000,000
4¼% Bonds due 1997 with Warrants

October 1993

POSCO
Pohang Iron & Steel Co., Ltd.

Pohang Iron & Steel Co., Ltd.
¥26,500,000,000
Samurai Bond

September 1993

HYUNDAI
ENGINEERING & CONSTRUCTION CO., LTD.

US$75,000,000
Floating Rate Notes due 1998

February 1993

Hansol Paper Co., Ltd.

(Incorporated in the Republic of Korea with limited liability)

850,000 Shares of Common Stock
(par value W5,000 per share)
evidenced by 1,700,000 Global Depositary Receipts
Offer Price: US$16.56 per Global Depositary Receipt

emerging capital markets, such as Hong Kong, China, Malaysia, Thailand, Singapore, and so on. The International Finance Department is also responsible for trading so-called Korean paper, ie CBs, BWs, and DRs issued globally by Korean firms. Active Korean paper trading is crucial, not only as a source of profit, but also as a means of supporting global underwriting.

Key Coryo subsidiaries

Coryo Research Institute (CRI)

Since its establishment in January 1987 as a subsidiary of Coryo Securities, CRI has developed a reputation as a leading research institute by performing quality research on the Korean stock market, industries, and economy. CRI's research also covers futures, options, commodities, and so on. CRI has long been preparing for the opening of the Korean capital markets, and has been training its staff to become specialists in their respective fields.

CRI divides its activities into three areas – economic research, industry analysis and securities research, and publishes a guidebook bi-annually in Korean, as well as in English and Japanese.

Coryo Investment Management Corp (CIMCO)

CIMCO was established in February 1988, also as a wholly owned subsidiary of Coryo Securities, to meet the need for professional investment management services particularly in the Korean market, and has become an undisputed leader in the Korean investment management business.

CIMCO provides asset management services, and a range of other services, including a variety of information on the Korean economy and capital market. CIMCO designates a fund manager who, armed with sophisticated information process, designs an efficient portfolio according to each client's unique characteristics and investment objectives.

Corporate Headquarters
Coryo Daeyungak Center
25-5, 1-ka
Chungmuro
Chung-ku, Seoul
Korea
Tel: (02) 771-3600
Fax: (02) 771-3213
Telex: COSCO K23817

Coryo International (UK) Ltd
2nd Floor
85 London Wall
London EC2M 7AD
United Kingdom
Tel: (071) 628-4400
Fax: (071) 628-9293

Coryo International (HK) Ltd
Suite 2015
Jardine House
1 Connaught Place
Central
Hong Kong
Tel: (852) 521-2326
Fax: (852) 868-5232

Tokyo Branch
1-21-5, Nihonbashi
Chuo-ku, Tokyo 103
Japan
Tel: (03) 3279-2628
Fax: (03) 3279-2629

New York Office
36th Floor
Carnegie Hall Tower
152 W. 57th Street
New York, NY 10019
United States
Tel: (212) 315-3600
Fax: (212) 315-3607

Zurich Office
3rd Floor
42 Talaker Strasse
Zurich 8001,
Switzerland
Tel: (01) 212-5512
Fax: (01) 212-5519
Telex: 812061

Korea Development Securities Co., Ltd.

A wholly-owned subsidiary of the Korea Development Bank (KDB)

Since commencing business on 21 June 1991, Korea Development Securities Co., Ltd. (KDS) has rapidly established itself as a major player in Korean securities markets. KDS is a wholly-owned subsidiary of the KDB, a state-run industrial bank with assets equivalent to US$34.5 billion as of the end of 1992.

KDS has concentrated on international business, acting as an expert financial intermediary for foreign investment in the newly liberalised Korean equity market. In addition, the development of the domestic bond market is another vital mission of KDS. To attain these goals, additional capital of US$127 million was provided to KDS by its parent in the second fiscal year, bringing the total paid-in capital to US$315 million. With a philosophy based on client satisfaction and the backing of a prestigious financial institution, KDS is now poised to take its place among the leaders in the Korean securities business, both domestically and internationally.

Headquarters in Seoul

Korea: the investors' choice for 1994

According to the poll taken at the end of 1993 by *World Equity*, a new IFR publication, 100 leading intermediate market fund managers chose Korea as the most attractive place for equity investment in 1994. *World Equity* said that the main reasons why most investors believe that the Korean stock market will outperform any other intermediate markets in 1994 are the expectation of the higher ceiling for foreign investment next year and the brighter outlook for the Korean economy.

Despite the fierce competition in international brokerage faced by KDS during its short history, KDS brokered nearly half a trillion Won of Korean stocks during 1993. It has continued to expand its market share in equity brokerage services. In helping sophisticated clients meet their needs, KDS has intensified its efforts to promote the brokerage business by strengthening research, execution, settlement, and custodial services.

Major participant in Korean equity fund business

KDS has continued its efforts to develop on- and off-shore funds which will give foreign investors long-term capital appreciation through investment in a portfolio consisting primarily of equities and equity-related securities. KDS successfully lead-managed the launch of two on-shore funds, Korea Strategic Trust (US$30 million) in August 1992 and the Seoul Access Trust (US$50 million) in August 1993. KDS also participated as placing agent in the New Korea Growth Fund (US$25 million) and in the New Korea Trust (US$100 million) last year.

Lead manager for Samsung Heavy Industry: the largest offering in the history of the Korean stock market

KDS was chosen as the lead manager for Samsung Heavy Industry's initial public offering, worth W150 million: the largest offering in the history of the Korean stock market. KDS was also nominated as the lead manager for the initial public offerings of Agabang, Seoul City Gas, Dae Han Paper, and Sam Woo. To fulfil its role as an intermediary in equity funding, KDS will more actively participate in public offerings in the primary market as well as in the OTC market. In addition, as the corporate fund-raising market becomes more complex, KDS will continue to meet the diverse needs of its corporate clientele.

Top: staff help foreign investors to pick stocks
Bottom: enjoying the bullish market

Successful Euro-issues for Kia Steel and Sam Yang Co., Ltd.

KDS has also performed superbly in international primary markets. During last year, KDS continued its active participation in primary markets and jointly lead-managed Euro-issues for Kia Steel and Sam Yang Co., Ltd.

The convertible bond issue for Kia Steel will be remembered as one of the most successful Korean issues because it hit the mark despite the bear market. KDS also completed its second deal as a joint lead-manager for a Sam Yang bonds-with-warrants issue, which was well received by investors worldwide. Because of its international investor base and its access to the KDB network, KDS has been in an excellent position to place Korean paper. As a result KDS was the top underwriter for Korean corporate issues during 1992 and 1993.

KDS's achievements in international underwriting

First Korean securities house in the Yankee bond market

In addition to underwriting activities in the Euromarkets, KDS has also played a major role in encouraging Korean companies and public institutions to raise funds in the US capital markets.

As a result of its efforts to diversify capital-raising sources for those institutions, KDS became the first Korean securities house to enter the Yankee bond market. It participated in all Korean Yankee bond issues in 1992, making it the top Korean Yankee bond underwriter. In 1992, the total amount raised by Korean issuers in the US bond markets was US$1.45 billion. Issuers included KDB, KEPCO, POSCO, Korea Telecom, and Samsung Electronics.

Quality information

The main focus of our service is research. KDS publishes pages KDSA–E on Reuters, providing up-to-date investment information on the Korean securities market and the economy. KDS also puts out a semi-annual Company Handbook and other publications on corporate analysis and major market news. Our research is based on fundamental analysis of information gained from direct interviews with target companies about their operating strengths and weaknesses and their long-term prospects. Because of this effort,

KDS has continued to build a fine reputation for quality research. We believe that KDS will be rated number one for research on the Korean stock market in the near future.

Quick response to meet the customers' needs

Financial advisory services

KDS has been as on active financial advisor for Korean public institutions. In 1992, KDS was designated as the financial advisor to the Seoul Metropolitan Government (SMG) for the SMG subway construction project; to the Korea Airport Authority for the new international airport project; to the Korea High-Speed Rail Construction Authority and to Korea Telecom. We are now faithfully acting as financial adviser by providing analysis and introducing new financial tools to help raise funds for these projects.

Head Office

Korea Development Securities Co., Ltd.
25-12, Yoido-Dong
Youngdeungpo-Ku
Seoul 150-010
Korea
Tel: +82 (2) 786 5050, 368 2114
Fax: +82 (2) 368 2872/2873
Telex: K22288KDSEC

Overseas network

London Representative Office
A/2/B Plantation House
31-35 Fenchurch Street
London
EC3M 3DX
United Kingdom
Tel: +44 (71) 626 2616/3135
Fax: +44 (71) 626 2606

Hong Kong Representative Office
Suite 3109, 31st Floor
Citibank Tower Building
Citibank Plaza
3 Garden Road
Hong Kong
Tel: +852 868 2909; 524 0211
Fax: +852 868 2198

Korea Exchange Bank:

The guide to the right directions in the rapidly changing Korean financial market

Korea Exchange Bank (KEB) was established in 1967 under the "Korea Exchange Bank Act" as a state-owned bank specialising in foreign exchange transactions and trade financing. Until the mid-1970s, the Bank served as the nation's major financial window to the world and hence one of the most important tasks of the Bank was to raise foreign capital to finance the development of Korean industries. As Korea's economic growth accelerated, however, the demand for diversified banking services increased, and KEB has expanded its business beyond its original scope, becoming a full service commercial bank with an extensive network both at home and abroad. Today, KEB offers a wide range of retail, wholesale, investment banking, trust, leasing, credit card, investment management consultant, and securities services through its wide branch and subsidiary network both in local and international markets.

Mr Joon Huh, Chairman and President

KEB has now grown to be one of the largest commercial banks in Korea with total assets of W27 trillion (US$34 billion) as of the end of 1993. The Bank is still expanding its international network, with 32 offices in major financial centres around the world, far surpassing those of its domestic peers. In addition, the Bank has caught up in domestic operations as the number of domestic branches increased to 265 as of the end of 1993.

At the end of 1989, the "Korea Exchange Bank Act" was revoked, and the Bank entered a new era of privatisation. In late 1991, KEB successfully completed the premiere share issue to the general public. As of the end of 1993, private shareholders own 33.06 per cent of the Bank, while the remaining shares are held by the Korean government (1.65 per cent), and the Bank of Korea (65.29 per cent). The Bank's shares that have been traded in the over-the-counter market, will be listed on the Seoul Stock Exchange during the first half of 1994. The privatisation allowed the Bank to increase its shareholders' equity from W769 billion to W1,082 billion and enabled the Bank to achieve a dramatic strengthening of its capital base. Along with the asset revaluation in 1993, the ratio of capital to risk-adjusted assets reached 9.23 per cent, well beyond the BIS threshold requirement of 8 per cent.

The Bank's net profit surged 35.3 per cent to W83 billion in 1993, and the value of total domestic deposits, the most important funding source to strengthen the Bank's competitiveness, increased by 37.2 per cent to W10,733 billion. Such a strong performance could be attributed to the improvement in asset quality and successful efforts to develop and market new financial products and services, as well as the enhancement of productivity by rationalising management and operations. KEB achieved the most outstanding improvement in asset quality, financial structure, and recorded the highest growth in earnings. Furthermore its productivity per employee was ranked top among the big six on the *1993 Commercial Bank Management Performance Assessment* conducted by the Office of Bank Supervision at the Bank of Korea.

With highly qualified manpower, the Bank will be able to maintain its present outstanding performance, continue to expand its business and provide the most advanced and excellent service to local and international customers. KEB will therefore maintain its position not only as the strongest domestic retail bank but as the nation's main financial window to the world.

Consumer banking

Commitment to service quality has allowed the Bank to enjoy competitive advantages in consumer banking. Since 1992, the Bank has adopted the "Customer Service Monitoring System" to improve customer service and has developed the Customer Satisfaction (CS) Index, a composite measure of the quality of services of the Bank.

To meet the ever-widening range of customer needs, KEB became the first bank to develop the on-line system in Korea. Since the Bank introduced an on-line passbook account system in 1972, KEB has worked hard to keep its dominant position in this area by investing heavily in both hard and software, setting up a wide ATM network throughout the country and by developing various computer-backed customer services.

In 1992, the Bank launched its private banking services with the opening of the Rose Service Center. Professional staff at the Center offer consultant services on tax matters, legal affairs, and fund and asset management to customers. Thus far, the main component of the Bank's drive to expand its consumer banking base has been its "5 Million Accounts" campaign in 1993. To further improve our customer satisfaction, the Bank will continue to introduce new products and services that best meet customer needs.

Korea Exchange Bank Head Office, Seoul

Corporate banking

KEB has been keen to strengthen relationships with thousands of corporate customers and is especially focused on small- and medium-sized companies. As of the end of 1993, the balance of loans to such customers grew 3.7 per cent to ₩2,620 billion: 47 per cent of the bank's total won-denominated loan portfolio.

In 1992, the Bank embarked on a consulting service to provide information for local firms intending to make direct investments in foreign countries. The Bank has also continued to arrange meetings between bank officers, specialists and small business customers on various issues to provide managerial information.

The Bank also launched a firm-banking system, KEB NET PC SERVICE as a part of the bank's ongoing drive to improve its data processing capabilities and electronic banking. The service is currently available to 4,034 corporate customers, and allows them to make transaction enquiries, transfer funds, and economic and financial information from PC terminals. At the same time, larger corporate customers now have easier access to even more sophisticated market information through an "Electronic Data Interchange (EDI) System" that is capable of furnishing a wide range of services.

KEB offers lease and merchant banking services to corporate customers through KEB Leasing Co Ltd, and Korea International Merchant Banking Co Ltd, the Bank's domestic subsidiaries.

International operations

Because of its original purpose, international banking business has been an area in which KEB has had a particularly strong competitive edge. Today, with years of experience and a worldwide network, KEB maintains the reputation of leading international commercial banking in Korea.

As an integral part of the Bank's global banking strategy, KEB continued to expand overseas network while improving productivity, developing skills and new products. In 1993, KEB opened branches in Bangkok, Thailand, and Tianjin, China, both being the first Korean bank branch in each country. As of the end of 1993, KEB's overseas network consists of 21 branches, nine subsidiaries with 15 branches, two representative offices, five affiliates throughout 19 countries, and more than 3,000 correspondent banks in 126 countries.

Previously, KEB's international banking activities have been concentrated on Korean enterprises operating overseas. However, as the Korean economy developed and its globalisation accelerated, the Bank's range of customers and business activities has expanded enormously. Recently, international investment banking has become the focus of the Bank's strategic category on which the management puts most emphasis. The Bank delivers the full spectrum of capital market services including loan syndications, debt financing, project finance, leasing and cross border M&A.

KEB already holds a dominant position in foreign debt issues of leading Korean corporations. The Bank has maintained a strong record of serving foreign institutional investors through the coordinated operations of the Bank's investment banking or securities arms based in London, Hong Kong, Zurich, Luxembourg, and Sydney. In 1993, KEB's overseas investment subsidiaries participated in 17 international bond issues amounting to more than US$800 million. KEB also packaged 22 syndicated loans totalling US$1.6 billion, ranking the Bank as the leading arranger of syndicated loans among Korean institutions.

Since the opening of the Korea stock market to non-resident investors in 1992, KEB has served as a bridge between domestic and overseas capital markets. In 1992, KEB structured a synthetic equity note (SEN) issue offered to foreign investors in the Korean stock market. In addition, KEB developed innovative "clique bonds," a type of FRN with detachable clique warrants. The US$70 million three-year notes were syndicated while the detached warrants were placed privately. The issue allowed the borrower, the Korea Index Fund, sub-Libor funding and the investor a high return.

The increasing participation of foreign institutional investors in the stock market has produced greater demand for the Bank to provide custodian services. The Bank has built a substantial custodian service system and promoted the service in the international market. Since the opening of the Korean stock market in 1992, the contract amount reached US$1 billion. In recent performance evaluations carried out by major global custodians, KEB's custody operation was rated top for its flawless execution, responsiveness, knowledgeable staff, and other services.

As the opening of the Korean financial and capital markets accelerates, KEB's role will significantly increase. The Bank will be able to meet the needs of the investors both at home and abroad with its skill and experience.

Data processing and interbank clearing system

The Bank launched its third phase computer system development plan in 1992, aiming to consolidate its electronic banking and information services. The new system will include Management Information, Branch Office Management, and Strategic Information Systems. Furthermore, the Bank is currently building a Global Network, that links the overseas branch network with digital, voice and visual information. The development will allow the Bank not only to adapt more effectively to the rapidly changing environment, but also to introduce new financial products, and strengthen its competitiveness.

KEB is the only bank in Korea operating Interbank Clearing Services. The Bank holds current accounts with all the banks operating in Korea in 25 designated currencies including Korean Won. The member banks are comprised of 38 Korean banks, 50 foreign bank branches, and 36 overseas correspondent banks. The total of 124 bank customers with 1,092 accounts constitutes a clearing system encompassing both domestic and overseas banks. The Bank also introduced the non-resident Free Won Accounts clearing service through its Interbank Clearing System.

KEB's new spirit

Since privatisation in 1991, KEB has endeavored to create a new corporate culture. This is reflected in the Bank's "SUPER KEB 21" campaign to firmly position itself as the leading international commercial bank in Korea and to perform effectively in a rapidly changing financial environment.

The recent changes in the Korean financial market, such as the easing of interest rates and foreign exchange controls, are expected to trigger fierce competition and force them to be exposed to greater risks.

To face these challenges, the Bank will further improve its overall productivity, broaden its customer base, and diversify its sources of earnings. KEB's new corporate culture has now taken full effect at all levels of its organisation, and the Bank will continue to encourage the staff to devise innovative solutions in response to the challenges of the post-privatisation era.

THE WORLDWIDE NETWORK OF KOREA EXCHANGE BANK

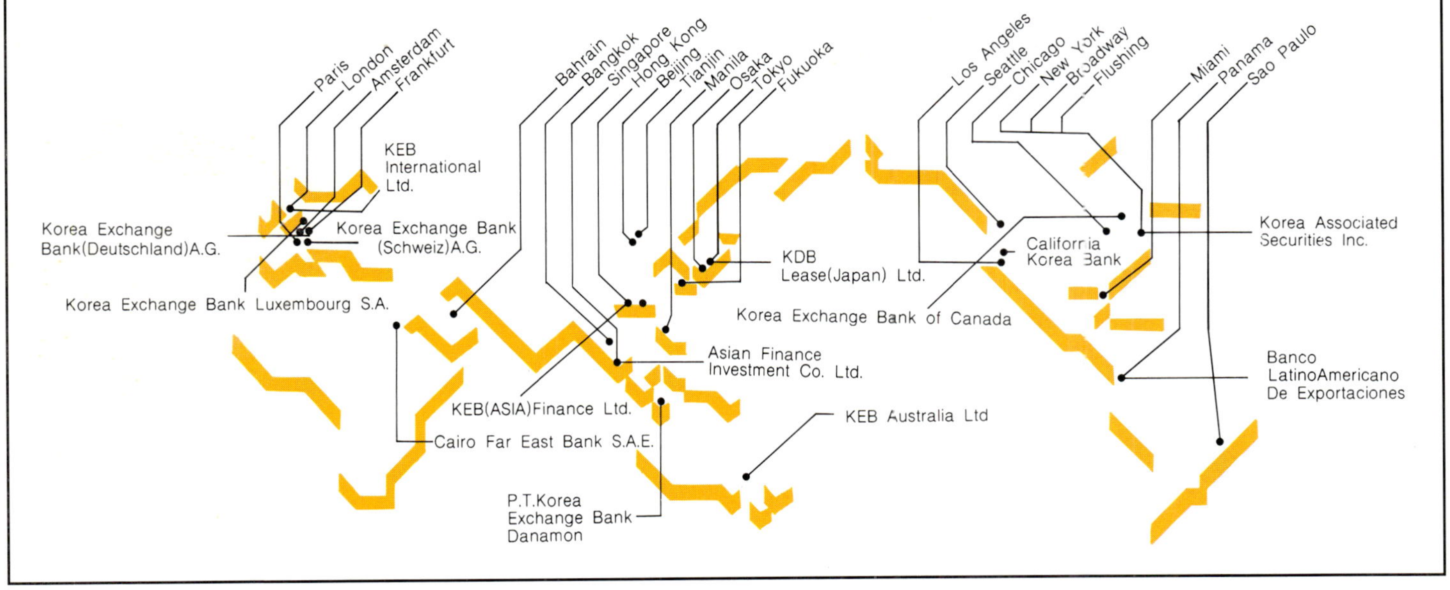